Congress,
Courts,
and Criminals

Recent Titles in Contributions in American History
Series Editor: Jon L. Wakelyn

Reform and Reformers in the Progressive Era
David R. Colburn and George E. Pozzetta, editors

History of Black Americans: From the Emergence of the Cotton Kingdom to the Eve
of the Compromise of 1850
Philip S. Foner

History of Black Americans: From the Compromise of 1850 to the End of the Civil
War
Philip S. Foner

The Southern Enigma: Essays on Race, Class, and Folk Culture
Walter J. Fraser, Jr., and Winfred B. Moore, Jr., editors

Crusaders and Compromisers: Essays on the Relationship of the Antislavery
Struggle to the Antebellum Party System
Alan M. Kraut, editor

Boston 1700-1980: The Evolution of Urban Politics
Ronald P. Formisano and Constance K. Burns, editors

The Great "Red Menace": United States Prosecution of American Communists,
1947-1952
Peter L. Steinberg

At Home on the Range: Essays on the History of Western Social and Domestic Life
John R. Wunder, editor

The Whiskey Rebellion: Past and Present Perspectives
Steven R. Boyd, editor

Law, Alcohol, and Order: Perspectives on National Prohibition
David E. Kyvig, editor

The Line of Duty: Maverick Congressmen and the Development of American
Political Culture, 1836-1860
Johanna Nicol Shields

Propaganda in an Open Society: The Roosevelt Administration and the Media,
1933-1941
Richard W. Steele

Congress, Courts, and Criminals

The Development
of Federal
Criminal Law,
1801-1829

Dwight F. Henderson

Contributions in American History, Number 113

Greenwood Press
Westport, Connecticut • London, England

Library of Congress Cataloging in Publication Data

Henderson, Dwight F., 1937-
  Congress, courts, and criminals.

  (Contributions in American history, ISSN 0084-9219 ;
n.113)
  Bibliography: p.
  Includes index.
  1. Criminal law—United States—History. 2. Courts—
United States—History. I. Title. II. Series.
KF9219.H39 1985   345.73   84-28960
ISBN 0-313-24600-9   (lib. bdg.)   347.305

Copyright © 1985 by Dwight F. Henderson

Library of Congress Catalog Card Number: 84-28960
ISBN: 0084-9219
ISSN: 0-313-24600-9

First published in 1985

Greenwood Press
A division of Congressional Information Service, Inc.
88 Post Road West, Westport, Connecticut 06881

Printed in the United States of America

The paper used in this book complies with the
Permanent Paper Standard issued by the National
Information Standards Organization (Z39.48-1984).

10 9 8 7 6 5 4 3 2 1

Contents

Tables

Preface

The development of the federal criminal justice system is one of the most important but least studied areas in American legal history. The purpose of this study is to fill part of that void by tracing the evolution of the federal system, excluding the District of Columbia and the territories, from its inception to 1829. Hundreds of years of European experience, in particular that in Great Britain, and 150 years of colonial modifications presented the founding fathers with a complicated maze of crimes and punishments, courts and procedures. The basic question was whether there would be a federal criminal justice system. The Constitutional Convention said that there could be one; the first Congress under the new government decided that there would be one.

Despite the centuries of evolution Sir William Blackstone in his *Commentaries on the Laws of England* found that it had "happened that the criminal law is in every country of European ('with the exception of France perhaps') more rude and imperfect than the civil."[1] In addition to starting with an imperfect model, the founders also would have to cope with several problems found in all criminal justice systems. Roscoe Pound in *Criminal Justice in America* found difficulties inherent in all "attempts to order human conduct and adjust human relations by any system of prosecution and penal treatment through legal or administrative machinery which the wit of man has been able to set up." Among these difficulties are "the close connection of criminal law and the administration of criminal justice with politics," the need to adjust to social and economic change, and the necessity to define crimes carefully in order to protect society but not to oppress it.[2]

Testing the system established by the first Congress and expanded and developed under the Federalists and Republicans against the inherent difficulties raises a number of interesting questions. How well did the system protect society? Did the system evolve in relation to social and economic change? What was the role of politics? Did oppression occur? Answers to these questions will be attempted in the pages which follow.

This study was a long time in the making, and a number of organizations and people played a role in its completion. My thanks go to the staff at the National Archives; the Federal Records Centers at Waltham, Massachusetts, East Point, Georgia, Suitland, Maryland, and Fort Worth, Texas; the Virginia State Library; the Indiana University–Purdue University at Fort Wayne library; and The University of Texas at San Antonio library. To Marci Irey at Indiana University–Purdue University at Fort Wayne and Marjorie Present and Charlotte Urrutia at The University of Texas at San Antonio goes my sincere appreciation for typing drafts of the manuscript. David Johnson and Steven Boyd rendered frequent encouragement and assistance, including reading parts of the work. Finally to my wife, Connie, without her help with the research, her careful reading and editing of the manuscript, and her gentle prodding, the work would not have been completed.

NOTES

1. J. W. Ehrlich, *Ehrlich's Blackstone*, 2 vols. (New York, 1959), II: 282.
2. Roscoe Pound, *Criminal Justice in America* (reprint, New York, 1972), 51, 65-67, 75.

Congress,
Courts,
and Criminals

1

The Federalists and the Beginning of the Criminal Justice System

The current federal criminal justice system is the product of centuries of evolution. The colonists brought concepts of law, particularly the English common law including its definition of crimes, criminal procedures, and courts, with them to the new world. In each location they adapted and modified the common law to accommodate their unique needs and circumstances.[1] When the Constitutional Convention met in 1787, the framers had no single model to copy but multiple examples of laws, structures, definitions of crimes, and punishments. The framers did not try to resolve this complex problem in the convention, instead they gave considerable latitude to the Congress to establish inferior courts, to define crimes and stipulate punishments, and to provide for modes of process and procedures to be used in the courts.

The Constitution authorized Congress to "constitute tribunals inferior to the supreme court, . . . to provide for the punishment of counterfeiting the securities and current coin of the United States, [and] . . . to define and punish piracies and felonies committed on the high seas, and offenses against the law of nations." The Constitution defined only the crime of treason—limited to "levying war against them [the United States], or in adhering to their enemies, giving them aid and comfort." In order to be convicted of treason there must be "two witnesses to the same overt act" or the person must confess. The Constitution authorized Congress to declare the punishment of treason but with the proviso that "no attainder of treason shall work corruption of blood or forfeiture, except during the life of the person attained."

The Constitution forbade Congress to suspend the privilege of the writ of *habeas corpus* unless "when in cases of rebellion or invasion the public safety may require it" and to pass a "bill of attainder or *ex post facto* law." Finally the Constitution required that the "trial of all crimes, except in cases of impeachment," should be by jury and should be held "in the state where the said crimes" were committed; but when "not committed within any state, the trial" should be at "such place or places as the Congress may by law have directed."

Objections to the judicial provisions followed quickly upon publication of the Constitution in September 1787. They were raised in newspapers and state assemblies but received the fullest expression in the state ratifying conventions. Opponents repeatedly condemned the lack of a Bill of Rights. Robert Whitehill in the Pennsylvania ratifying convention perhaps best summarized their objection: "There is no Security for People's Houses or Papers by the Constitution—All depends on the good Will of Congress and the Judges." It was "a solemn Mockery of Heaven to say that our rights are secured by the Constitution."[2]

The Anti-Federalists also objected strongly to the creation of inferior federal courts. They feared that the state courts would be wholly superseded.[3] Federalists in several states responded that the inferior federal courts and the state courts would have concurrent jurisdiction in all enumerated cases.[4] Anti-Federalists responded that even if they accepted that interpretation, which they did not always do, an appeal would still lie to the federal Supreme Court. Furthermore the appeal of cases, both as to law and fact, to the Supreme Court would deprive a defendant "of the benefit of a jury from your vicinage, that boast and birthright of a freeman."[5] These objections did not prevent the adoption of the Constitution, but they influenced the first Congress, which in 1789 established the federal judicial system and recommended amendments to the states that would become the United States' Bill of Rights.

In the fall of 1788 the several states that had ratified the Constitution elected Representatives, Senators, and electors. The House was organized in New York City on April 1, 1789; the Senate, five days later. To set the government in motion a revenue system, executive departments, and a judiciary were needed; and the Congress quickly went about enacting legislation to establish them. In addition Congress undertook consideration of amendments. To bring in a bill for organizing the judiciary, the Senate appointed a committee consisting of Oliver Ellsworth of Connecticut, William Paterson of New Jersey, William Maclay of Pennsylvania, Caleb Strong of Massachusetts, Richard Henry Lee of Virginia, Richard Bassett of Delaware, William Few of Georgia, and Paine Wingate of New Hampshire. Six days later Charles Carroll of Maryland and Ralph Izard of South Carolina were added. The story of their labor and the resulting congressional actions has been well portrayed by historians.[6] The approved act established the structure of the federal courts, designated their jurisdictions, created the court officials, and specified the procedures to be used in the handling of cases.

Each of these areas would have an important bearing on the development of federal criminal law in the period from 1789 to 1829 and will be explored further herein. The act established a three-tiered structure of courts, with the Supreme Court, to consist of six justices, at the top; district courts, to have a single judge, at the bottom; and circuit courts, to be made up of any two justices of the Supreme Court and the district judge of the district, in the middle. Each of the eleven states that had ratified the Constitution was given a district court, and in addition district courts were established in Kentucky, then a part of Virginia, and in Maine, then a part of Massachusetts. In each district, except Kentucky and Maine, a circuit court was to be held, with the states arranged into three circuits.

The act gave criminal jurisdictions to both district and circuit courts. Specifically, the district court was given cognizance of all crimes and offences committed within their jurisdiction or upon the high seas "where no other punishment than whipping, not exceeding thirty stripes, a fine not exceeding one hundred dollars, or a term of imprisonment not exceeding six months" was to be inflicted. The circuit courts were given exclusive cognizance of all crimes and offences cognizable under the authority of the United States "except where the act otherwise provides, or the laws of the United States shall otherwise direct, and concurrent jurisdiction with the district courts of the crimes and offences cognizable therein." The act did not spell out what these crimes were or which court should try those who committed crimes carrying lesser penalties.[7] Two things may be inferred from this omission: that Congress would enact a law detailing federal crimes or that the writers of the bill were assuming that the common law definition of crimes was being accepted as a part of federal criminal law. The district courts of Kentucky and Maine, which were not included in a circuit, were authorized to exercise circuit court jurisdictions.

The offices of clerk, marshal, and district attorney were created and regulated in Sections 7, 27, and 28. The Supreme Court and district courts could appoint clerks for their respective courts, with the clerk of the district court also becoming the clerk of the circuit court for that district. Marshals, appointed for terms of four years, were to execute all lawful precepts issued under the authority of the United States. If the need arose, deputies could be appointed, removable by the judge of the district court. The district attorney, a "meet person learned in the law," should be appointed to prosecute delinquents and to represent the United States in civil actions.[8]

The procedural sections of the act may be grouped into three categories: procedures for the orderly conduct of court business; requirements for the handling of criminal trials; and the process of arrest, confinement, and bail. Several sections of the act gave to the courts the right to issue writs, grant new trials, impose and administer oaths, punish all contempts of authority, and to "make and establish all necessary rules for the orderly conducting business in the said courts, provided such rules are not repugnant to the laws of the United States." The section permitting new trials carried a strange wording. It stipulated that courts of the United States could grant new trials in cases where there had been a trial by jury "for reasons for which new trials have usually been granted in the courts of law. . . ." This provides another implication that the framers of the legislation were assuming that the English common law was part of the new federal system.[9]

In criminal cases where the death penalty could be imposed, the act mandated that the trial had to be in the "county where the offence was committed, or where that cannot be done without great inconvenience twelve petit jurors at least shall be summoned from thence." The same section authorized the marshals to summon jurors, who "shall be designated by lot or otherwise in each State respectively according to the mode of forming juries therein now practiced." No other procedural provisions were included, probably because the legislators were simultaneously considering amendments which would provide such security. The most important feature of the act was an omission—the act did not provide for appeals in criminal cases.[10]

The most complex area concerned the arrest of offenders. Section 33 provided that an offender may be arrested by any justice or judge of the United States or "by any justice of the peace, or other magistrate of any of the United States," agreeable to the "usual mode of process against offenders in such state." The offender, at the expense of the United States, could be imprisoned or bailed. In all cases except capital crimes, bail could be admitted by a federal judge; or if there were no federal judge in the district, it could be taken by "any judge of the supreme or superior court of law of such state." In capital cases bail could be admitted only by a federal judge.[11]

The first Congress during its deliberations also approved twelve amendments to the Constitution which were submitted to the states for ratification. In 1791 a sufficient number of states had ratified ten of these amendments to make them part of the Constitution commonly known as the federal Bill of Rights.[12] Articles IV, V, VI, and VIII pertained to criminal proceedings. Article IV prohibited unreasonable searches and seizures; Article V mandated an indictment by a grand jury for a capital or otherwise infamous crime, prohibited trying a person twice for the same crime, and forbade compelling a person in any criminal case to be a witness against himself. Article VI repeated the safeguards contained in the Act of 1789 by guaranteeing the accused a speedy and public trial

by an impartial jury of the State and District wherein the crime shall have been committed. . . and to be informed of the nature and cause of the accusation; to be confronted with the witnesses against him, to have compulsory process for obtaining witnesses in his favor, and to have the assistance of Counsel for his defence.

Article VIII stipulated that "excessive bail shall not be required, nor excessive fines imposed, nor cruel and unusual punishments inflicted." The meaning of these procedural guarantees was not clear. All had been included in colonial and state bills of rights, but the meaning had differed from colony to colony and from state to state. It would be the federal inferior courts that would interpret these constitutional procedural safeguards.

In the closing days of the session the final action of the first Congress pertaining to the judiciary was the passage of a temporary Process Act. The act required that the forms of writs and the mode of process in the circuit and district courts in suits at common law were to follow those of the several states.[13]

The missing link of the criminal system—the definition of crimes and the establishment of punishments—was considered by the Congress. On August 31, 1789, the Senate passed a carefully worded bill defining crimes and offences that should be cognizable under the authority of the United States and their punishment, but the House took no action.[14] The following year Congress enacted a general Crimes Act, defining seventeen crimes ranging from obstruction of process to treason. (See Table 1.) The act established death by hanging as a penalty for six crimes—treason, murder, piracy, accessories to piracy, forgery, and rescue of a person found guilty of any capital crimes. Among additional crimes defined were misprision of treason, rescue of a body ordered for dissection, misprision of felony, confederacy to become pirates, maiming, stealing or falsifying any record or process, larceny, perjury, and bribery of a judge. Sections 25 to 28 offered protections for ambassadors and other public ministers. Any writ or process against such a person was declared null and void, and the person who sued forth or prosecuted the writ, including attorneys and officers who executed the writs, were liable to be imprisoned not exceeding three years and fined at the discretion of the court. A similar penalty was provided for any person who should violate a safe-conduct or passport or who should commit any violence to the person of a public minister or ambassador. The list of crimes was consistent with the constitutional authority of Congress. The punishments assigned to the crimes excluded the district courts, except those without a circuit, from trying any of the statutory criminal cases.[15]

The act also provided several procedural safeguards among which were a requirement that at least three days before the trial in cases of treason, at least two days in other capital offences, the accused was guaranteed a copy of the indictment and a list of the jury and witnesses, and he should be allowed to make "his full defense by learned counsel either of his own choosing or assigned by the court." If a person indicted for treason should stand mute or refuse to plead or should challenge "preemptorily above the

Table 1.
Crimes and Punishment under the Crimes Act of 1790

CRIME	ONLY PUNISHMENT
Treason	Death
Murder, on United States' property	Death
Piracy and felony	Death
Accessories to piracy before the fact	Death
Forgery and counterfeiting	Death
Rescue of a person convicted of a capital crime	Death

CRIME	MAXIMUM PUNISHMENT (imprisonment, fine, other)
Misprison of treason	7 years, $1,000
Rescue of a body ordered for dissection	1 year, $100
Misprison of murder or felony on United States' property or the high seas	3 years, $500
Manslaughter on United States' property	3 years, $1,000
Accessories to piracy after the fact	3 years, $500
Confederacy to become pirates	3 years, $1,000
Maiming on United States' property or on the high seas	7 years, $1,000
Stealing or falsifying a record or process	7 years, $5,000, 39 stripes
Larceny on United States' property or on the high seas	4 times the value of property, 39 stripes
Receiving stolen goods	4 times the value of goods, 39 stripes
Perjury	3 years, $800, 1 hour in the pillory
Bribery of a judge	Fine and imprisonment at the discretion of the judge
Obstruction of process	1 year, $300
Rescue of a person before trial	1 year, $500
Suing an ambassador or foreign minister	3 years, fined at discretion of the court
Violation of safe conduct, or violence to ambassador or minister	3 years, fined at discretion of the court

number of thirty-five of the jury" (twenty in other capital cases), the court should proceed to try the person as if he or they had pleaded not guilty. Section 32 established the statute of limitations on treason as three years and for all other crimes two years. The method of executing those convicted of capital crimes was hanging by the neck "until dead." The act prohibited the use of the benefit of clergy in all capital executions.

Congress had defined crimes and established punishments, but where were federal prisoners to be detained and imprisoned? Congress recommended on September 21, 1789, that the state legislatures authorize the keeping of federal prisoners in local jails. By 1800 all but two states had formally complied with the resolution.[16] The small number of federal prisoners during most of the period would have made a federal facility extremely expensive. In addition, federal prisoners benefited from the penal reform movements, particularly those in New York and Pennyslvania.[17] The system would prevail until 1894 when Congress provided "for the temporary conversion of the military prison at Fort Leavenworth into a civil prison and directed that a new prison be erected near that site."[18]

The passage of the Crimes Act and the adoption the following year (1791) of the Bill of Rights completed the initial structure of the federal criminal justice system. Changes and additions to this system became commonplace in the 1790s. The Supreme Court justices were unanimous in their objection to riding circuit. As early as 1790, Attorney General Edmund Randolph recommended to the House of Representatives that members of the Supreme Court cease being circuit judges.[19] The House took no action on Randolph's report at the time; however, three years later a bill came out of the Senate, approved by both houses on March 2, 1793, which reduced the number of Supreme Court justices from two to one for each circuit. The act also stipulated that if the two judges divided in opinion the cause should continue to the succeeding court; and should the same thing happen a second time with a different judge of the Supreme Court, the district judge adhering to his former position, then the opinion of the Supreme Court justice would prevail.[20] Although the new system was less onerous, the justices continued to request total relief. After several aborted attempts, the Federalist Congress in 1801 granted their plea by abolishing circuit riding. The Judiciary Act of 1801 created five circuits with three judges each and a sixth circuit—consisting of Tennessee and Kentucky—with three judges to include one circuit judge plus the district judges of Kentucky and Tennessee. The act should have been considered a major reform piece of legislation. However, when President John Adams attempted to fill the new judgeships with Federalists, the act came to be viewed as a political ploy, and the Republicans repealed it in 1802.[21]

The Process Act of 1789 was reenacted as a temporary measure in 1790 and again in 1791. Finally in 1792 Congress approved a permanent act which incorporated the act of 1789 but permitted "such alterations and additions as the said Court respectively shall, in their discretion, deem expedient," and "such regulations as the Suprme Court of the United States shall think proper, from time to time, by rule, to prescribe to any Circuit or District Court concerning the same."[22]

The number and types of officials remained the same until the Judiciary Act of 1801 expanded the number of judges. The advent of political parties, however, affected the replacement process for officials who either resigned or died in office. President Adams consistently refused to appoint

Hamiltonians or Republicans for the few positions of district attorney, marshal, or judge that he had to fill. The use of these judicial positions as patronage on which to maintain or build a political party was quickly absorbed into the American political process.[23]

From time to time Congress added additional crimes to the statutory list. The first addition was Section 17 of "An Act to establish the Post Office and Post Roads within the United States," approved February 20, 1792. The act made robbing a mail carrier or stealing mail punishable by a fine up to $300, or imprisonment up to six months, or both. The act appears consistent with the Crimes Act of 1790 since Congress had specific authority to establish post offices and post roads under the Constitution. By implication Congress could protect an institution it had the authority to create.[24]

The second addition to the list of crimes had a more complicated history. Following Washington's issuance of the Neutrality Proclamation in 1793, Gideon Henfield and John Singleton, officers aboard the *Citizen Genet*, were arrested by the United States Marshal for Pennsylvania on May 30, 1793. The same day Attorney General Edmund Randolph advised Secretary of State Thomas Jefferson that Henfield was punishable "because treaties are the supreme law of the land; and by treaties with three of the Powers at war with France, it is stipulated that there shall be a peace between their subjects and the citizens of the United States." He was also "indictable at the common law, because his conduct comes within the description of disturbing the peace of the United States." In the summer of 1793 the petit jury acquitted Henfield although the court declared that the act with which Henfield had been charged was punishable under law.[25]

To clarify the situation Congress in 1794 approved the Neutrality Act which defined and established punishments for specific violations of neutrality making the prosecution of offenders much easier than it had been. The act covered the types of activities that Citizen Edmond Genêt had commenced in 1793. It prohibited the acceptance of a commission to serve a foreign prince (maximum fine of $2,000 and maximum imprisonment of 3 years), enlisting in the service of a foreign prince ($1,000, 3 years), fitting out and arming or attempting to fit out and arm a vessel to be employed in the service of a foreign prince ($5,000, 3 years, forfeiture of vessel and equipment), increasing or augmenting the force of any ship of war of a foreign prince ($1,000, 1 year), and setting on foot a military expedition or enterprise ($3,000, 3 years). The act specifically noted that prosecutions for treason and piracy were not prohibited. Finally the act was limited to two years. The right of a nation to declare and enforce neutrality was clearly part of international law. It was both necessary and proper for Congress to assist in the enforcement of foreign policy by the passage of this act. In March 1797 Congress extended the act for another two years. Later in that year, Congress prohibited citizens of the United States from privateering against nations at peace with the United States or our own citizens. The punishments provided were the stiffest for any non-capital crime during the decade—a fine not exceeding $10,000 and imprisonment not exceeding ten years. In 1800 Congress made the Neutrality Act permanent.[26]

A number of other common law cases occurred in the 1790s, among which were the cases of Robert Worrall and Isaac Williams. Williams was charged in Connecticut with accepting a commission from the French Republic. He admitted the deed but in his defense offered to prove himself a duly naturalized citizen of France. Chief Justice Ellsworth denied the right of expatriation, using a definition of citizenship out of the English common law. The jury convicted Williams, and the court sentenced him to pay a fine of $1,000 and to suffer four months' imprisonment.[27]

Robert Worrall was found guilty before the Pennsylvania circuit court on charges of having offered to split the profits of a proposed contract for the construction of a lighthouse with a treasury official, Tench Coxe. Alexander James Dallas, the defense attorney, moved for an arrest of judgment claiming that Congress had the power "to make a law which would render it criminal to offer a bribe to the commissioner of the revenue; but, not having made the law, the crime is not recognized by the federal code, constitutional or legal, and consequently is not a subject on which the judicial authority of the Union can operate." Justice Chase asked the district attorney if he meant to support the indictment solely at common law; if he did, "the indictment cannot be maintained in this Court." When William Rawle, the district attorney, replied affirmatively, Chase delivered an opinion holding that the United States did not have a common law. District Judge Richard Peters took the opposite position, declaring that "the power to punish misdemeanors is originally and strictly a common law power; of which I think the United States are constitutionally possessed." The court being divided, it became doubtful if sentence could be adjudged. After a short consultation, however, the court sentenced the prisoner to three months in prison and a fine of $200. The sentence has a distinctly common law stamp.[28]

In 1797 Marquis de Casa Yrujo, Spanish Minister to the United States, complained to the Secretary of State about a number of slanderous articles in *Porcupine's Gazette*, a Federalist newspaper edited by William Cobbett. Yrujo requested that the case be brought to the Pennsylvania state court, but Timothy Pickering ordered the federal district attorney in Pennsylvania to commence a prosecution in the circuit court. The court accepted jurisdiction, but a grand jury failed to indict Cobbett. A few months later, Benjamin Franklin Bache in Pennsylvania and John Daly Burk in New York were arrested and charged with libeling the President of the United States in certain publications, specifically the Philadelphia *Aurora* and the New York *Time Piece*. Both charges were based on the common law. Neither case was brought to trial. Bache died on September 10 and thus abated his case, while the charge against Burk, an alien, was dropped following acceptance of an agreement, negotiated by Aaron Burr, for Burk to leave the country. In fact he never left, but the prosecution was ended.[29]

The difficulty of securing convictions under the common law has been suggested by at least one historian as a factor in bringing about the passage of the Sedition Act. The act, the fourth of the famous Alien and Sedition Acts, was approved July 14, 1798. The measure contained only four sections. The first section defined conspiracies with intent to oppose any measure or measures of the government. The second section defined the crime of libel, and the third section permitted a person prosecuted under the act to give as evidence in his defense "the truth of the matter contained in the publication charged as a libel." The fourth section provided that the act would expire on March 3, 1801.[30]

Republicans in Congress opposed the law, particularly sections two and three. The Republicans conceded that "when belief and opinions are put into action, they are liable to the limitations which apply to other actions." They questioned however the necessity for this particular law since they claimed that the nation already had laws "which punished this offense." Republican opposition to the other sections centered on the nature of the freedom of speech and jurisdiction. Senator Harrison Gray Otis contended that since the states had jurisdiction over libels the federal government must also. The Republicans countered that the "federal government had only delegated powers, and since the power to pass a law punishing political libels was neither enumerated nor necessary and proper to carry any delegated power into execution, it followed that this power was reserved to the states or to the people" under the Tenth Amendment. The Republicans also contended that the First Amendment prohibited the "punishment of words for their supposed injurious tendencies."[31]

The difficulties with France during the late 1790s also produced another criminal act. "An Act for the punishment of certain crimes therein specified," more commonly known as the Logan Act, was approved January 30, 1799. Dr. George Logan, a Quaker, had gone to Paris to try to break the impasse that had resulted following the disclosure of the XYZ dispatches. Logan returned with information that led to the reopening of diplomatic relations between the two countries. The Federalist majority, stimulated by Secretary of State Pickering, censured Logan and enacted the law which provided a fine of up to $5,000 and imprisonment from six months to 3 years for any "American who on his own corresponded with a foreign government on a matter in dispute with the United States with the intent of influencing the conduct of that government."[32]

The original Crimes Act defined forgery and counterfeiting of government securities. The Congress did not provide similar protection to the Bank of the United States when it was chartered in 1791. In June 1798 Congress made it a federal violation to falsely make, alter, forge, or counterfeit bills, orders, or checks of the Bank of the United States. Penalties provided included confinement at hard labor for not less than three nor more than ten years or imprisonment for a period not exceeding ten years and a fine not exceeding $5,000. The final section of the act stipulated that "nothing contained shall be construed to deprive the courts of the United States of a jurisdiction under the laws of the several states over the offences declared punishable by this act." This was the first of what would become a number of acts granting concurrent jurisdiction to state and federal courts in criminal matters.[33]

The final addition to the crimes list related to the slave trade. In 1794 Congress passed an "Act to prohibit the carrying on the slave trade from the United States to any foreign place or country." The penalties included forfeiture of vessels and money but no criminal sanctions. In 1800 Congress added to the act, making it unlawful for any citizen of the United States to serve on board any vessel of the United States "employed or made use of in the transportation or carrying slaves from one foreign country or place to another." Upon conviction a person could be fined up to $2,000 and imprisoned for up to two years.[34]

The criminal law system was tested repeatedly under the Federalists. From 1789 to 1801, 426 criminal charges were brought into the federal courts. The most common early cases were assault and battery aboard ship. There was a scattering of cases for forgery and counterfeiting and for violation of the Postal Act. The first major set of cases resulted from the Whiskey Rebellion. To the Pennsylvania circuit court fell the task of punishing rebels. Before the April 1795 session the district attorney submitted thirty-five indictments for treason. The grand jury returned twenty-five as true bills. Nine people were actually tried for treason, and two—John Mitchell and Philip Vigol (Weigel)—were convicted. The Weigel case involved no dispute on a question of law but rested on the proof of the overt act by two witnesses. The trial of Mitchell did involve a major question of law—specifically, what constituted treason? The Constitution stipulated that treason shall consist only in levying war against the United States or in adhering to their enemies, giving them aid and comfort. What constitutes levying war? The district attorney, turning to the British law, found it uniformly and clearly declared that "raising a body of men to obtain by intimidation or violence the repeal of a law, or to oppose and prevent by force or terror the execution of the laws" was an act of war as was also an "insurrection with an avowed design to suppress public offices." Furthermore if "any of the conspirators actually levy war, it is treason to all persons that conspired . . . for in treason all are principles."[35]

Mitchell's counsel contended that the defendant, though not guiltless of any description of crime, had not committed treason. His acts were in the nature of a misdemeanor. Justice Paterson instructed the jury that the purpose of the insurrection had been to wage war against the United States and that, although there were not two witnesses placing Mitchell at the spot of an overt act, he was among the conspirators, which might itself be deemed treason. The jury returned a verdict of guilty on May 25, 1795. On June 5 the court sentenced Weigel and Mitchell to be hanged, but President George Washington pardoned both after being informed by several Pennsylvanians that neither was in his right mind.[36]

In addition to the twenty-five indictments for treason, indictments were sought against four of the other insurgents for misprision of treason and misdemeanor (the grand jury returned "ignoramus" in each case), one for felony in the robbing of the Pittsburgh mail (the grand jury returned a true bill) and thirteen for misdemeanors (the grand jury returned one ignoramus and twelve true bills). Thomas Wilson, one of those against whom true bills were returned, was charged with the misdemeanor of sedition for reportedly saying "any man who supported the Excise law is a damned rascal and . . . wished for his sword that he could shiver [meaning that he would kill] any man who would oppose him and that he . . . could in six hours raise five hundred men who would support him . . . in contempt of the constitution. . . ." Similarly, Robert Lusk, indicted at the October session of the court, was charged with a misdemeanor for writing a certain malicious and seditious letter to William Morehead on August 26. Only two charged with lesser offences were brought to trial before Washington issued a general amnesty. That case, *U.S.* v. *Robert Philson and Herman Husbands*, ended in an acquittal.[37] The government had successfully prosecuted people for treason. The insurrection, however, had exposed the difficulty of obtaining convictions against all participants. The attempt to indict under the common law for sedition was not tested because of Washington's amnesty proclamation.

The second major set of criminal cases arose as a result of the Sedition Act. Under the third section of the act at least eighteen persons were charged either of uttering or of publishing libelous matters. Most of these trials have been well documented and need not be repeated here.[38] Historians of the Alien and Sedition Acts have restricted their inquiries to prosecutions under the second section of the act. As a matter of fact, the first section was used as the basis of prosecutions. The occasion was the affair known as the Fries's Rebellion.

The "rebellion" was against the tax acts Congress passed in 1798 in anticipation of a war with France. When tax assessors entered Northampton and certain other counties of eastern Pennsylvania to compile information, several of them were attacked and deprived of their assessment rolls. As a result the Federal Marshal ordered into the disaffected region by the district judge arrested twenty-three men and took them to Bethlehem. Part of them were released on parole. Then a mob led by John Fries removed the others. By proclamation President Adams called upon the insurgents to desist. Surprisingly enough the opposition did cease, allowing the law to be carried into execution.[39]

The grand jury of the federal circuit court of Pennsylvania returned true bills for treason on April 22, 1799, against John Fries, Frederick Hearny, and Anthony Stahler. Between April 22 and April 30 the jury was given twenty-two additional bills of indictment containing the names of ninety-five persons. Eleven persons were indicted for treason, five for seditious combinations, one for seditious expressions, forty-six for conspiracy, and twenty-six for conspiracy, rescue, and obstruction of process. Only six of the bills were returned ignoramus. The petit jury convicted Fries of treason; however, the court granted him a new trial because one of the jurors had "declared a prejudice against the prisoner after he was summoned as a juror in the trial."[40]

The second trial of John Fries came on at the session of April 1800, Associate Justice Samuel Chase and District Judge Peters presiding. Fries's lawyers promptly withdrew because the judges "laid down their opinions as to the law before hearing counsel." Thus Fries, charged with treason, his life at stake, was left without counsel. Judge Chase instructed the prisoner that he could ask any questions of the witnesses or the court and that the court "will be your counsel, and give you every assistance and indulgence in their power." The jury returned a verdict of guilty. Four days later juries also convicted John Gettman and Frederick Hearny. They along with Fries were sentenced on May 2 to be hanged.

Meanwhile verdicts of guilty had been brought in against thirty men; eighteen for conspiracy; eleven for conspiracy, rescue, and obstruction of process; and one for prison break and conspiracy. They were sentenced to pay fines from $40 to $800 and to serve terms of between four months and two years in prison.[41] On May 21, 1800, President Adams instructed Charles Lee, acting Secretary of State, to issue pardons for Fries, Hearny, and Gettman.[42]

The Sedition Act and the trials were one of the factors which led to the defeat of the Federalists in the election of 1800. The Federalists had initiated the federal criminal justice system. They had established a court structure and then drastically modified it in 1801. Congress' initial Crimes Act and the addition of protective clauses for the post office and the Bank of the United States were easily justified. The Federalists, however, also had introduced some dangerous precedents. The offices of judge, district attorney, and marshal had become part of the patronage system. The Federalists also had prosecuted opponents of government policy under the common law. When common law prosecutions were rejected, particularly in regard to seditious utterances, they enacted the Sedition Act which was a clear violation of freedom of speech and of the press contained in the First Amendment. When an ordinary citizen intervened to promote peace between the United States and France, the Congress made such interference illegal. Finally the court procedures established under the Federalists did not permit an appeal in criminal cases to the Supreme Court. This prevented that court from interpreting procedural and civil liberty safeguards, leaving such interpretation to the circuit or district judges. The Federalists had not developed a theory of how the criminal justice system should work. The system, if it can be called that, was a mixture of constitutional and statutory provisions, state practice, and the common law. The Republicans faced a challenge. Would they be able to establish a system or would they merely expand upon what they inherited? Would they, when their policies were opposed, react with invidious legislation? Would they depoliticize the system or continue with the precedents established by the Federalists? Finally, would they attempt to codify the system to provide a true national, uniform system of justice, or would they keep the compromises of the first and subsequent Congresses that left such things as process and jury selection dependent upon state practice?

NOTES

1. See Bradley Chapin, *Criminal Justice in Colonial America, 1606-1660* (Athens, 1983); Oliver P. Chitwood, *Justice in Colonial Virginia* (Baltimore, 1905); Julius Goebel, Jr., and T. Raymond Naughton, *Law Enforcement in Colonial New York: A Study in Criminal Procedure, 1664-1776* (reprint, Montclair, N. J., 1970); George Lee Haskins, *Law and Authority in Early Massachusetts: A Study in Tradition and Design* (New York, 1960); William E. Nelson, *Americanization of the Common Law: The Impact of Legal Change on Massachusetts Society, 1760-1830* (Cambridge and London, 1975); Arthur P. Scott, *Criminal Trials in Colonial Virginia* (Chicago, 1930); Raphael Semmes, *Crime and Punishment in Early Maryland* (reprint, Montclair, N. J., 1970); and George A. Washburne, *Imperial Control of the Administration of Justice in the Thirteen American Colonies* (New York, 1923).

2. John Bach McMaster and Frederick D. Stone, eds., *Pennsylvania and the Federal Constitution, 1787-1788* (Lancaster, 1888), 368-401. For a complete discussion of the judiciary in the constitutional and ratifying conventions see Julius Goebel, Jr., *The Oliver Wendell Holmes Devise History of the Suprme Court of the United States*, vol. I, *Antecedence and Beginning to 1801* (New York and London, 1971), 196-412; and Dwight F. Henderson, *Courts for a New Nation* (Washington, D.C., 1971), 5-19.

3. See "The Address and Reasons of Dissent of the Minority of the Convention of Pennsylvania to Their Constituents," published in the Pennyslvania *Packet and Daily Advertiser*, December 18, 1787, and reprinted in Herbert J. Storing, ed., *The Complete Anti-Federalist* (7 vols., Chicago and London, 1981), III:145-161; and "Essays of Brutus," published in the New York *Journal*, October 1787-April 1788, and reprinted in ibid., II:358-452.

4. Alexander Hamilton even suggested in the Federalist No. 81 that federal and state judges "may hold circuits for the trial of causes in several parts of the respective districts." *The Federalist* (Modern Library Edition, New York, 1941), 528.

5. "Address by Cato Uticensis," published in the Virginia *Independent Chronicle*, October 17, 1787, reprinted in Storing, *The Complete Anti-Federalist*, V:122-123.

6. See Charles Warren, "New Light on the History of the Federal Judiciary Act of

1789," *Harvard Law Review* 37 (November, 1923), 49-132; Goebel, *History of the Supreme Court*, I:457-458; and Henderson, *Courts for a New Nation*, 20-26.

7. U. S. Congress, *Statutes at Large of the United States of America, 1789-1873* (17 vols., Boston, 1850-1873), I:73-79, (hereafter cited as *U.S. Statutes at Large*).

8. Ibid., 76, 87-88.

9. Ibid., 76, 81-83, 88-93.

10. Ibid., 88.

11. Ibid., 91-92.

12. On the origin and adoption of the Bill of Rights see Robert Allen Rutland, *The Birth of the Bill of Rights, 1776-1791* (Chapel Hill, 1955); and Edward Dumbauld, *The Bill of Rights and What It Means Today* (Norman, 1957).

13. 1 *U. S. Statutes at Large*, 93-94; and Goebel, *History of the Supreme Court*, I:509-551.

14. U. S. Congress, Senate, *Journal of the Executive Proceedings of the Senate of the United States, 1789-1905* (90 vols., Washington, D. C., 1828-1919), I:25, 68, 82, 84, 106, 108-109, 131.

15. 1 *U. S. Statutes at Large*, 112-119.

16. *Del. Law*, 1789, pp. 957-958; *Penn. Laws* (Dallas, 1789), 760-761; *Md. Laws*, 1789, chap. 30; 13 *Vir. Statutes at Large* (Henning, 1789), 3; *Mass. Laws*, 1790, p. 59; *R. I. Laws*, 1790, p. 616; *N. H. Laws*, 1790, p. 146; *Vt. Session Laws*, 1792, p. 116; *Ky. Acts*, 1798, p. 42; *Conn. Acts and Laws*, 1792, p. 224; *N. J. Laws*, 1799, p. 82; *S. C. Acts*, 1800, pp. 342-344; *Journal of the Senate*, I:84, 311.

17. See David J. Rothman, *The Discovery of the Asylum: Social Order and Disorder in the New Republic* (Boston, 1971); W. David Lewis, *From Newgate to Dannemora: The Rise of the Penitentiary in New York 1796-1848* (Ithaca, 1965); and Michael S. Hindus, *Prison and Plantation: Crime, Justice and Authority in Massachusetts and South Carolina, 1767-1878* (Chapel Hill, 1980).

18. Blake McKelvey, *American Prisons: A History of Good Intentions* (New York, 1977), 194.

19. U. S. Congress, *American State Papers* (38 vols., Washington, D. C., 1832-1861), *Miscellaneous*, I:21-36.

20. 1 *U. S. Statutes at Large*, 333-335.

21. 2 *U. S. Statutes at Large*, 89-100. The interpretation of the significance of the act given in Max Farrand, "The Judiciary Act of 1801," *American Historical Review* 5 (July, 1900), 682-686, is revised by Kathryn Turner, "Federalist Policy and the Judiciary Act of 1801," *William and Mary Quarterly*, 3rd ser., 22 (January, 1965), 3-32.

22. 1 *U. S. Statutes at Large*, 123, 196, 275-279.

23. Henderson, Courts for a New Nation, 90-94.

24. 1 *U. S. Statutes at Large*, 237.

25. "Opinion of Randolph," May 30, 1793, *American State Papers, Foreign Relations*, I:151; Pennsylvania circuit court, Minute Book, 1792-1795, (Federal Records Center, Suitland, Maryland), 25, 29; Pennsylvania circuit court, Criminal Cases, 1791-1883, file box 1791-1794; Francis Wharton, *State Trials of the United States during the Administrations of Washington and Adams* (Philadelphia 1849), 49-89; Goebel, *History of the Supreme Court*, I:624-627.

26. 1 *U. S. Statutes at Large*, 381-384.

27. Wharton, *State Trials*, 652-654.

28. George Mifflin Dallas, *Life and Writings of Alexander James Dallas* (Philadelphia, 1871), 59-61; Wharton, *State Trials*, 195-196; Goebel, *History of the Supreme Court*, I:631-632.

29. A full discussion of the two cases may be found in James Morton Smith, *Freedom's Fetters: The Alien and Sedition Law and American Civil Liberties* (Ithaca, 1956), 188-220; and John C. Miller, *Crisis in Freedom: The Alien and Sedition Acts* (Boston, 1951), 60-68, 96-102. See also Goebel, *History of the Supreme Court*, I:632-633.

30. Smith, *Freedom's Fetters*, 139; 1 *U. S. Statutes at Large*, 596-597.

31. Smith, *Freedom's Fetters*, 131-155.

32. Alexander DeConde, *The Quasi-War: The Politics and Diplomacy of the Undeclared War With France 1797-1801* (New York, 1966), 155-174; 1 *U. S. Statutes at Large*, 613.

33. 1 *U. S. Statutes at Large*, 573-574.

34. 1 *U. S. Statutes at Large*, 347-349; 2 *U. S. Statutes at Large*, 70-71; W. E. Burghardt Du Bois, *The Suppression of the African Slave Trade to the United States of America 1638-1870* (reprint, Williamstown, Mass., 1970), 80-84.

35. Henderson, *Courts for a New Nation*, 67-70; Pennsylvania circuit court, Minute Book, 1793-1795, pp. 85, 88-90, 92, 117-123; Pennsylvania circuit court, Criminal Cases, 1791-1883, file box 1795; Wharton, *State Trials*, 177-178.

36. Wharton, *State Trials*, 175-176; Pennsylvania circuit court, Criminal Cases, 1791-1883, file box 1795.

37. *U. S.* v. *Thomas Wilson*, *U. S.* v. *Robert Lusk*, and *U. S.* v. *Robert Philson and Herman Husbands*, Pennsylvania circuit court, Criminal Cases, 1791-1883, file box 1795.

38. See Miller, *Crisis in Freedom*; Smith, *Freedom's Fetters*; and Frank Maloy Anderson, "Enforcement of the Alien and Sedition Laws," American Historical Association *Annual Report 1912* (Washington, D. C., 1914), 120. Maloy found that twenty-four or twenty-five people were arrested and at least fifteen indicted. Smith verified at least fifteen indictments and uncovered an additional five unverified indictments. This researcher was able to verify all of the former and two of the latter in addition to finding at least two new unverified indictments: one against the editor of the Newark *Centinel of Freedom* and the other against Alexander Martin, editor of the Baltimore *American*.

39. 1 *U. S. Statutes at Large*, 580-591, 597-604; *American State Papers, Miscellaneous*, I:187-188.

40. Pennsylvania circuit court, Minute Book, 1796-1799, pp. 30-33, 36-39, 46-47, 50-51, 74; Wharton, *State Trials*, 608-609, 612.

41. Pennsylvania circuit court, Minute Book, 1796-1799, p. 80; Minute Book, 1799-1800, pp. 16-18, 77, 90, 94-116, 122.

42. Adams to Charles Lee, May 21, 1800, John Adams, *Works*, Charles Francis Adams, ed. (10 vols., Boston 1850-1856), IX:60-61. Though several of those convicted of lesser crimes petitioned for pardon, Adams refused their requests. See petition of June 5, 1800, Microfilm of the Adams Papers (608 reels, Boston, Massachusetts Historical Society, 1954-1959), reels 120, 398.

2
An Overview of the Republicans and the Criminal Justice System

The first issue to confront the Republicans after they assumed office in 1801 was what to do about the Judiciary Act of 1801. Shortly after taking the oath of office Thomas Jefferson ordered Secretary of State James Madison to hold all undelivered commissions issued either under the Judiciary Act or the act concerning the District of Columbia. Republicans were puzzled, however, about what could be done about the judges who already had their commissions. The solution they reached was to abolish the courts by repealing the Act of 1801.[1] The mechanics, motivations, and Republican divisions over the repeal of the act have been brilliantly portrayed by Richard E. Ellis in the *Jeffersonian Crisis: Courts and Politics in the Young Republic.* The repeal act, enacted on March 8, 1802, restored the 1789 system as amended. In the congressional debates the Federalists repeatedly criticized the unconstitutional nature of abolishing the circuit judgeships. They "warned that the Supreme Court would declare such an act unconstitutional."[2] Federalists already were looking to a pending case, *Marbury* v. *Madison,* to serve that purpose. The case contested Jefferson's right to refuse to deliver commissions to four justices of the peace appointed under the District of Columbia act. The Supreme Court was scheduled to meet in June, a month before the repeal act was due to take effect. Not only would the Court be able to dispose of the *Marbury* case, but it would have the opportunity "to consider the constitutionality of the repeal act before it became operative."[3]

To avoid this head-on collision the Senate appointed a special committee on March 18, 1802, "to re-examine the federal court system and recommend any necessary changes."[4] The committee reported a bill on March 26 which, with subsequent amendments, the Senate approved on April 29, 1802. This act not only altered the times for sessions of the Supreme Court, delaying the Court's next meeting until February 1803, but also restructured the 1789 court system.

Section 4 formed the districts (excepting Maine, Kentucky, and Tennessee) into six circuits in a manner not unlike that provided in the Act of 1801 but, significantly, without separate circuit judges. Section 6 contained an important procedural change. It required that any point of disagreement between the judges, upon request of either party or their counsel, would be certified to the Supreme Court to be finally decided. The decision of the Supreme Court would then be remitted to the circuit court and recorded. There were two exceptions: one that a cause should proceed, "if, in the opinion of the court, farther [sic] proceedings can be had without prejudice to the merits" and another "that imprisonment shall not be allowed, nor punishment in any case inflicted, where the judges of the said court are divided in opinion upon the question touching the said imprisonment or punishment."[5] This section would require clarification by over fifty Supreme Court decisions, and it would be the nearest the system would come to permitting full Supreme Court review of criminal cases until 1889.[6]

The major organizational deficiency of the act was the lack of a western circuit. In 1807, through a bill sponsored by Henry Clay, Congress created the seventh circuit and added a new associate justice residing in that circuit to the Supreme Court.[7] This addition was the closest the judicial system came to offering a circuit court in each state until 1837. Presidents Madison, James Monroe, and John Quincy Adams from time to time urged the Congress to undertake a reorganization of the court structure. Between 1812 and 1828 the topic arose nine times in either the House or the Senate. The Senate twice approved bills, in 1819 and 1820, but the House failed to act. The only expansion to occur came in 1820 when Congress added Maine to the first circuit when it was admitted as a state.[8]

The Republicans made very few changes in procedures used in the courts. Senator William Branch Giles of Virginia introduced a resolution in February 1809 requesting that a committee be appointed to inquire into the expediency of amending the previous process acts in order that circuit and district courts of the United States "shall be subjected to, and be regulated by, the laws of the several States in which they shall be held, which are now in existence, or may hereafter be enacted, regulating the issuing of process, the proceedings thereon, and the suspension thereof."[9] Although nothing came of the motion, the issue was not forgotten. The matter surfaced again in 1825 when the seventh circuit court certified two cases—*Wayman* v. *Southard* and *The Bank of the United States* v. *Halstead*—to the Supreme Court. Both cases dealt in part with the issue of process. When Congress convened in December 1825, Representative Charles A. Wickliffe of Kentucky offered a resolution in the House requesting that "a law ought to pass prescribing more specifically what processes ought to be used in the courts of the United States."[10] The Senate referred the matter to the Judiciary Committee, chaired by Daniel Webster, which reported on February 13, 1826. The committee found some difficulty in recommending a law to render execution process uniform in all the courts of the United States.[11] Although the matter was not continued during the session, it arose again in January 1828. This time a new act emerged, approved on May 19, 1828. Section 1 stipulated that the forms of mesne (intermediate) process held in the states admitted since 1789 and in those of common law "shall be the same in each of the said states, respectively, as are now used in the highest court, or original and general jurisdiction of the same. . . ." The section permitted United States' courts to make such alterations and additions as the courts deemed expedient and subject "to such regulations as the Supreme Court of the United States shall think proper, from time to time, by rules, to prescribe to any circuit or district court concerning the same." Section 3 provided that writs of execution and other final process issued on judgments and decrees should be the same as were "now adopted by the legislatures of the respective states for the state courts." The final section excluded the federal court of Louisiana from the operation of the act. Undoubtedly the process bill was a victory for the states' rights advocates. It reinforced the close ties through procedure between the state and federal courts.[12] Although the Republicans were reluctant to alter the structure or procedures of the court, they were not hesitant when it came to the personnel.

During the balloting by the House of Representatives to elect a president, Thomas Jefferson wrote to Dr. B. S. Barton that "no man who has conducted himself according to his duties would have anything to fear from me. . . ."[13] To obtain an appointment, however, would be different. "The Republicans," Jefferson maintained, "have been excluded from all offices from the first origin of the division into Republican and Federalist. They have a reasonable claim to vacancies till they occupy their due share."[14] Shortly after his inauguration Jefferson indicated that a few removals would be indispensable, but that they would be "chiefly for real malconduct, & mostly in the offices connected with the administration of justice."[15] With a set policy in the offing, Jefferson wrote to William Branch Giles on March 23, 1801, that the following principles had been the subject of conversation but not determination:

(1) All appointments to *civil* offices *during pleasure*, made after the event of the election was certainly known to Mr. Adams, are considered as nullities. (2) Officers who have been guilty of *official* malconduct are proper subjects of removal. (3) Good men, to whom there is no objection but a difference of political principle . . . are not proper subjects of removal, except in the case of attorneys and marshals.

Jefferson singled out the latter because he felt that the courts were "so decidedly federal and irremovable" that Republican court officers were "indispensably necessary as a shield to the republican part of our fellow-citizens. . . ."[16] To Benjamin Rush, Jefferson explained what he meant by misconduct, and again he took the example from the judiciary:

The marshal in your city, who being an officer of justice, intrusted with the function of choosing impartial judges [jurors] for the trial of his fellow-citizens . . . selected judges [jurors] who either avowed, or were known to him to be predetermined to condemn. . . . The same practice of packing juries, and prosecuting their fellow-citizens with the bitterness of party hatred will probably involve several other marshals and attorneys.[17]

Jefferson's patronage policy did not go unopposed. Shortly after removing Elizur Goodrich from the post of collector, Jefferson received a remonstrance from a committee of merchants of New Haven. In his reply Jefferson sought to test his policy publicly. After indicating that the monopoly of office should not be continued in the hands of the minority he asked, "How are vacancies to be obtained? Those by death are few; by resignation none. Can any other mode than that of removal be proposed?"[18] The effect of his reply was greater than Jefferson had anticipated. "The Republicans," he lamented to Albert Gallatin, "hope for a great number of removals; the Federals also expect it." Jefferson desired the matter to end quickly.[19]

Carl Prince has pointed out that most historians have accepted these expressions of moderation as being the Jefferson policy. Prince discovered that Jefferson removed 146 of 316 second level officeholders (46 percent) "at least 118 (37 percent) of whom can be identified as hardcore Federalist party cadre occupying the most politically useful offices in their respective states." Andrew Jackson, who is generally accredited with the initiation of the spoils system, removed 252 of 610 incumbents or 41.3 percent. One may conclude that Jefferson, not Jackson, commenced the spoils system.[20]

It was natural, in view of Jefferson's stated policy and the feeling that the Federalists had "retreated into the judiciary as a stronghold," that the judicial system would be the subject of numerous removals. Of the 146 persons removed, thirteen were district attorneys and eighteen were marshals.

The judges presented a more difficult problem. Judges held office for life. Outright removal was impossible. The repeal of the Judiciary Act of 1801 eliminated fifteen circuit judges (the sixteenth judgeship was vacant and thus subject to Jefferson's appointment). Two district judges, Ray Greene of Rhode Island and Jacob Read of South Carolina, were displaced. Jefferson removed Greene on a technicality, claiming that Greene's commission was invalid because of a flaw. Read never held his office because

Thomas Bee, whom Adams appointed to the circuit court, declined that appointment. Jefferson refused to recognize Read's commission on the "grounds that no vacancy existed, inasmuch as Bee had never properly resigned." Even though Jefferson lacked the removal power, "eighteen of thirty Federalist partisans were cleared from the bench by 1803."[21]

Still this was not enough. John Pickering, district judge of New Hampshire, showed evidence of definite mental derangement a short time before Jefferson became president. Perhaps with Pickering or his predecessor on New Hampshire's district court, John Sullivan, in mind, the Judiciary Act of 1801 had authorized the circuit judges to appoint one of their number to "exercise the functions of any district judge who became incapacitated." Between 1802, when Congress repealed the Act of 1801, and 1809, when Congress finally approved a new law, there was no provision for dealing with cases such as Pickering's other than to resort to impeachment. The Constitution provided that the only impeachable offensives were treason, bribery, or other high crimes and misdemeanors. The strict constructionist Republicans would have to apply a broad interpretation to the Constitution to impeach Pickering. Nevertheless the House brought charges against Pickering, and the Senate convicted him. The roll call vote found nineteen Republican Senators approving his removal, while seven Federalist Senators opposed it. Thus Pickering became the first federal judge to be impeached, convicted, and removed.[22] William Plummer wrote on the day following the Senate's vote, "How far these proceedings will form a precedent to establish the doctrine, that when requested by a majority of the House, two-thirds of the Senate can remove a Judge from office without a formal conviction of high crimes and misdemeanors, time alone can develop."[23] The day Plummer wrote his missive, the House impeached Samuel Chase, associate justice of the Supreme Court. To a number of Republicans who had had some difficulty in subscribing to the impeachment of Pickering, the charges against Chase went too far. Six Republicans voted with nine Federalists to prevent the conviction of Chase by one vote.[24]

Jefferson completed the removals within the first two years of his administration; however, the problem of appointments was perennial. The one indispensable qualification was that a person should be a Republican. Of the seventy appointees of Jefferson to posts of judge, district attorney, and marshal, only one, Silas Lee, district attorney for Maine, was a Federalist.[25] Although Sidney Aronson[26] found a slight drop in the qualifications of Jefferson appointees compared with those of John Adams, the Republican personnel were well qualified for the positions they occupied.

Jefferson's successors—Madison, Monroe, and John Quincy Adams—did not have to face the issue of political removals. Each, however, confronted the more difficult problem of intraparty factionalism. For example, Madison encountered little difficulty in appointing two ex-Federalists to office,

William Davies as attorney in Georgia and David Howell as district judge of Rhode Island. The strife between the Smith faction, a group of hostile Senators led by Samuel Smith of Maryland, and Gallatin, an intraparty struggle, created numerous difficulties for Madison. The group forced Madison to appoint Samuel's brother Robert Smith to the post of Secretary of State instead of Gallatin.[27] Late in Monroe's second administration several members of the cabinet began vying for the Presidency. Monroe was forced, as he put it, either to distribute the offices among friends of the candidates "to avoid charges of favoritism" or to "take my own course and appoint those whom I knew & confided in, without regard to them." Monroe lamented that if he had pursued the former, "the office in my hands, for two or three years of the latter term, would have sunk to nothing." He therefore adopted the latter and steadily pursued it, believing that he had given "sufficient proof of respect for, and confidence in each of the members, of the administration by appointing and continuing him in his place."[28] Monroe also attempted to carry out a policy of assimilation. He wrote to Andrew Jackson on December 14, 1816, that his administration would "rest strongly on the Republican party," but he hoped to bring the whole Union into "the Republican fold as quickly as possible." In 1818 he nominated William B. Irish, "an out and out Federalist," for the post of marshal for the western district of Pennsylvania. Although several Republicans opposed Irish, the Senate confirmed him. When Monroe recommended his appointment in 1822, however, the Senate rejected Irish 26 to 14.[29]

John Quincy Adams attempted to continue the policy of assimilating Federalists. Adams twice appointed Federalists to judicial posts. Following the death of Marshal Paul Bantalou of Maryland in 1826, Adams recommended Thomas Finley, a Federalist, for the position. Before Adams submitted the nomination to the Senate, Peter Little, long-time Congressman from Maryland, warned him that Finley's appointment would have an unfavorable effect upon the administration. Adams bitterly wrote in his diary:

It is upon the occasion of appointments to office that all the wormwood and the gall of the old party hatred oozed out. Not a vacancy to any office occurs but there is a distinguished Federalist started and pushed home as a candidate to fill it—always well qualified, sometimes in an imminent degree, and yet so obnoxious to the Republican party that he cannot be appointed . . . without offending one-half of the community—the Federalists, if their associate is overlooked; the Republicans, if he is preferred.

The Senate confirmed Finley.[30] Again in 1828 Adams appointed a Federalist, John Duer, as district attorney for the southern district of New York—this time without major opposition. By 1828, however, with a new Presidential campaign in progress, the old rancor between Republicans and

Federalists had been replaced by new competition between Adams and Andrew Jackson. Friends of Adams strongly pressured him to use his patronage power at least to reward the faithful if not to displace the disloyal. Adams resisted the pressure—according to Samuel Bemis, he "would do nothing to build up a political machine to keep himself in power." In fact, in one case where the man was delinquent in his duties, Adams refused to replace him because it was impossible to prove that the removal was not done in retribution for the appointee's stand against Adams.[31]

Madison, Monroe, and Adams made a total of 150 judicial appointments, only five of whom were Federalists. The general qualifications for office, aside from party affiliation, appear to be compatible throughout the Jeffersonian period.[32] Comparing these appointees to Aronson's study of John Adams, Jefferson, and Jackson does not reveal major differences. (See Table 2.) The marshals of the former groups do not appear to merit the title of elite; the attorneys apparently do. Generally the attorneys and judges compare favorably to the elite of the latter Presidents. Two categories—federal service and military service—reveal some discrepancies. The decline in federal service perhaps demonstrates that a bureaucracy had gradually developed under the Jeffersonians, providing fewer and fewer people with the opportunity for prior service. The decline in military service may be attributed to the gradual elimination of Revolutionary veterans due to advanced age or death.[33]

Table 2.
Qualifications of Appointees

APPOINTIVE PRESIDENT	COLLEGE EDUCATION	PROVINCIAL OR STATE SERVICE	FEDERAL SERVICE	MILITARY SERVICE
John Adams*	63%	72%	65%	57%
Jefferson	52%	62%	61%	53%
Jackson	52%	64%	62%	39%
Madison, John Quincy Adams and Monroe				
Judges	56%	61%	43%	17%
Attorneys	42%	71%	35%	24%
Marshals	10%	36%	18%	39%

*Data on John Adams, Jefferson, and Jackson taken from Aronson, *Status and Kinship*, pp. 104, 108, 124.

Jefferson and his successors faced numerous difficulties with the expansion of criminal jurisdictions. Two interesting and controversial episodes revealed the opinion of Congress on the concepts of seditious libel, free press, and the common law. The first episode began in Connecticut in 1806 when Pierrepont Edwards, recently appointed as federal district judge, charged the circuit court grand jury "to examine the newspapers to see if nothing had appeared against the officers of the General Government." According to both the contemporary newspaper and later historical accounts, the grand jury had been carefully picked by the Republican marshal. At the April term of the court, the grand jury found indictments under the common law against Judge Tapping Reeve for articles he had published in the Litchfield *Monitor*; against Thomas Collier, the editor of the Litchfield *Monitor*, for the following sentence: "There is (says an energetic modern writer) a point of profligacy in the line of human impudence, at which the most disguised heart seems to lose all sensibility to shame; and we congratulate the American public that our chief magistrate has so completely arrived at this enviable point"; and against Thaddeus Osgood, a candidate for the ministry. In the fall the grand jury returned indictments against Hudson and Goodwin, editors of the Connecticut *Courant* of Hartford, and against the Rev. Azel Backus of Bethlehem. During the session the district attorney moved for a warrant against Judge Reeve, but Judge Edwards refused to issue it allegedly because Edwards was related to Reeve by marriage. The court scheduled the trials of the other five defendants for April 1807.[34]

Jefferson did not institute the prosecutions, yet he did not disapprove of or halt the proceedings. The trials received national attention early in 1807. Late in 1806 the President requested the House to formulate new legislation on illegal expeditions. A bill was shortly thereafter presented, discussed, and recommitted. The revised report came to the House on January 2, 1807. Representative Samuel W. Dana of Connecticut seized the opportunity to reveal the Connecticut prosecutions to the public. After a few general and somewhat inaccurate remarks, Dana offered a resolution requesting the formation of a committee to

inquire whether prosecutions at common law should be sustained, in the courts of the United States, for libelous publications, or defamatory words, touching persons holding offices or places of trust under the United States, and whether it would not be proper, if the same be sustained, to allow the parties prosecuted the liberty of giving the truth in evidence. . . .

Dana moved to refer the resolution to the committee of the whole. Taken aback, the Republicans did not defend or explain the Connecticut cases but disputed the necessity of referring the resolutions to the Committee of the Whole. Representative William Ely of Massachusetts suggested two substitute resolutions:

Resolved, That the common law of England is not a part of the law of the United States, except so far as it has been adopted by the laws of the United States or of the individual states; and that the prosecution of a person at common law for libel is a violation of the freedom of the press, and contrary to the Constitution of the United States, [and] Resolved, That in all prosecutions, whether criminal or otherwise, it is the natural right of the citizen to give in evidence the truth.

The House eventually approved Dana's original resolution and referred it to the Committee of the Whole. It does not appear that the issue was brought up during the remainder of the session. The Federalists continued their attack, however, by introducing into the debates over the new act concerning expeditions references to the unconstitutional nature of the Sedition Act of 1798 and the indictment of Luther Baldwin of New Jersey under that act.[35]

The scene shifted back to Connecticut in April. When the cases were brought up for trial, Judge Edwards discovered defects in the indictments of several of the defendants. The district attorney entered a *nolle prosequi* (will not further prosecute) in the case of Osgood. The grand jury immediately found new bills against Hudson and Goodwin and Backus. The defense counsel made two motions: one questioning the jurisdiction of the court over common law crimes and the second requesting a postponement until a member of the Supreme Court joined the district judge. Judge Edwards dismissed the motions but soon discovered that the marshal had impaneled the petit jury contrary to the laws of Connecticut. Thus the court dismissed the petit jury and postponed the cases until September.[36]

When the defense made similar motions concerning the jurisdiction of the court and the necessity of having a member of the Supreme Court on the bench in September, Judge Edwards (to the surprise of the defendants) ruled (except in the case of Backus) that "a decision on the plea to the court's jurisdiction should not be made until he was joined by a member of the Supreme Court." Backus insisted on being tried. Edwards countered that it was not "in his [Backus's] best interest to be tried." Edwards postponed the trial over the protest of the defendant. Leonard Levy claims that Edward's turnabout occurred because Jefferson had finally discovered the exact nature of the Backus libel.

The libel in question concerned the "Walker affair," of 1768, when Jefferson seems to have attempted the seduction of a friend's wife. . . . Since the Reverend Backus had the facts on his side and had already subpoenaed the lady's husband, as well as James Madison and other Virginians, the decision to prevent the trial from occurring was understandable.[37]

In 1808 the district attorney dropped the prosecutions against Backus, Collier, and Reeve "but arranged for the appeal of the cases of Hudson and

Goodwin, prior to trial, to the Supreme Court on their plea to the jurisdiction of the Circuit Court."[38]

Because of the failure of the clerk of the Connecticut circuit court to forward the certificate, the Supreme Court did not take up the case in 1809. A few months after Jefferson left office, John Randolph of Roanoke renewed the question of the previous session, calling upon the House to appoint a committee "to inquire whether any and what prosecutions have been entertained by the courts for the United States for libels at common law, and to report such provisions as in their opinion may be necessary for securing the freedom of speech and of the press." In his preface to the resolution Randolph asserted the absolute interpretation of the First Amendment, i.e., that Congress had no right to pass any law at all on the subject. Recalling the objection to the Sedition Act, he claimed that it was not "to the nature of the law that we objected, but to the having a federal law of libel at all. . . ." Randolph voiced even greater opposition to the common law.

If Congress or the courts below, can at once saddle us with the common law of England, there is no necessity for prohibiting the abridgement of the freedom of speech, or of the press. We know what the common law of England is—an unlimited license to print, and an almost equally unlimited license to punish.

The House approved the motion unanimously.[39]

Two days later on May 27 Richard Stanford of North Carolina proposed to expand the inquiry to include prosecutions conducted under the Sedition Act and the "expediency of remunerating the sufferers under such prosecution." Although most history texts commonly and falsely assert that Jefferson refunded the fines of those convicted under the Sedition Act, the fines had not been restored. Mathew Lyon, one of the "sufferers" and now a member of the House from Kentucky, confirmed the fact. A rather extended debate ensued over Lyon's case specifically and the general issue of whether Congress had the power to remunerate the sufferers. The House finally approved a motion to postpone consideration indefinitely, 69 to 50. The session ended before the committee reported on Randolph's resolution.[40]

With the decision of the Supreme Court still pending, in November 1811 Mathew Lyon petitioned Congress for the repayment of his fine with interest as well as his pay as a member of Congress which had been withheld while he was in prison. There was discussion whether the petition should be referred to the Committee of Claims or a select committee to include an inquiry into the gist of Randolph's resolution proposed in 1809. The House agreed to the amendment and referred the petition to a select committee of seven. The committee made no report during the session.[41]

The Supreme Court finally issued its opinion on the jurisdictional question in 1812. Neither William Pinkney for the United States nor

Samuel W. Dana for the defendants argued the case. Justice William Johnson wrote the brief opinion of the court and concluded that certain implied powers

must necessarily result to our courts of justice from the nature of their institution. But jurisdiction of crimes against the state is not among those powers. To fine for contempt, imprison for contumacy, enforce the observance of order, etc., are powers which cannot be dispensed within a court, because they are necessary to the exercise of all others; and so far as our courts no doubt possess power not immediately derived from statute; but all exercise of criminal jurisdiction in common law cases, we are of opinion, is not within their implied powers.[42]

The scene shifted back to Congress in 1814 when the House instructed the Judiciary Committee to inquire whether the Constitution required the United States "to extend the jurisdiction of the courts of the United States to cases now provided for by law; and, also, the expediency of such extension." Charles Jared Ingersoll of Pennyslvania reported a bill for the committee in March. Section 11 granted jurisdiction to the circuit court "over all common law and admiralty and maritime crimes and offences, which under the Constitution, are cognizable by the judicial power of the United States" and provided that where no other punishment was prescribed by law to levy a fine of not more than $1,000 and imprisonment of not more than one year or both. On April 5 the House indefinitely postponed the bill.[43]

Two years later in 1816 Justice Joseph Story wrote a bill that would have given general jurisdiction to punish crimes committed against the Federal Government to the United States' courts. In a lengthy manuscript prepared for use of a friend in Congress, Story argued that "few, very few, of the practical crimes . . . are now punishable by statutes, and if the court have [sic] no general common law jurisdiction . . . they are wholly dispunishable." Story contended that the United States had an uncontestable right to provide for all crimes against the United States.

The only question is, whether this is to be done by passing laws in detail respecting every crime in every possible shape, or shall give the Courts general jurisdiction to punish wherever the authority of the United States is violated, and leave the Courts to settle this by legal constructions, upon common law principles.

Story felt it was impractical to legislate for each specific crime. "Crimes are so various in their nature and character, and so infinitely diversified in their circumstances, that it is almost impossible to enumerate and define them with the requisite certainty. An ingenious rogue will almost always escape from the text of the statute book." Congress was not persuaded and postponed the bill indefinitely.[44]

Whatever hope that proponents had that the common law might be adopted by the federal government was dealt a fatal blow in the period from 1817-1826 by a rising set of American jurists who seemed to capture the nationalism and expansionism of the post-war period. John Milton Goodenow, Peter S. Du Ponceau, Charles Jared Ingersoll, and William Duane all produced important works during the period. Goodenow captured the public's fancy when he declared that the English law was inadequate for the American frontier.[45]

The common law issue had apparently been laid to rest; however, the issue of refunding the fine of Mathew Lyon would not die. In 1818 he again petitioned the Senate for remuneration. In the course of the discussion over the report of the Judiciary Committee on the memorial, Senator John J. Crittenden introduced a resolution providing that all persons, prosecuted and fined under the second section of the Sedition Act, should be reimbursed and indemnified out of the public treasury. Crittenden explained that he "considered the sedition act as having been unconstitutional not only from a defect of power in Congress to pass such a law, but because its passage was expressly forbidden by the Constitution." Harrison Gray Otis of Massachusetts, the only remaining Senator to have voted for the Sedition Act, did not believe the act was unconstitutional. Every government, he maintained, has an inherent right to punish offences which endanger its existence; and this definition provided a justification for the law. Although Otis considered the law inexpedient, he did not consider it new in principle. He pointed out that similar provisions existed in several of the states. Finally, he contended that the judiciary, not Congress, should determine the constitutionality of the act. The Senate rejected Crittenden's resolution 20 to 17; however, it approved the report of the committee denying Lyon's compensation with twenty ayes.[46]

Lyon was not dissuaded. The following year he petitioned the President, who in turn sent the petition to Congress. Both the Senate and House referred the memorial to committees. Neither body reported during the session.[47] Lyon encountered initial success in 1821. Congress referred his petition to a select committee which reported in January 1821. The committee recommended by resolution that much of the Sedition Act of 1798 which pretended to prescribe and punish libels, was unconstitutional and that the fines collected under the act should be restored to those from whom they were exacted.

The debates over the resolution did not differ significantly from those of 1818. William Smith of South Carolina asserted more fully than Otis the right of the courts not Congress to judge the constitutionality of the acts. He told his colleagues:

You have the power to enact laws, but no power to sit in judgment upon those laws. It is expressly and exclusively given to the judges to construe the laws, and to decide upon their constitutionality. . . . You have power to punish judges for corruption, but none to revise and correct their decisions.

Although the common law again was discussed, no mention was made that the Supreme Court in the case of *Hudson and Goodwin* in 1812, and later in the case of *Coolidge* in 1816, had rejected the concept of a federal common law. On January 21 the Senate indefinitely postponed the resolution 24 to 191.[48]

Simultaneous with the action of the Senate, the House Judiciary Committee issued a report stating that they felt that law was unconstitutional and that Lyon should be reimbursed and added a strange statement: if the committee should be mistaken concerning the constitutionality of the law, Lyon should still be reimbursed because of the "peculiar circumstances of hardships attending" his case. The report was not acted upon during the session.[49]

Lyon's case appeared for a final time in 1827. Representative James Hamiton, Jr., of South Carolina proposed on January 18 that the fines exacted under the Sedition Act should be refunded. The House rejected the resolution 80 to 72.[50]

The consistent rejections from both Houses of Congress from 1811 to 1827 prompts one to conclude that a slim majority in Congress had accepted Otis's reasoning that the issue of constitutionality should be resolved by the courts and/or that every government has an inherent right to punish offences which endanger its existence. Both views have been consistently upheld by the Supreme Court in numerous cases until the present.

During the Jeffersonian period Congress enacted numerous acts expanding the federal criminal jurisdiction. Several of these will be treated in detail in separate chapters—such as acts pertaining to the embargo, neutrality, the War of 1812, and the slave trade. Congress enacted two acts concerning crimes relating to control of the Indian nations. The first of these, passed in 1802, prohibited hunting on Indian lands, using Indian lands as a range for cattle, entering Indian lands without a passport, selling goods to Indians without a license, purchasing Indian goods (including a separate category for horses), entering into illegal treaty negotiations, and committing crimes including murder on Indian territory. The penalites were mild for most of the crimes ranging from a fine of $50 and three months imprisonment for entering without a passport to a fine of $1,000 and imprisonment for twelve months for entering into illegal treaty negotiations. There were, however, two strange features. If a citizen should enter into any area under the control of a nation or tribe of Indians and commit "robbery, larceny, trespass, or any other crime against the person or property of any friendly Indian or Indians, which could be punishable, if committed within the jurisdiction of any State, against a citizen of the United States," the offender would forfeit a sum of $100 and suffer imprisonment of twelve months "and shall also, when property is taken or destroyed, forfeit and pay to such Indian or Indians, to whom the property taken and destroyed belongs, a sum equal to twice the just value of the property so taken or destroyed." If the offender could not pay the double value, whatever payment should fall short would be paid out of the treasury of the United States. The final stipulation was that no such Indian should be entitled to payment out of the treasury if he "or any of the nation to which he belongs, shall have sought private revenge, or attempted to obtain satisfaction by any force or violence." The second feature was that if a citizen should enter into any town of an Indian nation and commit murder, the offender, upon conviction, should suffer death.[51]

Two things should be noticed about the provisions. First, it is the only act during the period providing penalties plus monetary compensation to the offended party. Second, the penalties, except for murder, appear to be mild, considering the number of possible crimes covered. The possibility enters one's mind that the Congress did not consider crimes against Indians on the same level as crimes against other citizens. An act of 1817 brought Indians and other persons in the Indian territory under general federal criminal jurisdiction.[52]

Postal crimes sharply increased during the early 1800s. In 1810 Congress passed a Postal Act which revised and expanded the crimes and penalties contained in the Act of 1792. Penalties ranged from a $5 fine for concealing a letter in a newspaper to death for wounding a mail carrier in the commission of a robbery or for the second conviction of robbing the mail. Between the extremes were a large number of crimes, among which were obstructing the mail (fine of $100), operating a competing postal system (fine $50), counterfeiting frank (fine $50), and mutilating a mail bag (fine $500). If a postal employee should detain, delay, open, embezzle, or destroy a letter, he could be fined $300 and sentenced to six months imprisonment. If the letter contained a bank note or bill, he could be imprisoned for ten years. A non-postal employee could be sentenced to ten years imprisonment for the first offence of robbing the mail, three years for using force but not being successful in robbing the mail, seven years for stealing mail, and a fine of $500 for illegally opening the mail. The act protected newspapers with a separate listing of offences: including a fine of $50 for an employee who should destroy a newspaper, a fine of $20 for a nonemployee who should destroy a newspaper, and imprisonment of three months at hard labor for stealing a newspaper. The act also provided that all accessories to postal crimes would receive the same penalties as the principals.[53] The relative harshness of the penalties reflected Congress' view that the safety of the mails was a prime concern in a developing economy which depended upon safe, efficient communication as an important stimulus to growth.

Congress enacted a new act to provide protection to the Bank of the United States. In 1806 the Georgia grand jury indicted Baylis Corder and Zebulon Cantril for passing forged bills of the Bank of the United States. The jury convicted the men in separate trials; whereupon, their counsel moved an arrest of judgment contending: that the indictment was insufficient and repugnant, inasmuch as it charged the prisoner with having uttered and published as true a certain false, forged, and counterfeit paper, partly written and partly printed, purporting to be a bank bill of the United States for ten dollars, signed by Thomas Willing, President, and G. Simpson, Cashier &c.; and because the act of Congress of 1798 under which the prisoner was indicted "or so much thereof as related to the charge set forth in the indictment" was "inconsistent, repugnant, and therefore, void." The circuit judges divided in opinion relative to the construction of the act and thus certified the proceedings to the Supreme Court. Chief Justice John Marshall, without hearing argument and without reasons, issued the opinion of the court in 1807 in the case of Cantril and applied the ruling also to Corder. Marshall ruled that "the judgment ought to be arrested, for the reasons assigned in the record," and "directed the opinion to be certified accordingly." The prisoner was duly discharged by the circuit court. The court's ruling was equivalent to declaring the Act of 1798, which contained but a single section, unconstitutional.

Congress hastily rectified the situation in 1807 when it passed an act to punish frauds committed on the Bank of the United States. The act made it a crime to falsely make, forge, or counterfeit notes of the Bank of the United States or checks or orders thereon. Upon conviction for one of the crimes a person could be imprisoned and kept at hard labor from three to ten years and fined a sum not exceeding $5,000. A proviso stipulated that "nothing herein contained shall be construed to deprive the courts of the individual states of a jurisdiction under the laws of the several states, over the offense, declared unpunishable by this act."[54] When Congress established the second Bank of the United States in 1816, the chartering act contained a crimes section with similar definitions and penalties for criminal acts. The act added as a crime using plates to counterfeit notes with a penalty of five years imprisonment and a fine of $1,000.[55]

In addition to the acts dealing with specific types of crimes, Congress twice made additions to the general Crimes Act of 1790. In 1804 Congress added the crime of willfully and corruptly casting away, burning, or otherwise destroying any ship or vessel. The penalty upon conviction was death. The act provided the same penalty for an owner who should commit the crime. The act also established a five-year limit for trying a person guilty of any crime arising under the revenue laws or incurring any fine or forfeiture by breaches of the said laws.[56]

The massive evasion and violation of laws which occurred in the period from 1806 to 1812 (see Chapter 6) led to a movement to revise the penal code. In March 1812 Representative James Milnor of Pennsylvania proposed to the House that the Attorney General be directed to examine and recommend changes to the code. Milnor explained that in many instances crimes were not defined with sufficient precision; in other cases, such as assault and battery on the high seas, there was no court vested with jurisdiction to try the offence. Milnor also wondered whether the punishments inflicted by the laws of the United States "ought not to be accommodated to the prevailing sentiments of the time, as expressed by the Legislatures of the several States in regard to punishments."[57] The House approved the resolution, but the War of 1812 delayed consideration of the matter for several years. Attempts were made again in 1818 and in 1823. Late in 1824 the House commenced considering a bill "more effectually to provide for the punishment of certain crimes against the United States, and for other purposes." Congress intended the act to clarify jurisdiction between federal, state, and international courts over admiralty crimes; ameliorate the punishments assigned to crimes under previous acts; and add additional crimes not previously defined. The bill originally contained sixteen sections but ended up with twenty-six sections as approved on March 3, 1825.[58]

The act was conservative—seemingly out of touch with the reforms that had occurred in the states. The debates in the House revealed that not all Congressmen were unaware of the reform movement. Representative Wickliffe of Kentucky claimed that the new act contained sixteen additional capital crimes. Wickliffe approved of the death penalty for treason, murder, and rape but felt the large number of new crimes carrying the penalty were uncalled for. Representative William C. Ellis of Pennsylvania supported Wickliffe, stating that

it was easy for a legislator to say that those who broke through the salutary restraints which tend to preserve society are worthy of death; but, where it was found, on experience, that penalties of a milder form were equally effectual in the prevention or diminution of crimes, it would not do to insist on such doctrine.

Representative James Buchanan of Pennsylvania added,

We should, therefore, be careful not to inflict punishments of a nature more severe than the safety of society requires. In all cases where the character of the crime does not involve such a degree of moral depravity in the criminal as to preclude a reasonable hope of his reformation, it would be both unjust and cruel in the extreme, to deprive him of life.

The principal speaker against the act was Representative Edward Livingston of Louisiana who should be called the father of the movement to abolish capital punishment in the United States. Livingston moved to substitute a fine and imprisonment for death as a punishment for the burning of a dwelling house. He "avowed it was his solemn conviction that it was not proper to take away human life as a punishment for any crime whatever." Livingston identified three disadvantages to capital punishment. First, he claimed that in many instances it produced impunity. When death was the only penalty, "witnesses, judges, and jurors were reluctant to convict" with the result that the accused "was too often permitted to escape; or, even, if the evidence was such as to compel his conviction, a pardon interposed to prevent his punishment." Second, the effect on the mind of the public was often detrimental. If capital punishment were frequently used, it either gave a "ferocious character to our population, in cherishing and strengthening those feelings which, in Rome, led to the exhibition of gladiators" or it would lead to indifference. If frequently used, "the sufferer was by sympathy converted into a hero; his crime was forgotten, though of the deepest dye." Third, the punishment once inflicted was irrevocable and "if inflicted wrongfully, admitted of no redress."[59]

Webster defended the act throughout the debates. He regretted "as much as any of the gentlemen could do, the necessity of capital punishment," however "such was not the present system of our laws." He added that the "great object of human punishments is to deter, by example, from the commission of crimes. Laws do not or ought not to proceed on a vindictive principle. Offenders are punished, not to take vengeance of them, but that others may not offend in like manner." Representative George Kremer of Pennsylvania was more blunt. In responding to the third disadvantage of Livingston's he said, "It might as well be said that you must not have a razor to shave your beard, because, forsooth, you might chance cut your throat. What does the penitentiary system, after all, amount to? Experience had demonstrated that it produced a school for crime." He concluded that system was founded on a mistaken "feeling of humanity towards the wrongdoer." Consistently the opponents of capital punishment lost in their attempts to substitute imprisonment for the death penalty.[60]

The act supplanted twelve sections of the Crimes Act of 1790 and replaced one section each of the Piracy Act of 1819, the Piracy Act of 1820, and the Bank Act of 1816. New capital crimes included the burning of a dwelling house on United States property, murder and rape on the high seas, and willfully destroying a vessel. Other crimes added by the act fell into two categories—those committed on United States property or the high seas and those designed to provide additional protection to the national financial system. (See Table 3.)

For general comparison, the maximum imprisonment under the 1790 act was seven years; the maximum fine was $5,000; the maximum physical punishment was thirty-nine stripes and one hour in the pillory. The amount of the fine in several cases was left to the discretion of the court. Under the 1825 act the maximum imprisonment was ten years; the maximum fine, $10,000; and there were no physical or discretionary punishments.

The 1825 act included several new procedural sections. The new legislation gave the federal courts jurisdiction over crimes committed on board any ship or vessel belonging to any citizen or citizens of the United States lying in a port or place within the jurisdiction of any foreign state or sovereign, with the proviso that if the offender should "be tried for such offense, and acquitted or convicted thereof, in any competent court of such foreign state or sovereign, he shall not be subject to another trial in any

Table 3.
Crimes and Punishments under the Crimes Act of 1825

CRIME	ONLY PUNISHMENT
Arson on United States' property of a dwelling	Death
Murder and rape on the high seas	Death
Willfully destroying a vessel	Death

CRIME	MAXIMUM PUNISHMENT
Arson on United States' property of a non-dwelling	10 years hard labor, $5,000
Attack on a ship on the high seas	10 years hard labor, $5,000
Attempt to kill, rob, rape on high seas	5 years hard labor, $1,000
Buying or receiving stolen goods	3 years hard labor, $1,000
Plundering ship in distress	10 years hard labor, $5,000
Leaving mariners or officers on shore	6 months, $500
Extortion by officer of the United States	1 year, $500
Perjury	5 years hard labor, $2,000
Bank employee taking money etc.	10 years hard labor, $5,000
Forgery of treasury notes and other public securities	10 years hard labor, $5,000
Forging ships documents	3 years hard labor, $1,000
Forging gold or silver coin	10 years hard labor, $5,000
Forging copper coin	3 years hard labor, $1,000
Attempted murder on the high seas	3 years hard labor, $3,000
Conspiring to destroy a vessel	10 years hard labor, $10,000
Debasing of coin by an employee of the mint	10 years hard labor, $10,000

court of the United States." Section 14 stipulated that if a person, upon arraignment upon any indictment for any offence, not capital, shall stand mute, or will not answer or plead to such indictment, the court should proceed to the trial as if the person had pleaded not guilty, and upon a verdict being returned by the jury, may proceed to render judgment accordingly. For offences committed upon the high seas, the trial should occur in the district where the offender was apprehended or into which he might be brought first.

The resolution of 1790 requesting the states to authorize the use of their prisons by the United States was now made part of the statute. The final section provided protection to state jurisdiction over various crimes by stating that "nothing in this act contained shall be construed to deprive the courts of the individual states, of jurisdiction, under the laws of the several states, over offenses made punishable by this act." This section had a curious history. During the 1790s Congress had empowered state courts to try persons for violations of a variety of federal crimes.[61] Congress continued the trend in the early 1800s through an act of 1806 which granted certain county courts in New York and Pennsylvania "cognizance of all complaints and prosecutions for fines, penalties and forfeitures arising under the United States revenue laws." Congress extended the act in 1808 for an indefinite time period and included selected Ohio county courts. The Embargo of 1807; the Non-Intercourse Act of 1809; Macon's Bill Number 2 of 1810; and the Embargo of 1813 all made fines, penalties, and forfeitures recoverable in the state courts.[62] Finally an 1815 act provided that state and county courts within or the next adjoining any Federal direct or internal collection district might take cognizance of all complaints, suits, *and prosecutions* for taxes, duties, fines, penalties, and forfeitures arising under any of such laws, even though the cause of action or complaint arose within fifty miles of the nearest district court. The act further tried to regulate proceedings in the state courts and permitted appeals from state court decisions to United States circuit courts under the same provisions as appeals from United States district courts.[63]

There were no debates reported on the 1815 act. In 1818, however, several Congressman reacted when a proposed fugitive slave act contained provisions for enforcement by state officials. Senator David L. Morril of New Hampshire contended that the United States "cannot constitutionally demand, or employ, the agency of any other power than its own, to discharge duties and perform services, under criminal laws emanating from Congress." In the House, James Pindall of Virginia felt that Congress might have the power in some cases but not in this specific instance. Ezekiel Whitman of Massachusetts added that Congress would not "compel the State officers to perform this duty—they could only authorize it."[64] Political consideration led to the defeat of the bill.

There has been no study of the frequency of use of state courts to try offenders. State Supreme Courts occasionally confronted the issue with a mixed reaction as to its acception or rejection. Virginia denied the right in 1815, followed by Ohio in 1816, Maryland in 1817, New York in 1819, and Connecticut in 1828.[65] On the other hand, Pennsylvania and South Carolina specifically upheld the power.[66] The Supreme Court resolved the issue in 1842 in *Prigg* v. *Pennsylvania*, when it held that the Constitution "does not point out any state functionaries, or any state action to carry its provisions into effect. The states cannot, therefore, be compelled to enforce them."[67]

Another problem that Congress became involved with during the period, imprisonment for debt, bridged both civil and criminal jurisdiction. In accord with the humanitarian spirit of the post-Revolutionary period in 1792, Congress passed an "Act for the Relief of Persons Imprisoned for debt." This provided that if a prisoner swore that he had neither twenty dollars nor the amount of his debt, a federal judge could require the creditor to support the debtor, to a maximum of one dollar per week and if the creditor failed to furnish such weekly support, the debtor might be discharged from his imprisonment and "not be liable to be imprisoned again for the said debt." Congress approved renewals of this act in 1794, 1796, 1798, and 1800. The renewal acts increased the amount to $30 and provided a thirty-day waiting period after which time the debtor could take an oath that he had neither the $30 nor the amount needed to pay the debt after which the debtor would be released, although he would still be responsible for the debt if he should accumulate a future estate.[68]

The question appeared sporadically in Congress through 1820. In 1807 upon recommendation of Representative John Porter of Pennsylvania, who complained that a debtor must be imprisoned at least thirty days before he could obtain relief, the House appointed a committee to inquire whether the law needed an alteration. The committee reported a bill which the House rejected.[69] Congress in 1817 added a supplemental provision to the Act of 1798 permitting a person whose case was such that the Secretary of the Treasury could not authorize a discharge to appeal directly to the President.[70]

The numerous economic problems engendered by the panic of 1819 and the depression which followed prompted Congress again to address the problem. Representative Hugh Nelson of Virginia proposed on February 2, 1821, the formation of a select committee to "inquire" into the expediency of abolishing imprisonment for debt. Nelson asserted that the distress which pervaded the country was known to everyone. "It had already too long been a stain on the statute books of the country, that men were liable to be imprisoned, not for crime, but for their misfortune." The committee headed by Nelson reported in February. The report stated that the practice of imprisoning the body of a debtor, though sanctioned by very ancient usage, seemed to have had its origin in an age of barbarism and could only be considered an amelioration of that system by which the person of the debtor was subjected to being sold. In a strong humanitarian plea, the report continued:

This crying indifference to the miseries of the wretched; this cold insensibility to the distress and suffering of our fellow-creatures, has too long stained the annals of our country, and blurred with the imputation of incongruity our boast of independence, liberty, happiness, when contrasted with our practice of imprisonment for misfortune, not for crime.

The committee introduced a bill with certain stipulations abolishing imprisonment for debt on process issuing from the courts of the United States. The report was read twice and not brought up again during the session.[71]

The Senate took up the question on several occasions during the remainder of the 1820s. From 1823 to 1827 the Senate formed a committee to inquire into the expediency of abolition. The leader of the movement was Senator Richard M. Johnson of Kentucky. In February 1824 he made a lengthy speech pleading for consideration of abolition. Johnson considered imprisonment for debt a

flagrant violation of personal liberty. In a country free as ours, civil injury and crime should never be confounded. Punishment is a retribution for offense, and is solely the prerogative of the sovereign power of the State. Civil injury is repaired by pecuniary satisfaction, and this the injured person has a right to claim.

Johnson revealed studies which had been made in Massachusetts. In one jail male and female debtors were confined in a single room; in another, debtors enjoyed one comfortable meal in twenty-four hours. After a long incursion into the British antecedents of the system, Johnson concluded that imprisonment for debt was the "offspring of a barbarous age—the enslaving instrument of wealth, associated with the lover of power, and with principles base and sordid." On April 9, the Senate approved the bill, 24 to 19. The House did not concur.[72] In 1824 Congress made several slight modifications to the Acts of 1798 and 1800. The Senate defeated an abolition bill in 1825 but approved a bill in 1828. The House did not consider the Senate bill of 1828.[73]

In 1828 Daniel Webster introduced a resolution calling for the publication of Edward Livingston's *A System of Penal Law for the United States* by the House. The work modeled after Livingston's codes for Louisiana contained three principal parts—the penal code which included a list of offences, a code of procedure to be used in executing the laws of the United States, and the code of reform and prison discipline. Shortly thereafter Livingston lost his seat in the House but was chosen to represent the state in the Senate. In 1831 he proposed that the Senate consider his proposals, most important of which in Livingston's eyes was the abolition of capital punishment. When Livingston accepted the post of Secretary of State in 1831, the reforms "lay dormant in his absence."[74]

In reviewing the 2,718 criminal cases brought before the circuit courts for trial, one is struck by the lack of problems over jurisdiction and/or procedure in the numerous trials. Of the two, jurisdictional problems presented the most frequent difficulties. In April 1804 the New York Circuit Court tried Peter Vass for a felony on the high seas. The jury acquitted him on the basis that if the offence was committed, it was committed on an uninhabited island called St. Felix in the Pacific Ocean and not on the high seas as charged in the indictment.[75]

The petit jury in Massachusetts convicted Barnabas Howland and others of endeavoring to make a revolt. Their counsel moved for an arrest of judgment because of certain defects in the indictment and because the indictment did not allege that the crime was committed within the jurisdiction of the United States. The court denied the motion and sentenced the mariners to thirty days in jail and a $20 fine each.[76]

The same issue was met in 1818 in the case of William Bevans who was indicted for murder in Massachusetts. The indictment was founded in Section 8 of the Crimes Act of 1790. At the time Bevans allegedly committed the crime he was a seaman on board the United States' ship of war *Independence*, a ship lying at anchor in the main channel of Boston harbor. The jury convicted Bevans whereupon his counsel moved for a new trial, questioning: "1. Whether, upon the foregoing statement of facts, the offense charged in the indictment and committed on board the said ship as aforesaid, was within the jurisdiction of the state of Massachusetts, or of any court thereof. 2d. Whether the offense charged in the indictment, and committed on board the said ship as aforesaid, was within the jurisdiction or cognizance of the Circuit Court of the United States for the District of Massachusetts." When the judges, John Davis and Joseph Story, differed in opinion on the questions, they certified the case to the Supreme Court for an opinion. Daniel Webster, representing the defendant, argued before the Court that for the United States to have jurisdiction the crime had to be committed "on the high seas or in any river, harbor, basin or bay, out of the jurisdiction of any particular state." He maintained first that Boston Harbor was not the high seas and secondly that the state of Massachusetts had consistently exercised jurisdiction over the harbor. Next Webster pointed out that the delegation of admiralty jurisdiction to federal courts was exclusive; however, it must be shown that the offence was one over "which the admiralty has jurisdiction . . . [and] one which the admiralty has exclusive jurisdiction." Webster contended that common law as exercised by the state and the admiralty law as exercised by the federal government may overlap. To sustain the conviction, Webster concluded, "It must be shown, not only that it is a case of exclusive admiralty jurisdiction, but also that Congress has conferred on the circuit court all the admiralty jurisdiction that it could confer." Webster did not believe that Congress had conferred jurisdiction on the circuit court in such a case where a concurrent common law jurisdiction existed.[77]

Henry Wheaton for the United States countered that a national ship of war is a part of the territory of the sovereign or state to which she belongs. A state has no jurisdiction in the territory of the United States; therefore, it has no jurisdiction on a ship of war belonging to the United States. Wheaton also maintained that sea "includes ports and havens, rivers and creeks, as well as the sea coasts."

Chief Justice Marshall's opinion for the court generally accepted Webster's arguments, concluding that "a murder committed on board a ship of war, lying within the harbor of Boston, is not cognizable in the circuit court for the District of Massachusetts."[78]

Two years later the Supreme Court was again asked to interpret the Crimes Act of 1790. A man named Wiltberger had been indicted for manslaughter in the circuit court of Pennsylvania and found guilty. The jury, however, in returning its verdict stipulated that their verdict was conditional upon the court having jurisdiction in the case. The indictment charged Wiltberger with manslaughter committed on board the American ship *The Benjamin Rush* in the river Tigris in the empire of China off Wampoa, about one hundred yards from the shore. The defense counsel maintained that the Crimes Act of 1790 provided only for the punishment of manslaughter committed on the high seas and that the act did not include the river Tigris in that definition. Marshall, again speaking for the Court, sided with the defense and certified that "the offense charged in this indictment is not cognizable in the courts of the United States."[79]

The third case of this type occurred in Georgia. The grand jury of the Georgia circuit court indicted two men—Gillies and Donohue—for larceny. Gillies and Donohue were alleged to have committed the larceny on an American vessel lying alongside of and fastened to a wharf in the port of Havana. Judge Jeremiah Cuyler ruled that the "prisoners must be discharged for I do not think the case cognizable in the courts of the United States."[80]

The last case certified to the Supreme Court concerning the interpretation of the Crimes Act of 1790 originated in Pennsylvania. The grand jury indicted Kelly and others in 1824 for endeavoring to make a revolt on a vessel called *The Lancaster* on the high seas. The court found the defendants guilty, whereupon their counsel moved an arrest of judgment contending that the act of Congress did not define the offence of endeavoring to make a revolt and that it was not competent for the court to give a judicial definition of the crime. The Supreme Court, speaking through Justice Bushrod Washington, disagreed. Washington said that although "the act of Congress does not define this offense, it is nevertheless competent to the court to give a judicial definition of it."[81]

A rather complicated case concerning a counterfeited bank note came out of the district court of Maine. In December 1817 the grand jury indicted Paul Stone, Jr., and the petit jury convicted him for passing a counterfeited bank note. The motion to arrest the judgment contended that the indictment failed to identify properly that the district court of Maine was acting as a circuit court and failed to allege that the bill was passed to any particular person or persons or corporation, so that a conviction on said indictment could not be pleaded in bar to another indictment. The Court rejected the former plea but accepted the latter and ordered Stone discharged from the indictment. The grand jury reindicted Stone in February 1818, and the court tried him in June. Again the jury found Stone guilty, whereupon his attorney asked that the verdict be set aside and a new trial ordered because (1) one of the jurors "did before the said jury was impanelled . . . form and express a decided opinion against the said Stone," (2) the jury was not legally selected and returned, (3) the verdict was against the law and the weight of evidence in the trial, and (4) Stone had discovered new evidence. The court rejected the motion, stating that the reasons assigned for a new trial were insufficient. The attorneys thereupon moved for an arrest of judgment maintaining that (1) the first count of the indictment, which charged that the defendant did feloniously pass, utter, and publish as true, certain falsely altered bill and note issued by order of the President, directors and company of the bank of the United States was repugnant, inconsistent, and insensible, (2) no person was named in the indictment to whom the bill was uttered, (3) in the second count of the indictment it was not stated to whom the bill and note was uttered, and (4) the indictment was not countersigned by the district attorney nor by any law officer by special appointment authorized to prosecute offences in this court. The court rejected the motion and sentenced Stone to be imprisoned for two years and fined $50.[82]

Two cases concerning the Act of 1804 presented the courts with difficult problems concerning the interpretation of the act. In New York in 1817 Frederick Jacobson was indicted and convicted of willfully and corruptly destroying the ship *Aristides*. His attorneys contended that (1) the court did not have jurisdiction since Congress did not have the right to assign any justice of the Supreme Court to hold a circuit or inferior court, and (2) the jury convicted the prisoner of the first five counts of the indictment in which he was charged as not being the owner of record, as it appeared in the evidence that the owner was on board and that the prisoner probably acted under his directions and by his orders, and (3) he had not been guilty of any offence within the act of Congress. The judge denied the motion and ordered Jacobson to be hanged. Monroe pardoned Jacobson on April 16, 1818.[83]

In 1825 the Virginia circuit court indicted and convicted John B. Amedy for destroying a vessel with intent to prejudice the underwriters—in violation of the Act of 1804. His counsel moved for an arrest of judgment on the following grounds: (1) The exemplification of the acts of the legislature of the State of Massachusetts, incorporating the Boston Insurance Company, given at the trial was not admissible in evidence as a sufficient verification thereof; (2) before the policy of insurance underwritten by the Boston Insurance Company could be given in evidence, it was necessary to prove that the subscription to the stock and the payment of such subscription, as required by the act of incorporation, had actually been made; (3) the policy ought to have been proved to be executed by the authority of the company in such manner as to be legally binding on them; (4) the court instructed the jury that it was not material whether the company was incorporated or not; it was not material whether the policy were valid in law or not; that the prisoner's guilt did not depend upon the legal obligation of the policy but upon the question whether he had willfully and corruptly cast away the vessel, as charged in the indictment, with intent to injure the underwriters. The judges differed in opinion and thus certified the proceedings to the Supreme Court for an opinion. Justice Story delivered the opinion ior the Court. On the first question, Story regretted that "an exemplification so loose and irregular should have been permitted to have found its way into any court of justice." He pointed out, however, that under the Act of 1790, prescribing the mode in which the public acts, records, and judicial proceedings of each state shall be authenticated so as to take effect in every other state, the only formality required was the seal of state affixed to a document by the properly authorized officer. Since the documents had been authenticated by the Secretary of State of Massachusetts, the act required the court to accept the documents. Concerning the second and third questions, Story felt that since the corporation was not a party but was merely collaterally introduced, the only thing the government had to do was to prove that the company was de facto organized and acting as an insurance company and corporation. Upon the last question, Story felt the instructions of the court to the jury were proper. Finally Story dealt with another question, not raised in the court below but argued before the Supreme Court. The defense had maintained that a corporation was not a person within the meaning of the act of Congress. Story disagreed. "That corporations are, in law, for civil purposes, deemed persons is unquestionable." Amedy was sentenced by the circuit court in 1827 to be hanged. President Adams pardoned him on February 24, 1829.[84]

There were occasionally procedural difficulties in the criminal cases. The procedural guarantees contained initially in the Judiciary Act of 1789 and shortly thereafter in the first ten amendments to the Constitution are difficult to interpret. The Sixth Amendment guarantees the accused in all criminal prosecutions the right to a speedy and public trial. What is meant by a speedy trial? The circuit courts disposed of most cases rapidly. The interpretation of speedy, however, differed from court to court. Judge St. George Tucker of Virginia ruled in 1821 that the trial of John White, indicted for murder, had to proceed or the charges would have to be dropped. Due to the lack of prosecution witnesses, the district attorney dropped the charges. Judge William Stephens of Georgia, however, was more tolerant. In December 1805 the grand jury indicted Noyal Nelms for passing forged bills of the United States. He pleaded not guilty; but the district attorney was not prepared, and the court postponed the trial until the next term. The defendant was ill in May 1806 which caused another postponement. The district attorney received another postponement in December 1806. Finally in December 1807 when witnesses on the part of the United States failed to attend, the judge ordered Nelms discharged—two years after his indictment. A final example arose in North Carolina. The grand jury indicted Allen Twitty for counterfeiting in June 1806. The defendant asked for a continuance after pleading not guilty. In December the court granted another continuance provided the defendant would agree to have the depositions of witnesses on the part of the United States taken *de ben esse* (conditionally, in anticipation of future need) in Raleigh "whilst the defendants counsel are in town before one of the Judges of the Court or some Justice of the Peace." The defendant agreed to the terms, received a postponement, and the court bailed him in the sum of $10,000 on two separate indictments. Not until May 1809 did the trial occur. The jury found Twitty not guilty on one charge. The court remanded Twitty to jail until the next term to answer a charge upon the second indictment. The district attorney may have dropped the charges for no record of the trial on the second charge has been found.[85]

The modern view that procedural safeguards cannot be waived was not held during this period. The Pennsylvania grand jury indicted Thomas Thompson for murder on the high seas in October 1807. Thompson waived the service of a copy of the indictment and the lists of jurors and witnesses. The district attorney agreed to proceed to the arraignment and trial. The jury found Thompson not guilty.[86]

The requirement of an impartial jury contained in the Sixth Amendment encountered various problems in the period. An editorial in the New York *Post* of March 18, 1822, revealed a recurring problem in criminal cases. The newspaper commented:

A practice has of late come into use in our city, which, for the sake of that free and unprejudiced administration of justice which is the right of every citizen, ought to be abolished. I allude to publishing notices in the public journals respecting persons who have been (perhaps innocently) suspected of crime. Law and reason declare that every person is supposed to be innocent until the contrary be proven, and he is legally convicted by the judgment of his country; and the most guilty man that ever was brought before a court is entitled to as full and impartial a trial as the most innocent. And can a juror, after reading an open assertion respecting one who is committed for trial, that he is a "notorious dealer in counterfeit money, and has formerly been confined in the State Prison," enter a jury box without feeling some prejudice against a prisoner? A man who is placed in that situation is half convicted before he is legally put upon his trial. If this practice is tolerated, it may lead to the most dangerous consequences, and no person in the community will be safe.[87]

Although the federal courts did not seek to limit pretrial publicity, from time to time juries were ordered not to speak to any person concerning the trial during recess. When a jury violated such instruction in Massachusetts in 1809 in the trial of Alexander Trott, the court ordered a new trial.[88]

The interpretation of the Fifth Amendment's guarantees against self-incrimination was in its infancy during this period. The first use of the Fifth occurred in the trials of Samuel G. Ogden and William S. Smith (see Chapter 3). Several other cases appeared involving the use of "voluntary" confessions. In May 1818 Charles Jared Ingersoll, district attorney of Pennsylvania, requested the President to pardon John Alexander who had been convicted of robbing the mail. Ingersoll reported that Alexander did not confess immediately "but hesitated for some time, and was urged by his counsel and by me to make a confession." Ingersoll continued that though "I distinctly and repeatedly told him that I promised nothing, yet I have no doubt that his confession was made under the expectation that it would recommend his case to your clemency and I think that something like this was said at the time." Postmaster General Return Jonathan Meigs made a similar request to the President for a pardon for Felix McNamara, convicted of robbing the mail in Virginia and sentenced to prison for two years. Meigs reported that before the trial McNamara "was assured by this Department that if he would satisfactorily state the facts relating to the transaction, . . . he should be recommended to the clemency of the Court." Meigs did not know if his agent who handled the inquiry informed the court; however, Meigs knew that McNamara was still in prison. Meigs concluded that McNamara was a fit object of clemency. Monroe did not pardon either person. Another postal case occurred in 1826. The Virginia circuit court indicted James Poarch for a violation of the Mail Act. The only evidence used against Poarch was his own confession. The court noted that the confession was made voluntarily after the accused had been informed of the failure of an application to the Postmaster General for his discharge. The promise on the part of the mail contractor to make this application, however, had induced the accused to confess the offence for which he was charged when arrested. The court accepted the confession, the jury convicted him, and the court sentenced Poarch to ten years imprisonment but recommended him to the President for mercy. Adams refused to pardon Poarch.[89]

Two cases involving confessions were found in Louisiana. The confession of John Johnston was produced in a trial for murder in 1815. Johnston was found guilty, but the court arrested judgment on jurisdictional grounds. In 1821 the court quashed indictments against Thomas Orr and William Bell on motion of the district attorney because the confession of Orr was before the grand jury when the bill against Bell was found. The grand jury reindicted both men, and the petit jury convicted them.[90]

The final area of difficulty encountered by the courts concerned the trial of aliens and public officers. In 1806 the New York circuit court grand jury indicted John Thomas for murdering John Geon at sea. The marshal committed Thomas on September 2, whereupon he applied for a copy of the indictment and a list of the witnesses for the prosecution. Two days later his cousin filed a special plea praying that the court did not have jurisdiction because Thomas was a British subject and thus outside the jurisdiction of United States courts. The district attorney demurred, and the defendant joined the demurrer. The court rejected the plea. The defendant pleaded not guilty on the 6th and received a postponement until the 8th. Meanwhile the envoy of Great Britain interceded, claiming that the Thomas case did not come under the jurisdiction of the federal courts because Thomas and the vessel were British. On November 1, 1806, Jefferson ordered a *nolle prosequi* entered on the indictment.[91]

In 1825 the United States prosecuted Juan Gualberto de Ortego for assaulting and striking the Spanish Minister and for violating the law of nations. On October 25 the Pennsylvania circuit court convicted Ortego on both charges. His attorneys moved for an arrest of judgment and a new trial claiming that "the circuit court did not have jurisdiction of the matter, inasmuch as they were cases affecting an ambassador or other public minister, and that the defendant had been found guilty on two indictments when Evidence was given of only one offense." The judges differed in opinion on the first point, whereupon they certified the case to the Supreme Court.[92]

The Supreme Court rendered its opinion in 1826. Justice Brockholst Livingston divided the question into two parts: whether this is a case affecting an ambassador or other public minister within the meaning of the second section of the third article of the Constitution of the United States; and if it be, then whether the jurisdiction of the Supreme Court in such cases is not only original but exclusive of the circuit courts under the true construction of the above section and article. Livingston said the Court need not answer the second part since it was clearly of the opinion that this was not a case affecting a public minister within the plain meaning of the Constitution. He felt that the case was merely a

public prosecution, instituted and conducted by and in the name of the United States, for the purpose of vindicating the law of nations, and that of the United States, offended, as the indictment charges, in the person of a public minister, by an assault committed on him by a private individual. It is a case then which affects the United States and the individual whom they seek to punish: but one in which the minister himself, although he was the person injured by the assault, has no concern, either in the event of the prosecution or in the costs attending it.

Thus the Court certified that the circuit court had jurisdiction.[93]

A total of 2,718 criminal indictments were returned by circuit courts from 1801 to 1828.[94] Juries found 596 of the defendants guilty and 479 not guilty. *Nolle prosequis* were entered in 902 cases, and 741 were disposed of by other means. The other category included 661 cases where no disposition was recorded, and 80 cases which were either abated, quashed, discharged, discontinued, or the prisoner escaped. (See Appendix I.)

Pennsylvania provided the most cases (1,119), followed by Louisiana (341), Massachusetts (219), Georgia (196), Vermont (184), and New York (121). Delaware, with only one recorded case, had the lowest number. (See Appendix II.)

Admiralty and maritime crimes (murder on the high seas, assault and battery on the high seas, revolt, piracy,) accounted for 820 cases. Counterfeiting, forgery, and other cases related to banks accounted for 357. (See Appendix III.)

The court imposed a variety of punishments. (See Appendix IV.) The courts sentenced sixty-six persons to be hanged, but only thirty-two were actually executed. To ameliorate the punishments permitted by law, Article II, Section 2, of the Constitution gave the President the power to grant reprieves and pardons for all crimes except impeachment. Only twice during the period were attempts made to give the President the power to commute a sentence. The first proposal came in 1821. (See Chapter 8, pp. 146-147.) Late in the debates over the revision of the Crimes Act in 1825 Representative Arthur Livermore of New Hampshire offered as an amendment a new section of the bill which would have required that the name and conduct of a prisoner be reported to the President from time to time "who should have power to shorten the term of confinement, as the good conduct of the prisoner might appear to him to merit." Webster approved of the principle of the amendment but "apprehended, as the United States have no penitentiaries of their own, some difficulty might arise from the introduction of new rules in a penitentiary borrowed from one of the states." The amendment was decided in the negative.[95] From 1801 to 1829 this power was used 1,098 times, including 148 criminal pardons and 83 respites.[96]

Jefferson early established a procedure of referring petitions for pardons to the district attorney who prosecuted and the judges who sentenced the person. If the district attorney and judge recommended mercy, Jefferson usually pardoned the person. The practice appears to have been followed by succeeding Presidents, although Adams added a requirement that the clerk of the court should submit a statement of the indictment upon which the person was convicted.[97] For persons convicted of capital crimes, the Presidents often issued an initial reprieve, followed by several additional reprieves, and then a pardon.

The majority of criminal pardons occurred after the prison sentence had been fulfilled. Often the criminal was unable to pay either the fine assessed or the costs of prosecution. The President would thus pardon the payment of those items. When part of the prison sentence was pardoned, the President often conditioned the pardon upon payment of costs.[98]

Other conditions were seldom placed upon pardons; however, two exceptions are worth noting. President Monroe pardoned Thomas Jefferson Gurnett and William Wood on July 19, 1822, both of whom had been convicted in Pennsylvania for stealing and embezzling money from the mail. As part of their petition the men said they would atone for their crime by enlisting in the Navy. Monroe made their request a condition of the pardon, requiring that prior to their discharge from confinement they should make an agreement with a responsible naval officer that "they will immediately enter into the naval service of the United States, and continue therein until the expirations of the terms prescribed by the sentence of the Court for their imprisonment." On September 8, 1824, Monroe pardoned Patrick Smith on condition that "he forthwith leave the United States and never thereafter return to the same."[99]

Presidential pardons often had the support of various citizens, although on occasion the pardon evoked some public outcry. When Monroe pardoned Joseph Maurice and Doctor Dezeareau, convicted in New Jersey of mail robbery, the New York *Evening Post* opposed, saying "what use is it to bear the trouble and expense of having tribunals for trying criminals, and prisons for detaining them, if crime is to be fostered by a mistaken lenity."[100]

Monroe appears to have been the most lenient President. Of the 148 criminal pardons, Monroe issued seventy-two. Adams appears to have been the strictest, issuing only three. Adams revealed his attitude in his diary. When Mrs. West appealed to Adams for a pardon for her brother, Lewis Hare, who had served eight years of a ten-year sentence, Adams wrote: "Mail robbery is one of those offenses the full punishment of which in this country ought perhaps never to be remitted, and the sentence of ten years imprisonment was, in this case, itself a very mitigated penalty." Needless to say, Adams did not pardon Hare.[101]

The evolution of the federal criminal law from 1801 to 1829 differed little from the development of the criminal law under the Federalists. The Republicans failed to address to issue of structure, except for permitting cases to be certified to the Supreme Court when the judges differed in opinion on the law. Furthermore, the Republicans failed to create sufficient circuit courts to include all the districts.

Like the Federalists before them, the Republicans incorporated the judicial offices into the patronage system. Only a handful of Federalists would be appointed as marshal, district attorney, or judge under the Republicans.

The expansion of federal criminal laws under the Republicans closely paralleled the social and economic trends in the nation as a whole. The concern of the government in protecting the postal system and the Banks of the United States reflected concerns and needs of the country in communication and finance. The Republican use of criminal laws to enforce foreign policy was similar to that of the Federalists in the 1790s. Because of their overwhelming majorities in Congress, the Republicans were able to enact such laws without major opposition. The extensive nature of these attempts will be covered in the chapters which follow.

NOTES

1. 2 *U. S. Statutes at Large*, 132.

2. Richard E. Ellis, *The Jeffersonian Crisis: Courts and Politics in the Young Republic* (New York, 1971), 58.

3. Ibid., 59.

4. Ibid.

5. 2 *U. S. Statutes at Large*, 156-167.

6. Ibid. 159-162.

7. U. S. Congress, *Debates and Proceedings in the Congress of the United States, 1789-1824 [Annals of Congress]* (42 vols., Washington, D. C., 1834-1856) XVI: 27-28, 46, 74, 485-486, 499-500; 2 *U. S. Statutes at Large*, 420-421, 477-478, 516.

8. *Annals of Congress*, XXIII: 1086; XXX: 357-358; XXXI: 135; XXXIII: 31, 91-96, 100-101, 103-110, 160, 178, 596-598, 703-704; XXXVI:477, 498-499, 585-586; XXXVII:1823; XL:236-237, 293-294, 298, 1173-1175; XLI:21, 32, 38, 339, 419; XLII:1701-1702; U. S. Congress, *Register of Debates in Congress, 1825-1837 [Congressional Debates]* (29 vols., Washington, D. C., 1825-1837), I:527-536, 603-616, 618-620, appendix 63-65; II:884-925, 927-953, 1014-1018, 1020-1029, 1037-1040, 1042-1055, 1061-1075, 1081-1116, 1119-1149; III:424-571, 668-671, 691-692, 698-704; IV:2303, 2514-2519, 2578-2586, 2601-2605; VII:2-349. See also Curtis Nettels, "The Mississippi Valley and the Federal Judiciary, 1807-1838," *Mississippi Valley Historical Review*, 12 (September, 1925), 202-226; Robert J. Remini, *Martin Van Buren and the Making of the Democratic Party* (New York, 1959), 114; Claude M. Fuess, *Daniel Webster* (2 vols., Boston, 1930), I:328-329.

9. *Annals of Congress*, XIX:412-413.

10. Henry Wheaton, *Reports of Cases Argued and Adjudged in the Supreme Court, 1816-1827* (12 vols., Philadelphia, 1816-1827), X:150, 66 (1925); *Process of Execution: United States' Courts*, U. S. 19th Congress, 1st session, House Document 71 (1826), 1, 3-25.

11. *Process of Execution*, 1-2.

12. *Congressional Debates*, V:90-95, 201-203, 327, 343; VI:2619, 2651; 4 *U. S. Statutes at Large*, 278-282.

13. Thomas Jefferson, *Works*, ed. Paul Leicester Ford (12 vols., New York, 1904-1905), X:199.

14. Ibid., 200.

15. "Jefferson Papers," *Massachusetts Historical Society Collection*, 7th series (10 vols., Boston, 1900), I:92-93.

16. Jefferson, *Works*, X:238-239.

17. Ibid., 242.

18. Ibid., 272.

19. Albert Gallatin, *Writings*, ed. Henry Adams (3 vols., Philadelphia, 1879), I:33.

20. Carl E. Prince, "The Passing of the Aristocracy: Jefferson's Removal of the Federalists, 1801-1805," *Journal of American History*, 57 (December, 1970), 565-566.

21. Ibid., 567-568.

22. Lynn W. Turner, "The Impeachment of John Pickering," *American Historical Review*, 54 (April, 1949), 504-505.

23. Ibid., 505.

24. *Annals of Congress*, XIV:92, 100-165, 200, 203-205, 207, 251-267, 313-493, 556, 560-562, 582-662, 665-669, 675-676, 1213.

25. Data compiled from Letters of Application and Recommendation during the Administration of Thomas Jefferson 1801-1809 (12 reels, National Archives, Record Group 59, Microcopy 418).

26. Sidney H. Aronson, *Status and Kinship in the Higher Civil Service: Standards of Selection in the Administrations of John Adams, Thomas Jefferson and Andrew Jackson* (Cambridge, Mass., 1964).

27. Irving Brant, *James Madison* (6 vols., Indianapolis, 1941-1961), V:52-54, 265-287, 403-405; Leonard D. White, *The Jeffersonians: A Study in Administrative History, 1801-1829* (New York, 1961), 36.

28. James Monroe, *Writings*, ed. S. M. Hamilton (7 vols., New York, 1898-1903), VII:11-12.

29. Carl R. Fish, *The Civil Service and the Patronage* (reprint, New York, 1963), 61; U. S. Congress, Senate, *Journal of the Executive Proceedings of the Senate of the United States, 1789-1905* (90 vols., 1828-1919), III:140-141, 274.

30. John Quincy Adams, *Memoirs*, ed. Charles Francis Adams (8 vols., 1874-1875), VII:207-208.

31. Samuel F. Bemis, *John Quincy Adams and the Union* (New York, 1956), 135.

32. Data compiled from Letters of Application and Recommendation during the Administration of James Madison, 1809-1817 (8 reels, National Archives, Record Group 59, Microcopy M 438): Letters of Application and Recommendation during the Administration of James Monroe, 1817-1825 (19 reels, National Archives, Record Group 59, Microcopy M 439); and Letters of Application and Recommendation during the Administration of John Quincy Adams, 1825-1829 (8 reels, National Archives, Record Group 59, Microcopy M 531).

33. Aronson, *Status and Kinship*, 104, 108, 124.

34. New York *Evening Post*, April 25, and October 2, 1806; Leonard Levy, *Jefferson and Civil Liberties: The Darker Side* (Cambridge, 1963), 61; Connecticut circuit court, Docket 1800-1815 (Federal Records Center, Waltham, Mass.), 123, 143, 145. See also Randall Bridwell and Ralph U. Whitten, *The Constitution and the Common Law: The Decline of the Doctrines of Separation of Powers and Federalism* (Lexington, Mass., 1977), 1-60.

35. *Annals of Congress*, XVII:180, 217-220, 247-252, 282-284.

36. Connecticut circuit court, Docket 1800-1815, pp. 160, 182; New York *Evening Post*, May 15, 1807; Levy, *Jefferson and Civil Liberties*, pp. 63-64.

37. New York *Evening Post*, October 2, 1807; Levy, *Jefferson and Civil Liberties*, 64-66.

38. Levy, *Jefferson and Civil Liberties*, 66.

39. *Annals of Congress*, XX:75-89.

40. Ibid., 119-134.

41. Ibid., XXIII:345-348.

42. William Cranch, *Reports of Cases Argued in the Supreme Court of the United States, 1801-1815* (9 vols., Washington, D. C., 1804-1817), VII:108-112.

43. *Annals of Congress*, XXVI:1768-1770.

44. W. W. Story, ed., *Life and Letters of Joseph Story*, (2 vols., Boston, 1851), I:297-300.

45. The first assault on the common law occurred in St. George Tucker, *Blackstone's Commentaries: with notes of reference, to the Constitution and Laws, of the Federal Government of the United States; and of the Commonwealth of Virginia* (Philadelphia, 1803). Tucker felt it would be impossible to digest the conflicting and diverse interpretations of the common law in the different states into a single system. In the law lectures of David Hoffman *Course of Legal Study* (Baltimore, 1817), he criticized the dependence on the memorization of *Blackstone's Commentaries* and attempted to establish the principle that "legal decisions should rest on principles and doctrines of which the cases are mere evidence and example." See also John Milton Goodenow, *Historical Sketches of the Principles and Maxims of American Jurisprudence . . .* (Steubenville, Ohio, 1819); Peter S. Du Ponceau, *A Dissertation on the Nature and extent of the Jurisdiction of the Courts of the United States . . .* (Philadelphia, 1824); William Duane, writing under the pseudonym of William Sampson, *Sampson's Discourse, and Correspondence with various Learned Jurists, upon the History of the Law and the Addition of Several Essays, Tracts and Documents, Relating to the Subject*, ed. Pishey Thompson (Washington, D. C., 1826); and Charles Jared Ingersoll, *A Discourse Concerning the Influence of America on the Mind* (Philadelphia, 1823). For views of historians on this period see Perry Miller, *The Life and Mind in America* (New York, 1965), 105-109; Nelson, *The Americanization of the Common Law*, 165-174; Morton J. Horwitz, *The Transformation of American Law, 1780-1860* (Cambridge and London, 1977), 1-30; and Gerhard O. W. Mueller, *Crime, Law and the Scholars A History of Scholarship in American Criminal Law* (Seattle, 1969), 21-25.

46. *Annals of Congress*, XXXIII:47-58, 60-64.

47. Ibid., 23, 48, 710.

48. Ibid., XXXVII:185, 191-212, 405-430.

49. Ibid., 478-486, 682.

50. *Congressional Debates*, IV:716-717, 746.

51. 2 *U. S. Statutes at Large*, 139-146.

52. 3 *U. S. Statutes at Large*, 983.

53. 2 *U. S. Statutes at Large*, 592.

54. Georgia circuit court, Minute Book, 1798-1806 (Federal Records Center, East Point, Ga), 531, 539-540, 546; Minute Book, 1806-1816, p. 29; Cranch, *Reports*, IV:167-168; 2 *U. S. Statutes at Large*, 423-424.

55. 3 *U. S. Statutes at Large*, 275-276.

56. 2 *U. S. Statutes at Large*, 290-291.

57. *Annals of Congress*, XXIII:1236-1238.

58. Ibid., XXXIII:34, 176, 213-214; XLI:757, 762; XLII:6, 152; *Congressional Debates*, I:154-156, 165-169, 348-355, 713; 4 *U. S. Statutes at Large*, 115-123.

59. *Congressional Debates*, I:155-159, 335-341, 348-355, 363-365.

60. Ibid., 355.

61. The "Act laying duties and licenses . . ." approved June 5, 1794, provided that where a fine, penalty or forfeiture should

have been incurred, and where the cause of action on complaint shall arise or accrue more than fifty miles distant from the nearest place by law established for the holding of a district court . . . such suit and recovery may be had before any court of the state holden within the said district having jurisdiction in like cases. ''

1 *U. S. Statutes at Large*, 378.

62. *2 U. S. Statutes at Large*, 354, 453, 473, 489, 499, 506, 528, 550, 605, 707; 3 *U. S. Statutes at Large*, 88, 92.

63. 3 *U. S. Statutes at Large*, 244.

64. *Annals of Congress*, XXXI:245, 827, 839.

65. *Jackson* v. *Row*, 2 *Virginia Cases*, 34-38 (1815);*Maryland* v. *Rutter* (Almeida's case), 12 *Niles Weekly Register*, 114, 118, 232, April 19, 1817; *United States* v. *Lathrop*, 17 *Johns.* (N. Y.) 4 (1819); *Davison* v. *Champlin*, 7 *Conn.* 244 (1828).

66. *Buckwalter* v. *United States*, 11 *Serg. and Rawle*; *Ex parte Rhodes*, 12 *Niles Weekly Register*, 264, 266-267, June 21, 1817.

67. Richard Peters, Jr., *Reports of Cases Argued and Adjudged in the Supreme Court, 1828-1842*, 17 vols. (Philadelphia, 1828-1843), XVI:539, 615 (1842).

68. 1 *U. S. Statutes at Large*, 265-266, 370, 482-483, 562; 2 *U. S. Statutes at Large*, 4-6.

69. *Congressional Debates*, V:1229; VI:1463.

70. 3 *U. S. Statutes at Large*, 399.

71. *Annals of Congress*, XXXVII:1224-1227.

72. Ibid., XLI:258-274, 504.

73. 4 *U. S. Statutes at Large*, 1, 19-20; *Congressional Debates*, I:230; IV:90.

74. Edward Livingston, *A System of Penal Law for the United States of America* (Washington, D. C., 1828); William B. Hatcher, *Edward Livingston: Jeffersonian Republican and Jacksonian Democrat* (Baton Rouge, 1940), 226-282; and Philip English Mackey, "Edward Livingston and the Origins of the Movement to Abolish Capital Punishment in America," *Louisiana History*, 16 (Spring, 1975), 145-166.

75. New York circuit court, Minute Book, 1790-1808, (Federal Records Center, Suitland, Md., 234, 237, 239-240; New York circuit court, Case Files, Box 5.

76. Massachusetts circuit court, Record Book #2, 1806-1811, (Federal Records Center, Waltham, Mass.), 259-262.

77. Wheaton, *Reports*, III:348-375.

78. Ibid., 386-391.

79. Ibid., V:76-106.

80. Georgia district court, Minute Book, 1813-1843, (Federal Records Center, East Point, Georgia), 179.

81. Wheaton, *Reports*, XI:417-419.

82. Maine district court, Minute Book, 1815-1818 (Federal Records Center, Waltham, Mass.), Dec. term 1817, June term 1818.

83. New York Circuit court, Minute Book, 1813-1819, pp. 244, 250; New York *Spectator*, September 23, 1817; B. Livingston to John Quincy Adams, February 16, 19, 26, 1818, Miscellaneous Letters of the Department of State, 1789-1906 (1,310 reels, National Archives, Record Group 59, Microcopy M 179), reel 40; Copies of Presidential Pardons and Remissions, 1794-1893 (7 reels, National Archives, Record Group 59, Microcopy T 967), reel 1, vol. II, p. 102.

84. Virginia circuit court, Order Book #12, 1825-1831, (Virginia State Library, Richmond, Va.), 47, 50, 57-61, 79-88, 119, 151-152, 170; Wheaton *Reports*, XI:392-413; (Microcopy T 967), reel 1, vol. IV, pp. 216-217.

85. Virginia circuit court, Order Book #11, 1820-1824, p. 290; Georgia circuit court, Minute Book, 1790-1806, p. 521; Minute Book, 1806-1816, pp. 12, 72; North Carolina circuit court, Minute Book, 1791-1808 (Federal Records Center, Suitland, Md.), 541, 557; Minute Book, 1809-1835, pp. 1, 21, 35; Charleston *Courier*, May 24, 1809.

86. Pennsylvania circuit court, Minute Book, 1805-1808, pp. 281-282.

87. New York *Post*, March 18, 1822.

88. See case of *U. S.* v. *Johns*, Pennsylvania circuit court, Minute Book, 1805-1808, p. 121-123; Massachusetts circuit court, Record Book #2, 1806-1811, p. 352-355.

89. Ingersoll to Monore, May 14, 1818 (Microcopy M 179) reel 41; R. J. Meigs to Monroe, May 26, 1818 (Microcopy M 179), reel 41; Virginia circuit court, Order Book #12, 1825-1831, pp. 119-124.

90. Louisiana district court, Docket Book, 1815-1820 (Federal Records Center, Fort Worth, Texas), 62, 68, 91; Docket Book, 1820-1830, pp. 74, 140, 149-150, 156, 162, 178.

91. New York circuit court, Minute Book, 1790-1808, pp. 383-385, 389, 394, 403-404, 406-407; New York circuit court, Case Files, Box 5; Madison to Sanford, October 23, 30, November 1, 1806, Domestic Letters of the Department of State, 1784-1906 (171 reels, National Archives, Record Group 59, Microcopy M 40), reel 13, pp. 163-164.

92. Pennsylvania circuit court, Minute Book, 1820-1828, pp. 207-208, 210, 212, 234.

93. Wheaton, *Reports*, XI:467-469.

94. Compiled from records of circuit and district courts for Connecticut, Georgia, Louisiana, Maine, Maryland, Massachusetts, New Hampshire, New Jersey, New York, North Carolina, Pennsylvania, Rhode Island, South Carolina, Tennessee, Vermont, and Virginia; and *A Statement of Convictions, Executions, and Pardons*, U. S. 20th Congress, 2nd session, House Document 146 (1829), 1-211.

95. *Congressional Debates*, I:365.

96. The residue of pardons, remissions, and reprieves were distributed as follows: 398 pardons for criminals in the District of Columbia, 11 for criminals in the territories, and 53 from sentences of court martials; 188 discharges of debtors, 206 remissions of fines, forfeitures and penalties, and 20 miscellaneous. (Microcopy T 967), reel 1, vols., I-IV.

97. Jefferson, *Works*, XI:254-255; John Quincy Adams, *Memoirs*, VII:407.

98. (Microcopy T 967), reel 1, vol. III:29.

99. Ibid., 106.

100. New York *Post*, July 10, 1823. On June 17, 1823, Monroe pardoned Joseph Maurice and Henry Nublette, both of whom had been convicted of robbing the mail in 1819. Dr. Dezeareau was probably an alias for Henry Nublette. (Microcopy T 967), reel 1, vol. III: 56-57.

101. John Quincy Adams, *Memoirs*, VII:197.

3
Neutrality and Treason: Miranda and Burr

Neutrality presented the Jefferson administration and courts with a series of intricate, diverse, and delicate problems. The administration inherited the Neutrality Act of 1794 which provided the legal basis for enforcing a neutrality policy, particularly in respect to Europe. The policy appeared to have less utility in dealing with the intrigues against Spain, either in South America or the Southwestern portion of the United States. When war resumed between Britain and France in 1803, Jefferson's message to Congress on October 17 outlined the policy which the government intended to pursue:

In the course of this conflict let it be our endeavor, as it is our interest and desire, to cultivate the friendship of the belligerent nations by every act of justice and of innocent kindness; to receive their armed vessels with hospitality from the distresses of the sea, but to administer the means of annoyance to none; to establish in our harbors such a police as may maintain law and order, to restrain our citizens from embarking individually in a war in which their country takes no part; to punish severely those persons, citizen or alien, who shall usurp the cover of our flag for vessels not entitled to it, infecting thereby with suspicion those of real Americans and committing us into controversies for the redress of wrongs not our own; to exact from every nation the observance toward our vessels and citizens of those principles and practices which all civilized people acknowledge; to merit the character of a just nation, and to maintain that of an independent one, preferring every consequence to insult and habitual wrong. Congress will consider whether the existing laws enable us efficaciously to maintain this course with our citizens in all places and with others while within the limits of our jurisdiction, and will give them the new modifications necessary for these objects.[1]

In regard to the European conflict, the courts tried and convicted a variety of neutrality violators. The first case occurred in Pennsylvania where the grand jury indicted James Medcalfe for the illegal outfit of the brig *Friends* to serve Great Britain against Holland and the French Republic. Medcalfe pleaded guilty. Judge Richard Peters fined him $100 and imprisoned him for three months.[2] Between 1804 and 1812, the courts tried seventeen other cases resulting in five convictions—four in South Carolina and one in Massachusetts.[3] Between 1804 and 1806 both the British and French Ministers to the United States bombarded the State Department with reports of alleged violations. Madison faithfully investigated the allegations, requesting information from the district attorneys and occasionally collectors and ordering that prosecutions should be instituted if sufficient evidence was found.[4]

The intrigues in the Southwest were more difficult to handle. Since the Treaty of Paris of 1783, conspiracies and rumors of conspiracies filled the Southwest. The first illegal act recorded under the Jefferson administration occurred in 1803, when the Spanish Minister reported an alleged hostile expedition against Louisiana, supposedly led by a man named Wilson.[5]

More serious in nature and more complete in its execution was the scheme of Francisco Miranda. On April 17, 1806, the grand jury of the federal circuit court for the district of New York returned indictments against Francisco Miranda, Samuel G. Ogden, William S. Smith, Thomas Lewis, and William Armstrong, charging that on January 10, 1806, the defendents had started a military expedition against Spain, a country at peace with the United States.[6]

The originator of the "military expedition" was General Francisco de Miranda. A Venezuelan by birth, Miranda had spent most of his mature years as a soldier of fortune in Europe. He had twice visited the United States and retained a keen interest in her affairs. In 1798 he proposed to President John Adams that the United States should assist in securing the independence of South America.[7] Although Adams dismissed the proposal, Alexander Hamilton wrote to Rufus King, United States' Minister in London, that "he wished the United States 'to furnish the whole land force necessary' to Miranda's project."[8] Miranda held frequent interviews with King and also developed contacts with Christopher Gore of Boston and Colonel William S. Smith, son-in-law of President Adams.[9] While he cultivated the Americans, Miranda also sought support from the British.[10] The British toyed with Miranda for over a decade, but their vacillating policy toward the Spanish possessions in the new world finally forced Miranda late in 1805 to turn again to the United States. The timing was propitious—the United States and Spain seemed headed for a war. Sailing on the *Polly* from Gravesend, Miranda disembarked at New York on November 9, 1805, "bearing a letter from Privy Counsilor Nicholas Vansittart to Rufus King" and a letter of credit in "favor of a fictitious

George Martin for 800 sterling."[11] Miranda soon contacted King and Colonel Smith (now surveyor of the port of New York) to inform them of his plans and to seek advice and assistance in implementing them. Smith put Miranda in contact with Commodore Jacob Lewis, commander of several armed vessels which had recently returned from Santo Domingo, and with Samuel G. Ogden, owner of the vessels. Ogden was interested in Miranda's propositions and even was willing to risk some of his own money provided that the government approved of the project. King had predicted this reaction and encouraged Miranda to journey to Washington, D. C., to secure the necessary governmental approbation. In the meantime King transmitted to Secretary of State Madison parts of his correspondence with the South American, including a letter from Vansittart which gave an account of Miranda's relations with England.[12]

Travelling to Washington, D. C., via Philadelphia (where he met briefly with Aaron Burr), Miranda arrived in the capital on December 6. He met with Madison twice and sat next to President Jefferson at a dinner. There are conflicting accounts of what transpired at these meetings; nevertheless, Miranda returned to New York on December 29 and informed Colonel Smith that the project had the "tacit approbation and good wishes" of the government.[13]

Using effectively this alleged approval, Miranda secured three vessels from Ogden without a written contract. He dispatched the *Emperor* and the *Indostan* under Jacob Lewis to Haiti with instructions to join Miranda at Santo Domingo. He armed, equipped, and staffed the third vessel, the *Leander*, in New York. With Miranda aboard, Colonel Smith cleared the *Leander*, commanded by Thomas Lewis, from New York port on February 2, 1806.[14]

While Miranda was busily organizing his expedition, the Spanish Minister, Marquis de Casa Yrujo, aware that something was afoot requested Henry Stoughton, the Spanish consul in New York, to "watch the movements of Miranda and, if possible, to have a person of confidence in the same house to spy on him." Stoughton informed Yrujo late in January that Miranda was fitting out an expedition. Yrujo immediately dispatched warnings to various Spanish officials in South America. In a letter of February 4 to Madison he complained of the equipping and departure of the *Leander*. Unfortunately Yrujo had become a *persona non grata* because of other events and thus Madison returned the letter. Yrujo then asked the French Minister, General Louis-Marie Turreau, to talk with Madison concerning Miranda. On February 8 Turreau forwarded to Madison a formal protest from Yrujo.[15]

The day before Madison received this protest, he requested Nathan Sanford, federal district attorney in New York, to conduct a full investigation into the facts alleged to the fitting out and sailing of the *Leander*, and to report "whether any persons now within the jurisdiction of the

United States have thereby rendered themselves liable to a criminal prosecution. . . '' On February 17 Madison asked Sanford to prosecute without waiting for further instructions if reasonable evidence to convict could be found.[16]

Acting on information supplied by Sanford, district judge Mathias B. Talmadge asked Ogden and Smith to submit to "voluntary" examinations. The judge held the examinations, and he submitted copies of the results to Madison.[17] The information contained in the examinations amounted to confessions. Madison referred the documents to John Breckenridge, the Attorney General, with a request for his observations. Breckenridge commented that from the facts disclosed "there remains no doubt, but that the laws of the United States have been flagrantly violated." Madison sent Sanford the Attorney General's observations on March 21 with an authorization from the President for the retention of an assistant prosecutor.[18]

On April 1, Sanford, with Pierrepont Edwards as his assistant, appeared before the federal circuit court to commence the judicial proceedings. The grand jury empanelled by Marshal John Swartwout consisted of twenty-two Federalists and two others. The district attorney described the majority as being "men of the most decided and violent character in politics."[19] Sanford presented evidence against Miranda, Ogden, Smith, Thomas Lewis, William Armstrong, and John Fink. The proceedings quickly centered on Ogden and Smith. Five attorneys represented these men—Cadwallader D. Colden, Josiah Ogden Hoffman, Thomas A. Emmet, Washington Morton, and Richard Harison. In the course of the proceedings concerning Ogden, the prosecution read and filed the depositions that Judge Talmadge had taken, whereupon Mr. Colden moved that they be suppressed on the grounds "of their having been improperly and illegally taken. . . ." The district attorney rebutted the objection, and the court postponed the hearing on the motion until the 2nd.

The court continued the hearing through the 3rd when it denied the motion. On Monday, April 7, the grand jury separately indicted Ogden and Smith.[20] The following day Smith and Ogden, when called upon to plead to their indictment, entered a plea in abatement, contending again that the depositions presented to the grand jury had been taken illegally. The next day Sanford filed his demurrers and in the course of the debate stated that the defense pleas were "so frivolous, that he would have been jusitified in taking no notice of them as pleas." Mr. Colden in reply asked if it were frivolous "to allege that testimony, which the party was compelled to give against himself, has been laid before the grand jury which found the bills? We hope to be able to convince, *even this court*, that the plea is not frivolous." Judge Talmadge immediately asked Colden for an explanation and an apology. Colden replied that the words must speak for themselves; "he thought the court ought not, and could not examine him, so as to draw from him answers which might criminate himself, and that he was not prepared to give any explanation on the subject." The judge ordered Colden committed to the custody of the marshal for contempt. After consulting with several friends Colden apologized, and the court discharged him. The court thereupon adjourned for three hours.[21]

Following the brief adjournment, Sanford argued in support of his demurrer claiming that the plea "was a perfectly novel experiment, for which no precedent or authority could be found." Citing Lord Matthew Hale, he contended that pleas could be entered only upon the following issues: "1st. Such defects as arise upon the indictment itself, and the insufficiency of it. 2d. Such defects as are in matters of face, as *misnomer, false addition to the prisoner*; and 3d. By matter of record." The district attorney denied that acts of the grand jury could be brought into court and questioned in this way:

They are independent and irresponsible; they judge for themselves of the testimony upon which they ought to find indictments, and no one had a right to inquire, nor has he, without a violation of the grand juror's oath, the means of knowing what evidence they may have had before them. No injury can result from this; for it is the duty of the grand jury to decide on *ex parte* evidence; and if they decide wrong, or prefer a false charge, the natural and the only remedy is, that the accused will be acquitted on his trial before the petty jury.

The district attorney concluded his speech by presenting several formal objections to the plea.[22]

After briefly refuting Hale, the defense proceeded to consider the general principle on which the plea could be supported. Contending that it is a "fundamental doctrine in the law, that there is no wrong without a remedy, and no right without the means of enforcing it." The defense asked:

Is it not a wrong to be accused and subjected to prosecution on illegal evidence; to be injured in character, in peace of mind, and in the trouble and expense of defending one's self against an indictment, which by the rules of evidence and law ought not to have been found? If so, what is the remedy?

The defense acknowledged that grand juries ought to listen only to *ex parte* evidence,

but that should be of such a nature as would be received to support the prosecution before a petty jury. . . . The rules of evidence, are the result of accurate reasoning, and of a strict regard to the rights of those, whose persons or property are to be affected. That reasoning is equally accurate, and those rights ought to be equally sacred, whether the investigation be before a grand or petty jury. Those rules of evidence are not the result of any statutory regulations, but are adopted on account of their wisdom, justice, and universal applicability.

Why should the grand jury be excused from such rules? Are grand juries independent and irresponsible "judging for themselves as to the grounds on which they will prefer an accusation, and that no one has a right to investigate or to know what evidence they have had before them." No, the defense answered, "Grand Juries are the offspring of free government; they are a protection against ill founded accusations. . . ." The defense concluded by replying briefly to the formal objections.[23]

At this point the grand jury made an unusual presentment, representing to the court that

it does appear that the Honorable Matthias B. Tallmadge, Esq. . . . did on the examination of William Smith and Samuel G. Ogden, as witnesses and principals touching certain crimes said to have been committed against the Laws of the United States, proceed in a manner UNUSUAL, OPPRESSIVE AND CONTRARY TO LAW.[24]

The judge adjourned the court until the next day without replying to the grand jury.[25]

The court rejected the defense plea on the 10th, and after further maneuvering failed, the defendants severally pleaded not guilty. The district attorney moved for leave "to proceed to the trial of the several indictments." Mr. Colden countered, requesting that the trial be postponed until the next circuit court in order that the attendance of several material witnesses from out of the city, including James Madison, William Duncanson, and Doctor William Thornton of Washington, D. C., and Thomas Lewis and Jonathan S. Smith of the *Leander*, could be procured. The court ordered a postponement until July 14 when a special session of the court would be held.[26]

Although there were political overtones in the April proceedings, the decision of the court basically had turned upon the legal arguments. Shortly after the court adjourned, Josiah Quincy, representative from Massachusetts, presented to the House of Representatives memorials drafted by Ogden and Smith. The House received the memorials on April 21. Two points were emphasized: First that the memorialists had been "led into error by the conduct of officers of the Executive Government," and second, that the memorialists "have also experienced great oppression and injustice in the manner of conducting the said prosecution." Several House members immediately defended the administration and criticized an introduction of the petitions before the case had been tried. The House overwhelmingly passed a resolution offered by Representative Peter Early as follows:

Resolved, That the charge contained in the memorials of S. G. Ogden and William Smith, are in the opinion of this House, unsupported by any evidence which, in the least degree, criminated the Executive government of this country;—that the said memorials appear to have been presented at a time and under circumstances insidiously calculated to excite unjust suspicions in the minds of the good people of this nation against the existing Administration of the General Government, and that it would be highly improper in this House to take any step which might influence or prejudice a cause now depending in a legal tribunal of the United States. Therefore, *resolved*, That the said memorials be by the Clerk of this House returned to those from whom they came.[27]

The controversy over the memorials sporadically continued in the press until the 14th when the circuit court convened to hear the case of the *United States* v. *William Smith*, Associate Justice Paterson of the Supreme Court and district judge Talmadge in attendance. Sanford presented a list of sixty prosecution witnesses. Mr. Colden on behalf of the defendant requested calling twenty-three witnesses. The defense list included not only James Madison but several other government officials among whom were Albert Gallatin, Henry Dearborn, and Gideon Granger. Mr. Colden read a subpeona directed to Madison and served on May 18. He indicated that he had subpoenas for other witnesses who were not in attendance and trusted that the "court would not order the trail to proceed until the defendant has had the compulsory process of the court, to bring up the witnesses who have disobeyed the subpoena." Colden moved that an attachment be issued compelling the witnesses to attend and that the court adjourn until the process was completed. The district attorney refused to argue the issue of whether an attachment should issue or not, contending that the trial should proceed and that the issue should be taken up later. Judge Paterson proceeded to read to the assemblage a letter received from Madison, Dearborn, and R. Smith, indicating that they regretted that the President of the United States, "taking into view the state of our public affairs, has specially signified to us that our official duties cannot, consistently therewith, be at this juncture dispensed with." The officials involved agreed to submit written depositions taken by the district attorney.[28]

Colden indicated that he had received a copy of the letter but insisted that in the opinion of the defense counsels "they could not. . . dispense with the attendance of these witnesses, or consent to receive their testimony in the way it had been offered."[29] The argument on the issue commenced with Sanford contending that the defendant must show that the absent witnesses were material for his defense in the present cause. Judge Paterson agreed and instructed the defense to offer an affidavit showing in "what respect the witnesses are material."[30]

After a brief conference between the contending counsel, Mr. Colden declared that they had agreed to postpone further proceedings until tomorrow. He then moved on the motion for attachments. Sanford countered that by agreeing to a postponement, he had not waived the priority of his motion that the trial should proceed. The court decided that the two motions should be argued simultaneously the following day.[31]

On Tuesday the defense offered an affidavit by William S. Smith relating to the relevancy of the testimony that could be offered by James Madison, Robert Smith, Jacob Wagner, and Dr. Thornton. The thrust of the argument was that the witnesses could testify that the expedition had the "knowledge and approbation" of the President and Secretary of State. At the conclusion of the remarks by Colden and Hoffman, Judge Paterson expressed "some regret that it was not in the power of the parties to carry the present motion up to the supreme court for its opinion. . . ."[32]

Sanford read a counter affidavit, claiming that the offences laid in the indictments occurred in New York at a time when the witnesses were in Washington, D. C., and that the witnesses "have not . . . any personal knowledge of the offences charged in the said indictments. . . ." The prosecution spent the remainder of the day explaining the affidavit and rebutting the defense's opening statement. The defense counsels used the whole of Wednesday on the same issue. On Thursday, July 17, Judge Paterson rendered the court's opinion on the two motions. On the motion to postpone the trial, he stated that the subpoenas had been served and asked if the evidence to be given by the witnesses were material? The defendant's affidavit contended that the enterprise was "begun, prepared and set on foot with the knowledge and approbation" of the executive department of the government. The judge cautioned that the "president of the United States is bound by the constitution to 'take care, that the laws be faithfully executed.' " He presumed that the President "would not countenance the violation of any statute; and, particularly, if such violation consisted in expeditions of a warlike nature against friendly powers." Even if he should give his approval, did the Neutrality Act of 1794 grant him a dispensing power? No, the judge answered, "the President of the United States cannot control the statute, nor dispense with its execution, and still less can authorize a person to do what the law forbids." The judge admitted that the testimony might be offered to mitigate punishment but the "suggestion; that the evidence should be permitted to pass to the jury, that they may determine whether the offender ought to be recommended for mercy, is utterly destitute of foundation." The judge indicated that he and his colleague had split on the motion to issue an attachment. Under the law "either party may carry 'the issue' to the supreme court for an ultimate decision. . . ."[33]

Sanford immediately moved to bring on the trial. The defense counsel requested a delay for a few days or to the next term. Judge Paterson stated that the court had considered that point. He was inclined to grant a delay due to his own infirm health but relinquished the idea. He did not perceive "any benefit which could result to the defendant by granting the application." At this point Judge Paterson left the bench. The court agreed to postpone further proceedings until the next day "on condition that the defendant's counsel would make no other attempt to create delay." The defense consented; the court adjourned until the 18th.[34]

The trial opened the next day. Sanford addressed the court and jury, explaining the general nature of the charge and indicating that it seemed to resolve itself into four principal points.

1st. That a military expedition was set on foot in this city. 2d. That this military expedition, was destined to be carried on against the dominions of Spain, in South America. 3d. That the defendant was concerned in preparing the expedition, in some of the modes charged in the indictment; that is to say, either by beginning it, or by setting it on foot, or by providing men and money, as means for the expedition. —And, 4th. That at the time when this shall appear to have been done, the United States and the King of Spain were at peace. Sanford then summarized the substance of the testimony the prosecution intended to offer.[35]

The first witness called was Samuel G. Ogden. Ogden acknowledged knowing Colonel Smith, seeing him with Miranda, and being introduced to Miranda. When asked what was the object of the first meeting between himself, Smith, and Miranda, Ogden replied that the purpose "was to make me acquainted with Gen. Miranda as a man of science and a great traveller." Sanford then inquired "What was the object of the expedition that was fitting out at the time? Was it against the Spanish dominions in South America?" Ogden declined to answer the question. Sanford queried, "Did you ever hear Col. Smith speak of an expedition to the West Indies?" Mr. Hoffman interjected that to answer such questions as "would tend to criminate himself will not be required by the court." Ogden answered, "If you ask this as a particular question, I decline to answer. If you put it as a general quesiton, I answer yes."[36] Judge Talmadge declared that the question appeared proper and instructed Ogden that he must say if he knew "anything of a conversation or declaration of Mr. Smith, made relative to the matters charged in the indictment."[37]

Colden expressed the hope that the court would not compel the witness to give testimony "as to confessions or conversations of the defendant, which may be made use of against the witness when it comes to his turn to be a defendant, and which will tend to criminate him." The court again stated that it was proper that the witness answer the question. Colden countered that he hoped this was "not a positive decision of the court. . . . The court is now to make a decision of the utmost consequence, not only to this defendant and to the witness, but to every citizen, inasmuch as it involved a fundamental principle in the administration of justice. A witness is not bound to give testimony which may tend to criminate himself. . . ."[38]

Edwards proposed a new wording of the question, which Colden also opposed. The court then declared that the defense must show "how this tends to criminate Mr. Ogden." Colden then demonstrated that both men were indicted for fitting out in the *Leander* a military expedition against the Spanish colonies. For the prosecutor to prove his case, he must prove that the witness not only provided and prepared means which might be applied to a military expedition, "but he must show upon the trial of the witness, that the witness knew that the means he did provide were intended for a military expedition." If the witness in answering the question should indicate that he knew the means were to be used in an expedition against Caracas, "would not this tend to criminate the witness?" Colden objected to being asked to answer specifically how the testimony would criminate the witness, for if he answered "you would contravene the reason of the rule, and draw him from that protection which he ought to find under the rule." Colden concluded that the court must accept the witness's declaration that it would criminate him.[39]

Mr. Hoffman proposed that if the district attorney desired the testimony of Mr. Ogden on this point, he should first enter a *"nolle prosequi,* and discharge the witness from the prosecution." The court indicated that the witness merely had to state whether he had "heard any confessions or admissions on the part of the defendant . . . not . . . to say in what degree he may have been an accomplice." Hoffman again asserted that "Nothing can entitle the prosecutor to his testimony but a *nolle prosequi,* according to all the rules of the English law."[40]

Ogden then declined to answer. Sanford did not force the issue but stated he did not waive the right to call upon the court to enforce its decision hereafter. After answering several questions, Ogden declined to reply when asked if Miranda had applied to him to charter a vessel. Sanford rephrased the question, asking bluntly if the witness chartered a vessel to Miranda. Ogden was about to answer when Emmet objected. Following a brief debate between Emmet and Edwards, the court declared that it could not see how the question could criminate the witness, since the testimony "could not be given in evidence on his indictment. . . because it is not a voluntary confession on his part." Hoffman and Emmet both declared "that it could be given in evidence by a third person." Edwards again asked, "How could it be given in evidence against himself."[41] Ogden replied that his answer might "lead to the fountain-head; they might supply by other witnesses what is wanting in mine, and thereby fill up the chasm." Sanford asked no further questions of the witness, although he again reserved the right to call on the court to enforce its decision.[42]

Hoffman posed two questions. First, he asked if Ogden had seen General Miranda in company with Mr. Smith and others? Ogden replied that he had seen "Gen. Miranda frequently in company with the first characters in New York." The second question inquired whether Ogden knew that Miranda had dined with officers of the government and was known to Madison and the President? The court declared that the question was unnecessary since the evidence would be hearsay. Ogden then stepped down as a witness.[43]

The prosecution called a variety of other witnesses to the stand. They identified Smith as the purchaser of a quantity of military supplies, such as swords, pistols, and gun-powder, and a recruiter of men for the expedition.

The parade of prosecution witnesses continued until August 22 when the prosecution temporarily closed its case.[44]

Mr. Colden opened for the defense by stating that he had expected to be able to prove that the acts charged upon the defendant as crimes "were done with the sanction and approbation of the president of the United States." Even without the subpoenaed witnesses Mr. Colden still hoped to establish that the President and Secretary of State had knowledge of the expedition and were "intimately acquainted with all his views and designs." Finally, Mr. Colden called attention to the prosecutor's assertion that the cause could not be maintained unless the United States and Spain were at peace. He stated that he wished to show "the real situation of this country, in relation to the Spanish government" by reading, with the permission of the court, the message of the President of the United States to Congress and a variety of other documents.[45]

Sanford instantly objected. The court eventually upheld the objection, rejecting various defense contentions that a state of war could exist without a declaration from Congress.[46] The defense next moved to offer testimony "to show that the government had knowledge of the whole transaction." The bench refused to permit this line of testimony, considering it immaterial to the issue.[47]

As Mr. Colden was proceeding to address the jury, the district attorney interrupted him to say "that he should offer further testimony." Whereupon he called several additional witnesses and then finally rested the prosecution.[48]

Colden, Hoffman, Emmet, and Harison addressed the jury for the defense; Sanford and Edwards summarized the case for the prosecution. Judge Talmadge then charged the jury, concluding:

It is not a question of party politics. The people of the United States of all denominations are equally interested; and I have too much respect for the character of an American jury to anticipate a determination upon such grounds. The undertaking may of itself be a great and glorious one, worthy of the breast of a good man, glowing with desire for the universal emancipation of those oppressed by the weight of monarchical power; nevertheless, an upright and dignified course of conduct, a harmonious intercourse with foreign nations is worthy the attention, is the duty of our government to cultivate and maintain. The laws must be observed and enforced. Sympathy ought not to cloud the conception nor warp the judgment of a jury whose duty simply is to pronounce truly upon the facts in evidence. The attribute of mercy is in other hands, and no doubt will be discreetly exercised.[49]

The jury after two hours deliberation returned a verdict of not guilty. Smith was thereupon discharged.[50]

The trial of Samuel G. Ogden, which commenced on Friday, was anticlimatic. Judge Talmadge early ruled that attachments ought not to issue. During the process of drawing a jury, the defense challenged one juror as being partial, and another juror, Schuyler Livingston, asked to be excused "as having been one of the jurors who had passed upon the trial of William S. Smith." Mr. Colden insisted that this was not a legal excuse, but the judge decided that Mr. Livingston "was not a fit juror."[51]

Sanford addressed the jury and then proceeded to call a lengthy list of witnesses. The prosecution rested early on Saturday morning. Mr. Colden attempted to offer evidence that the expedition had the consent of the President, but again the court refused to accept this line of testimony. Colden, Hoffman, and Emmet summarized the issue for the defense; Edwards addressed the jury for the prosecution. Judge Talmadge charged the jury in a manner similar to that in the trial of Smith. After retiring for a short time the jury returned a verdict of not guilty. Thereupon the court ordered Ogden discharged.[52]

The two trials had finally ended. Various newspapers immediately praised the jury and condemned the President. The New York *Evening Post* called upon Jefferson to say whether he was "not fully informed that General Miranda came to this country for the express purpose of fitting out the expedition which has sailed for Caracas." Jefferson declined to answer publicly, but months earlier, in March, he had written to William Duane that such an assertion "is an absolute falsehood. To know as much of it as we could was our duty, but not to encourage it."[53]

Madison, attempting to discover whether the absence of government witnesses had affected the outcome, wrote Sanford on August 1 requesting a statement of why the trial had resulted in an acquittal. Pierrepont Edwards supplied the answer. He indicated that the attendance of the witnesses was neither desired nor expected.

> To disgrace the president and you and the present administration was the point aimed at from the start—and it is a course of infinite mortification to the friends of the administration here that conduct, springing from such motives, should be crowned with so much success and have such cause of triumph.[54]

"The verdict was not wholly partisan, for even the Republicans on the jury had voted for acquittal." Even though the prosecution ably presented the government's case, the implication that the government was behind Miranda and the general feeling that "nobody regarded it as a crime to aid a revolution against Spain" were the determining factors.[55]

There were a few immediate results. Before the grand jury issued the indictments, Jefferson removed John Swartwout, the Federalist marshal of the district who had empanelled the jurors.[56] The President late in August ordered Sanford to bring Thomas Lewis to trial. This was not done. The country quickly became absorbed with another and more famous enterprise, that of Aaron Burr, and soon forgot the aborted Miranda expedition.[57]

The history and interpretation of Burr's conspiracy is available in a variety of works.[58] The legal proceedings relating to the conspiracy occurred in federal courts in five states, three territories, the District of Columbia, and the Supreme Court. The legal proceedings involved fifteen different people, but the courts tried only two—Burr and Major Davis Floyd. The first investigation occurred in Kentucky where the grand jury in December 1806 refused to indict Burr and John Adair. On his arrival at New Orleans in January, Adair was arrested and transferred to Baltimore, Maryland, where state judge Joseph F. Nicholson released him because of the lack of evidence. General James Wilkinson had several people arrested in New Orleans during his so called "reign of terror." They included Peter V. Ogden, whom Judge James Workman of the territorial court released; James Alexander, who like Adair was transferred to Maryland where Judge Nicholson released him; and Judge Workman and Louis Kerr, freed by the federal district judge of Louisiana.[59] Samuel Swartwout and Justus E. Bollman were arrested in New Orleans and sent to the District of Columbia. The circuit court of the district rejected by a 2 to 1 vote a writ of *habeas corpus* to free the two men.[60] The Supreme Court heard the case of Swartwout and Bollman on appeal. For the only time during the period the full Court interpreted the treason clause of the Constitution.

John Marshall rendered the decision of the Court which ordered the two men freed. The interpretation of treason specified in the decision presented Marshall with several problems a few months later when he presided over the Burr trial. "To constitute a levying of war," the Court wrote, "there must be an assemblage of persons for the purpose of effecting by force a treasonable purpose. Enlistment of men to serve against the government is not sufficient." Furthermore,

any assemblage of men for the purpose of revolutionizing by force the government established by the United States in any of its territories, although as a step to, or the means of executing, some greater projects, amount to levying war. The travelling of individuals to the place of rendezvous is not sufficient; but the meeting of particular bodies of men and their marching from places of partial, to a place of general rendezvous, is such an assemblage as constitutes a levying of war.

Finally, Marshall wrote, "When war is levied, all those who perform any part, however minute, or however remote from the scene of action, and who are actually leagued in the general conspiracy, are traitors."[61]

Before the Supreme Court heard the case, Senator William Branch Giles of Virginia pushed through the Senate a bill that would have suspended the writ of *habeas corpus* for three months for persons charged with treason, misprision of treason, or other high crimes or misdemeanors, endangering the peace, safety, or neutrality of the United States. A less compliant House, rejected the bill 133 to 19 on January 26, the same day it received the bill from the Senate.[62] The House further stirred the waters when Representative James M. Broom of Delaware proposed a resolution that it was "expedient to make further provision for securing the privilege of the writ of *habeas corpus* to persons in custody under or by color of the authority of the United States." The House debated the resolution from the 17th to the 19th when it voted 60 to 58 to indefinitely postpone consideration. Although defeated by a concerted effort by Jefferson and his supporters, the debates evoked the first major consideration of civil liberties since the adoption of the Bill of Rights.[63]

The Mississippi Territory grand jury investigated Harman Blennerhassett, Comfort Tyler, Major Davis Floyd, and Ralston but discharged them. Among the seven persons the Virginia grand jury indicted were Blennerhassett, Tyler, and Floyd. In addition Burr, Jonathan Dayton, John Smith, and Israel Smith were charged in Virginia with treason and misdemeanor. The Ohio grand jury indicted Blennerhassett for treason, but he was never tried.[64]

The Indiana Territory grand jury indicted Floyd of a high misdemeanor. The petit jury convicted him, and the court sentenced him to three hours in jail and a fine of $20. Shortly after the trial the lower House of the territorial legislature elected him the clerk.[65]

The district attorney of Pennsylvania, Alexander Dallas, charged Bartholomew White with a misdemeanor in April, shortly after the Virginia grand jury began investigating the charges of treason against Burr and several other conspirators. In March 1809 Dallas asked Attorney General Caesar A. Rodney what should be done with White. Rodney sent the letter to Madison, argreeing with Dallas that "White is too small game for us to pursue." Dallas shortly thereafter dropped the prosecution.[66]

The conspirators were small game. The "big game" was Burr. Twice he appeared before the Kentucky district court grand jury, and twice the grand jury refused to indict him; and once in the Mississippi territory with the same result. In Virginia, however, the grand jury indicted him for treason and misdemeanor, and the court tried him on both counts. After acquittal in Virginia the grand jury of Ohio indicted him for treason, but the court did not try him.[67]

The trials of Burr in Virginia have been ably and extensively reported. Two things stand out that should be mentioned. First, Marshall clarified and elaborated upon the definition of treason enunciated in *Bollman and Swartwout*. The indictment charged Burr with treason in levying war which had taken place on the island belonging to Harman Blennerhassett. Although Burr was not physically present, the government charged that he was legally present, thus the question arose "whether in this case the doctrine of constructive presence can apply." Marshall conceded that a person could be legally present if he had procured men to meet for the purpose of levying war; however, Marshall continued,

If in one case the presence of the individual make the guilty of the assemblage his guilt, and in the other case the procurement by the individual make the guilt of the assemblage his guilt, then presence and procurement are equally competent parts of the overt act, and equally require two witnesses.

Marshall realized that "the advising or procurement of treason" was a secret transaction, but he said "that the difficulty of proving a fact will not justify conviction without proof," and "certainly it will not justify conviction without [one] direct and positive witness in a case where the constitution requires two." With this interpretation Burr's acquital was certain on the charge of treason.[68]

The second signifiant occurrence during the trial was the attempt to subpeona the President. Burr maintained that certain orders had been issued by the government to the army and navy, which he had seen in print. The Secretary of the Navy had refused to allow him or his counsel to see the actual documents, hence Burr felt that the court should subpoena the President requiring him to produce certain papers. Informed of the move by the district attorney, Jefferson responded:

Reserving the necessary right of the President of the United States to decide, independently of all other authority, what papers, coming to him as President, the public interests permit to be communicated, and to whom, I assure you of my readiness under that restriction, voluntarily to furnish on all occasions, whatever the purposes of justice may require.

When court opened on June 10, Burr renewed his request. After an acrimonious exchange between various counsel, Marshall ruled that a *subpoena duces tecum* (court commands a witness to produce a document or paper at a trial) "be issued, directed to Thomas Jefferson, President of the United States." Jefferson refused to obey the subpoena and even threatened to use force against the execution of the process. One of the letters; however, was secured by *subpoena duces tecum* from District Attorney George Hay, with such parts of the letter as the President believed confidential omitted. The President ignored a second subpoena. "And there this heated and dangerous controversy appears to have ended."[69]

The repercussions of the conspiracy lasted more than a year after the trial. In February 1808 the Senate approved a treason bill; however, the House, late in the session on April 15, voted to postpone consideration indefinitely.[70]

Senator John Smith of Ohio, although not convicted by any court, had to withstand a Senate attempt to expel him. The inquiry which began on November 27 ended on April 9, 1808, when the Senate voted 19 to 10 to reject the resolution of expulsion.[71]

Judge Harry Innes, who presided over the Kentucky grand jury in 1806, was the subject of a House inquiry into his conduct. That commenced on March 21 and ended on April 19, 1808, when the committee to investigate his conduct, cleared him of any wrongdoing.[72] Finally Wilkinson was tried before a court martial between January 11 and June 18, 1808. The court cleared Wilkinson of charges of having been employed by Spain.[73]

The trials of Smith, Ogden, and Burr provide numerous gems for the study of legal history: first use of the Fifth Amendment, the right of the courts to subpoena the President or other executive officers, and the power of the President or lack thereof to suspend the operation of a law. The trials also revealed one of the safeguards of the Anglo-American criminal justice procedure—the ability of adverse public opinion to blunt the prosecutorial powers of the executive branch. Jefferson and his successors faced the reverse problem of how can the federal government enforce a criminal law when the general population or the population of a particular section is opposed to the law. The government would confront the problem over and over again in its attempt to carry on economic warfare with Britain and France starting in 1806 and culminating with the Embargo of 1807.

NOTES

1. *Annals of Congress*, XIII:14-15.

2. Pennsylvania circuit court, Minute Book, 1802-1805, pp. 110, 127.

3. The trials surrounding the Miranda and Burr conspiracies have been excluded. In 1804-1805 the South Carolina circuit court convicted Colin Mitchell twice, Barnard Johnson, Duncan Stewart, and Isaac Laures. The court fined the men as follows: Mitchell, a fine of $100 and imprisonment for fifteen days; Johnson, a fine of $50 and imprisonment for one month; Stewart, a fine of $1,000; and Laures, a fine of $50 and imprisonment for three months. The Massachusetts circuit court convicted one person in 1808 for illegally fitting out a vessel and fined him $40. South Carolina circuit court, Minute Book, 1790-1809 (Federal Records Center, East Point, Ga.) 223, 225, 229, 239, 240-242, 249; *A Statement of Convictions, Executions, and Pardons*, U. S. 20th Congress, 2nd session, House Document 146 (1829), 20a.

4. See Madison to Zebulon Hollingsworth, district attorney Maryland, August 28, October 26, 1804; Madison to Nathan Sanford, September 19, 1804; Madison to David Gelston, July 17, 1805; Madison to Collector of St. Mary's, January 6, 1806; Madison to Thomas Newton, June 11, 1806; Madison to John Stephen, July 19, 1806; Madison to Collector of the Customs at Norfolk, July 19, 1806; Madison to John Stephen, October 25, 1806 (Microcopy M 40), reel 12, pp. 359, 367, 375, 378; reel 13, pp. 15, 65-66, 123, 136-137, 145, 163.

5. Madison to Governor McKean of Pennsylvania, February 18, 1803 (Microcopy M 40), reel 12, p. 127. Madison sent the same letter to the Governors of Kentucky and Tennessee.

6. New York circuit court, Criminal Cases, Boxes 1-4.

7. Henry R. Lemly, "A Forgotton International Episode," *Journal of the Military Service Institute of the United States*, 52 (May, 1952), 396-397.

8. Brant, *James Madison*, IV:325.

9. Lemly, "A Forgotten International Episode," 397; Joseph Francis Thorning, *Miranda: World Citizen* (Gainesville, 1952), 172.

10. Brant, *James Madison*, IV:325; William Spence Robertson, *The Life of Miranda* (2 vols., Chapel Hill, 1929), I:293; William Spence Robertson, "Francisco de Miranda and the Revolutionizing of Spanish America," American Historical Association *Report*, 1907 (2 vols., Washington, D. C., 1908), I:361.

11. Robertson, "Francisco de Miranda and the Revolutionizing of Spanish America," I:362; Brant, *James Madison*, IV:325.

12. Brant, *James Madison*, IV:325; Thorning, *Miranda*, 172-173; Robertson, "Francisco Miranda and Revolutionizing of Spanish America," I: 362.

13. Brant, *James Madison*, IV:326; Lemly, "A Forgotten International Episode," 398; Thorning, *Miranda*, 173-175; Robertson, *The Life of Miranda*, I:294-297; Robertson, "Francisco de Miranda and the Revolutionizing of Spanish America," I: 363-365.

14. Robertson, "Francisco de Miranda and the Revolutionizing of Spanish America," I: 366-368; Robertson, *The Life of Miranda*, I:297-300; Brant, *James Madison*, IV:328.

15. Robertson, "Francisco de Miranda and the Revolutionizing of Spanish America," I:369-373; Robertson, *The Life of Miranda*, I:300-301; Thorning, *Miranda*, 175; Brant, *James Madison*, IV:329-330.

16. Madison to Sanford, February 7, 17, 1806 (Microcopy M 40), reel 13, p. 90.

17. *The Trials of William S. Smith and Samuel G. Ogden*, . . . *in July 1806* (New York, 1807), xviii-xviv.

18. Madison to Sanford, March 21, 1806 (Microcopy M 40), reel 13, p. 97; Breckenridge to Jefferson, March 18, 1806, Letters From and Opinions of the Attorney General (1 reel, National Archives, Record Group 60, Microcopy T 326), reel 1.

19. Brant, *James Madison*, IV:335.

20. *Trials*, iii-vi.

21. Ibid., xxiv-xxvi.

22. Ibid., xxvi-xxvii.

23. Ibid., xxvii-xxxiii.

24. New York circuit court, Criminal Cases, file box 4.

25. *Trials*, xxxiii.

26. Ibid., xv-xvii.

27. *Annals of Congress*, XV:1085-1094.

28. *Trials*, 1-7; New York *Evening Post*, June 4-6, 1806.

29. *Trials*, 7-8.

30. Ibid., 8-9.

31. Ibid., 9-11.

32. Ibid., 11-26.

33. Ibid., 26-89.

34. Ibid., 89-90.

35. Ibid., 90-95.

36. Ibid., 95-96.

37. Ibid., 98.

38. Ibid.

39. Ibid., 96-98.

40. Ibid., 98.

41. Ibid., 98-100.

42. Ibid., 100.

43. Ibid.

44. Ibid., 100-128.

45. Ibid., 128-129.

46. Ibid., 129-147.

47. Ibid., 147.

48. Ibid., 147-152.

49. Ibid., 152-242.

50. Ibid., 242.

51. Ibid., 245-247.

52. Ibid., 247-287.

53. New York *Evening Post*, July 28, 1806; Jefferson to Willian Duane, March 22, 1806, Thomas Jefferson, *Writings*, ed. Andrew A. Lispcomb (20 vols., Washington, D. C., 1903), XI:96.

54. Madison to Sanford, August 1, 1806 (Microcopy M 40), reel 13, p. 142; Brant, *James Madison*, IV:337.

55. Brant, *James Madison*, IV:337-338.

56. Madison to Sanford, August 31, 1806 (Microcopy M 40), reel 13, p. 152.

57. On June 24, 1806, James Cheetham wrote to Jefferson enclosing a list of grand and petit jurors with their party affiliations. Cheetham felt that "a fair and impartial trial of the gentlemen indicted cannot be expected from any jury which that officer will select." According to Cheetham the grand jury contained sixteen Federalists, five Burrites, and three Repbulicans. The petit jury panel was composed of thirty-four Federalists, eleven Burrites, and three Republicans. (Micrcopy M 418), reel 10.

58. See Albert J. Beveridge, *The Life of John Marshall* (4 vols., Boston and New York, 1919), III:274-545; Thomas Perkins Abernethy, *The Burr Conspiracy* (reprint, Gloucester, Mass., 1968); Walter F. McCaleb, *New Light on Aaron Burr* (Austin, 1963); Nathan Schachner, *Thomas Jefferson: A Biography* (New York and London, 1957), 823-861; Dumas Malone, *Jefferson and His Time, Vol. V: Jefferson the President: Second Term, 1805-1809* (Boston, 1975), 215-370; and Milton Lomask, *Arron Burr, The Conspiracy and Years of Exile, 1805-1836* (New York, 1982) 3-298.

59. Samuel M. Wilson, ed., "The Court Proceedings in 1806 in Kentucky Against Aaron Burr and John Adair," *Filson Club Historical Quarterly*, 10 (January, 1936), 37-39; Beveridge, *Marshall*, III:332-337, 344-346; Abernethy, *The Burr Conspiracy*, 172-182, 227-228; Mary K. Bonsteel Tachau, *Federal Courts in the Early Republic; Kentucky 1789-1816* (Princeton, 1978), 138-145; Charleston *Courier*, January 10, 1807.

60. Beveridge, *Marshall*, III:332-334, 344-346; Abernethy, *Burr Conspiracy*, 172-182, 227-228; Charleston *Courier*, January 10, 1807.

61. Cranch *Reports*, IV:75-137.

62. *Annals of Congress*, XIV:44, 402-426.

63. Ibid., 502-590.

64. Abernethy, *Burr Conspiracy*, 220, 227-228, 258-259; Beveridge, *Marshall*,

III:465-466, 527; Virginia circuit court, Order Book #6, 1806-1807, pp. 200-202, 229, 231, 235-236, 246.

65. Isaac J. Cox, "The Burr Conspiracy in Indiana," *Indiana Magazine of History*, 25 (December, 1929), 275-280. Abernethy, *Burr Conspiracy*, 263, reported the fine as $10.

66. Pennsylvania circuit court, Minute Book, 1805-1808, pp. 254, 285, 316, 324-325; Pennsylvania circuit court, Criminal Case Files, Box 5, 1800-1814; Dallas to C. A. Rodney, March 19, 1809, C. A. Rodney to Madison, October 24, 1809 (Microcopy T326), reel 1.

67. Wilson, ed., "The Court Proceedings of 1806 in Kentucky," 31-38; Beveridge, *Marshall*, III:317-319, 363-365, 465-466, 524; Abernethy, *Burr Conspiracy*, 95-99, 209-210, 217-218, 240, 260.

68. Cranch, *Reports,* IV:500. See also Robert K. Faulkner, "John Marshall and the Burr Trial," *Journal of American History*, 53 (September, 1966), 247-258; and David Robertson, *Reports of the Trials of Colonel Aaron Burr in the Circuit Court of the United States* (2 vols., Richmond, 1808).

69. Beveridge, *Marshall*, III:433-451, 518-522.

70. *Annals of Congress*, XVII:207; XVIII:2279.

71. *Annals of Congress*, XVII:39-42, 55-63, 66-78, 81-98, 164-170, 178-180, 184-234.

72. *Annals of Congress*, XVIII:1858, 1860, 1886, 2197, 2247-2250, 2760-2790; Tachau, *Federal Courts in the Early Republic*, 145.

73. Abernethy, *Burr Conspiracy*, 265-274.

4

Economic Coercion and the Courts

The Jeffersonian courts not only had to deal with multiple domestic problems but also became deeply involved in the political struggles over foreign policy. The reopening of the European conflict in 1803 placed renewed stress on the United States' relations with France and Great Britain.

In the summer of 1804 Captain Bradley of H.M.S. *Cambrian*, trying to intercept Jerome Bonaparte, searched a number of ships in New York harbor. Jefferson referred to the incident in his Fourth Annual Message, pointing out that harassment of the commerce of neutral nations "have, in distant parts, disturbed ours less than on former occasions; but in the American seas they have been greater from peculiar causes, and even within our harbors and jurisdiction infringements on the authority of the laws have been committed which have called for serious attention." Congress responded with a bill for the more effectual preservation of peace in the ports and harbors of the United States and in the water under their jurisdiction. The bill became law on March 3, 1805.[1]

The act required a judge or justice of any court of the United States, upon satisfactory proof, to issue a warrant directed to a marshal to arrest the offender and bring him before "the judge or justice, to be dealt with according to law." The act permitted the marshal, if he anticipated the need for assistance, to ask the judge or justice to issue an order directing any militia or regular army officer or any commander of an armed vessel of the United States to assist the marshal. The marshal, either singly or with assistance, could demand the surrender of the offender. If the request were resisted, the marshal could use force to seize the person. If the marshal or a person assisting him were killed, the "persons engaged in resisting the civil authority" should be punished "as in cases of felonious homicide." If the marshal or his party should kill one of the persons resisting arrest, the killing was justified. This is the only instance of a federal law defining justifiable homicide. In addition Section 2 authorized a state Governor to use regular troops or armed vessels of the United States to execute a state process against a person who should flee to a foreign armed vessel in any port or harbor of the United States. Several members of the House, among whom were Joseph H. Nicholson and George W. Campbell, could not conceive that a state officer could go out of his jurisdiction to execute a process. The act provided for a fine not exceeding $5,000 for any officer who should refuse to obey the requisition.

Section 6 was unique. It permitted the President by proclamation to prohibit the entrance of any foreign officer (or ship he commanded) who had committed any trespass or tort or spoilation on board any vessel of the United States or "any unlawful interruption or vexation of trading vessels actually coming to or going from the United States." Furthermore, if such officer after the President's proclamation should be found in the United States, he could be arrested, indicted, and punished by fine and imprisonment. The act specified that the sentence should require the person after the payment of fine and expiration of the term of imprisonment to leave the United States, "never to return." If the person should return after the passing of sentence, he could again be indicted, fined, and imprisoned "at the discretion of the court."

Section 8 permitted any person sued for anything done in pursuance of the act to "plead the general issue and give this act in evidence." This section would later be included in the Enforcement Acts of 1809 and 1815. Finally, Congress limited the act to a term of ten years.

The reversal of the broken voyage doctrine in the *Essex* decision, an increase in impressment from American ships, and general harassment of neutral rights between 1805 and 1806 prompted the Republicans to undertake additional counter measures. On January 28, 1806, Representative Andrew Gregg introduced a resolution proposing that no products of Great Britain or her colonies be imported into the United States. Representative Nicholson softened non-importation with a counter resolution introduced on February 10 specifying a limited number of articles that would be banned. The House formulated the Nicholson approach into a bill which it approved on April 18.[2]

The act to prohibit the importation of certain goods, wares, and merchandise went into effect on November 15. If any of the specified merchandise should be imported after that date, the articles as well as the vessel would be forfeited, and the owner would forfeit treble the value of the articles. Double the amount of the value of goods would be assessed any person who should conceal or buy any illegal articles. Administration of the act would be the same as for the Collection Act of 1799, and remission would be handled under the Remission Act of 1797.[3]

Before the act went into effect, Jefferson instructed James Monroe and William Pinkney to undertake negotiations with the British to try to resolve outstanding differences. After several delays the negotiations finally got underway in August. As the November deadline approached, the discussions were still in progress. British exporters were concerned for the safety of the cargoes of the fall fleet due to leave England between August and the November deadline. The American consul in Liverpool cautioned the British that Congress might repeal the law in the next session, "yet that in all vessels of my own employ I refuse any article prohibited by the law in question."[4]

On the appointed day the custom officials enforced the law at American ports.[5] As quickly as the seizures occurred, Albert Gallatin started receiving petitions for remission of the penalties. The administration acted quickly. On December 3rd, Jefferson sent Congress a message requesting suspension of non-importation until July 1 and further authorizing the President to further delay implementation "if. . . the public interest should require it" until the second Monday of December. The act remitted all fines incurred from November 15 until the passage of the act.[6]

Shortly after passage of the Suspension Act, Monroe and Pinkney signed a treaty with the British. The treaty arrived in the United States early in March, but Jefferson rejected it because the impressment issue had not been resolved. Because a peaceful solution was still possible, on March 24 Jefferson prolonged the suspension of non-importation until December. Shifts in the British government doomed the negotiations. The Whig Ministry of All the Talents fell from power in March; and a Tory ministry, headed by the Duke of Portland with George Canning at the Foreign Office, replaced it. Relations between the United States and Britain became critical in June due to the *Chesapeake-Leopard* incident.[7] Disdaining war, Jefferson again attempted negotiation. The discussions continued through the summer and into the fall. Public opinion, so heavily anti-British immediately after the *Chesapeake-Leopard* affair, had begun to mellow. When Canning abruptly ended the negotiations in October, Monroe and Pinkney sailed for home.[8]

Jefferson faced two possibilities—war, which probably lacked public support, and economic retaliation through restrictions on trade. The latter appeared to be the favored course of action.

The Non-Importation Act was due to take effect in December. Neither the President nor Congress showed any disposition to further suspend or repeal the act. Congress recognized the defects in the ill-drawn measure of 1806. The House Committee of Commerce and Manufactures wrote Gallatin asking what should be done. Gallatin replied that he had been given the "task of administering a law so badly worded that it 'will give rise to much perplexity and numerous suits.' '' Although the administration introduced a new bill, the House delayed consideration until February, well beyond the implementation date of December 14.[9]

For ten weeks the original act remained in effect. Treasury officials seized numerous ships and cargoes for alleged violations.[10] Finally on February 27, 1808, the supplemental bill became law. It clarified the list of prohibited articles and permitted United States' ships which cleared before the 14th of December to return with any kind of cargo provided they returned within specified time limits. The supplemental act effectively suspended the operation of the act until June 14.[11]

Not content with mere non-importation, Jefferson on December 17 discussed an embargo with his cabinet. The following day he submitted a brief message to Congress describing the alleged dangers to American commerce and recommending that Congress take the appropriate steps to inhibit "the departure of our vessels from the ports of the United States." With amazing speed the Republican majorities in the House and Senate approved an embargo on December 22, 1807.[12]

The first section of the act prohibited the departure of any United States' ship to any foreign port or place, except "vessels under the immediate direction of the United States." The second section stipulated that "no registered or sea-letter vessel" should be permitted to depart from one port of the United States to another port of the United States unless bond were posted in the sum of double the value of the cargo and vessel that the cargo shall be relanded in some of the United States, the dangers of the sea excepted.[13] Thus the President had a two-edged sword to use against Great Britain. Under non-importation, certain British products could not be imported and with the embargo no American goods could be sent to Britain or any place in the world.

The embargo proved easier to pass than to enforce. Jefferson's determination to enforce it through state officials presented one problem. Secondly, the American merchantment were keenly aware of the ways and means of circumventing custom laws. Only six days after passage of the embargo, Representative Jacob Crowninshield proposed that the Committee of Commerce and Manufactures inquire into the expediency of amending the Embargo Act.[14] The loophole the merchantmen had discovered was that the act required registered or sea-letter vessels to post bond; however, no restrictions had been placed on vessels licensed for the coastal trade. Crowninshield revealed to the House on the 19th that he had a letter indicating that "certain vessels . . . were now changing their registers, and making out coasting licenses. . . ." While few Congressmen opposed the correction of this defect, several New England representatives wanted vessels engaged in fishing or whaling to be exempted. Representative John Montgomery of Maryland countered that one means of evasion had already been employed.

He hoped "the good sense of the House would not open more doors to fraud or evasion than already were open under the embargo law. He considered this proposition a mere tub to the whale; and hoped it would catch no person in the House."[15] The Supplementary Act, approved on January 9, 1808, closed the coastal trade loophole, stipulated that owners of fishing or whaling vessels should give bond four times the value of the vessel and cargo and that they would not proceed to any foreign port or place, and provided the first penalties for violating either the embargo or the supplementary act. Among the penalties (which applied to both American and foreign vessels, owners, and masters) were (1) if seized, forfeiture of vessel and cargo if a vessel should depart the United States without a clearance or permit; (2) forfeiture of a sum equal to double the value of the ship and cargo if the vessel were not seized; and (3) forfeiture by the master as well as all other persons who shall knowingly be concerned in such prohibited foreign voyage of not less than $1,000 and not more than $20,000 for every such offence.[16]

The acts tested the ingenuity of the American merchantmen, and they rose to the challenge. Difficulties occurred with the bonding procedure, and furthermore the embargo had not dealt with trade on land or on the Great Lakes. In February Congress took steps to close the new loopholes. The Committee of Commerce and Manufactures reported another supplemental bill on February 19. Congress adopted a few proposed changes, although it rejected one calling for the jury instead of the court to determine the amount of fines. New England representatives complained of the operation of the law upon fisheries, claiming that they would be compe led every week to travel fifty, eighty, or one-hundred miles to make oath before the collector that during their voyage they had not sold any of their fishing fare. Representative Mathew Lyon did not like "this string of oaths, required by the embargo laws. There was too much swearing." He also felt ashamed that the House could not adapt a plaster to a sore. "They were stretching the plaster over on to the sound flesh, and he feared it would end in a gangrene."[17]

After the minority had concluded their opposition, Congress approved the bill on March 12. The second supplemental act provided a penalty of $10,000 for each offence of exporting from the United States in any manner, either by land or water, in a vessel, raft, cart, wagon, sleigh, or carriage. The failure of a fishing master or mate to declare on oath or affirmative before a collector whether any part of the fishing fare had been sold during voyage could result in the mate or master forfeiting $100. Finally, Section 7 authorized the President to permit citizens of the United States to send vessels in ballast for property acquired before December 22 for the purpose of importing such property into the United States.[18]

Three weeks after passing the second supplemental act, Congress began discussing a resolution authorizing the President to suspend the operation of the embargo until the commencement of the next session of Congress. In April Congress approved the resolution as translated into a bill.[19]

While the resolution was under consideration, other methods of circumventing the embargo were brought to the attention of Congress.[20] Thus Congress enacted a third supplemental bill on April 25. The new safeguards included a requirement that the lading of a vessel "shall be made hereafter under the inspection of a proper revenue officer"; provided a penalty of $5,000 for departing without a clearance or before a manifest of the cargo was delivered to the collector or surveyor; brought flat boats on the Mississippi River under the act; authorized the collector to detain any vessel ostensibly bound with a cargo to some other port of the United States, whenever "in their opinions the intention is to violate or evade any of the provisions of the acts laying an embargo, until the decision of the President of the United States be had thereupon"; and authorized the collector to seize any unusual deposits of provisions, lumber, or other articles and to refuse to permit the articles to be removed until "bond with sufficient sureties shall have been given for the landing or delivery of the same in some port or place of the United States."[21]

Believing that they had closed every imaginable loophole in the embargo, Congress adjourned for the summer. The mood of the administration in the early summer was optimistic. Jefferson wrote Governor Charles Pinckney of South Carolina that the legislature

having found, after repeated trials, that no general rules could be formed which fraud and service would not elude, concluded to leave, in those who were to execute the power, a discretionary power paramount to all their general rules. This discretion was of necessity lodged with the collector in the first instance, but referred, finally, to the president, lest there should be as many measures of law or discretion for our citizens as there were collectors or districts.[22]

The early optimism faded as Gallatin received reports of repeated cases of violations, resistance, and fraud. Late in July Gallatin wrote to Jefferson stating that if the embargo remained,

two principles must necessarily be adopted in order to make it sufficient: 1st, that not a single vessel shall be permitted to move without the special permission of the Executive; 2nd, that the collectors be invested with the general power of seizing property anywhere, and taking the rudders or otherwise effectually preventing the departure of any vessel in harbor, though ostensibly intended to remain there; and that without being liable to personal suits. I am sensible that such arbitrary powers are equally dangerous and odious. . . . I mean generally to express any opinion founded on the experience of this summer that Congress must either invest the Executive with the most arbitrary powers and sufficient force to carry the embargo into effect, or give it up altogether. And in this last case I must confess that, unless a change takes place in the measures of the European powers, I see no alternative but war.[23]

Jefferson replied two weeks later that the embargo law was

certainly the most embarassing one we have ever had to execute. I did not expect a crop of so sudden and rank growth of fraud and open opposition by force could have grown up in the United States. I am satisfied with you that if orders and decrees are not repealed, and a continuance of the embargo is preferred to war, (which sentiment is universal here) Congress must legalize all *means* which may be necessary to obtain its *end*.[24]

The administration's concern carried over to the Republican congressmen when the second session of the 10th Congress commenced in November. William Branch Giles, chairman of the Senate committee to report on the part of the President's message dealing with the embargo, requested Gallatin to appear and give information on what measures were necessary to enforce the law and whether any further modification was expedient. The committee sent Gallatin several specific questions two days later. Gallatin hastily appealed to Jefferson for a decision contending "that we must (or rather you must) decide the question absolutely, so that we may point out a decisive course either way to our friends."[25]

On November 24 Gallatin, with permission from Jefferson, proposed an extensive plan to Senator Giles, which Giles introduced in the Senate on December 12. The Republican majority quickly pushed the bill through both Houses by January 9, 1809. The opponents of the previous supplemental acts had appeared to be protecting local interests; however, the debate on the Enforcement Act touched upon issues of civil liberties and constitutionality.[26]

The alleged unconstitutional sections may be grouped into six categories: (1) subordination of civilian to military authority; (2) excessive power delegated to the President; (3) illegal search and seizure provisions; (4) the taking of property without due process of law; (5) infringement upon the right to a trial by jury; and (6) denying the right to use state judicial processes.

Section 11 permitted the President or his designee to use either the regular military or militia forces to prevent illegal departure of a vessel, to guard a vessel or cargo which had been seized, and to prevent and suppress "any armed or riotous assemblage of persons, resisting the custom-house officers in the exercise of their duties, or in any manner opposing the execution of the laws laying an embargo. . . ." Senator James Hillhouse of Connecticut exclaimed, "We see the military called on, in the first instance, to execute laws—taking the lead under a military chief; not following in the train and under the direction of the civil magistrate. . . ." Representative Benjamin Tallmadge of Connecticut moaned that at "a single stroke you prostrate the civil power, and make it completely subservient to military force."[27]

Opponents found excessive presidential power in Section 4, which authorized the President to give instructions to the collectors concerning "a general permission" given to vessels employed previously on bays, sounds, rivers, or lakes to take on board certain articles of foreign or domestic growth, when it can be done without danger of the embargo being violated; in Section 10, which authorized the President to instruct collectors concerning their powers to refuse permission to put any cargo on board any vessel or to take into their custody any article for the purpose of preventing violations of the embargo; and in the provisions of Section 11 cited previously.

The need for search warrants appeared negated by Section 9, which boldly permitted collectors to take into their custody specie or any articles of domestic growth, produce, or manufacture found on board of any vessel

when there is reason to believe that they are intended for exportation, or when, in vessels, carts, wagons, sleighs, or any other carriage, or in any manner on their way towards the territories of a foreign nation, or the vicinity thereof, or towards a place whence such articles are intended to be exported. . . .

Senator Chauncey Goodrich exclaimed,

Without warrant founded on proof, from suspicion only, may this unbounded license be exercised. Our houses, heretofore our castles, and the secure abodes of our families, may be thrown open to the visits of collectors to search for and seize our money and goods, when even instigated by suspicion, prejudice, resentment, or party spirit.

Representative Lewis B. Sturges declared bluntly that these seizures "without warrant and without being obliged to show cause, and without oath or affirmation, are expressly contrary to the fourth article of the amendments to the Constitution. . . ."[28] Several of the opponents of the bill felt that the latitude permitted collectors to seize property in Section 9 also violated the due process clause of the Fifth Amendment.[29]

Section 7 aroused claims that it prevented use of a trial by jury. The section stipulated that in all cases where a bond had been given to reland a cargo within two months (unless in the case of a voyage from New Orleans to an Atlantic port or from an Atlantic port to New Orleans, in either case four months would be allowed) the judgment was ordered given against the defendant unless proof was given of relanding or of loss of the vessel at sea. "But neither capture, distress, or any other accident whatever shall be pleaded or given in evidence in any such suit: Unless such capture shall be expressly proved to have been hostile, and such distress or accident occasioned by no negligence or deviation" nor unless the crew and mate were all United States citizens. Furthermore the costs of the suits would be assessed on the defendants unless they would produce the certificate of relanding. Senator Hillhouse declared,

To deprive the party of the right to plead or give in evidence what would establish his innocence, is to deprive him of his trial; to require a court to render judgment on a bond against the defendant, who is prepared and offers his plea and evidence, to establish a complete and legal defense before a court and jury, is to deprive him of his trial by jury, and is a denial of justice.[30]

Finally Section 10 provided protection to collectors against suits in state courts by permitting collectors to plead the general issue and give the enforcement act and the instructions and regulations of the President in evidence for his justification and defense. Furthermore, if the court should rule in favor of the collector, the collector would be entitled to treble costs. Representative Sturges concluded that Congress designed the section to deprive a citizen of "his remedy before a court and jury of his state, however wantonly a collector may abuse his authority."[31]

The Republican majority permitted the opponents to present their case. William Branch Giles offered the only comprehensive rebuttal in the Senate. The thrust of Gile's speech was that the bill offered nothing new or unique, "but that every provision it contains is amply justified by precedents in pre-existing laws, which have not been found to be so destructive to the rights of the people, as gentlemen strenuously insist similar provisions in this bill will be, if they receive the sanction of law."[32]

Historians have viewed the Enforcement Act with mixed reactions. It has been labeled as infamous and described as draconian.[33] Charles Warren asserted in his *The Supreme Court in United States History* that the statements of the opponents of the bill were seditious. Leonard Levy, however, called the act the "most repressive and unconstitutional legislation ever enacted by Congress in time of peace."[34]

Whether fortunate or not, the Supreme Court never ruled upon the act's constitutionality. On March 1 Congress repealed the Enforcement Act along with the embargo. It would appear that Jefferson, like his British predecessors during the decade prior to the American revolution, discovered the utter frustration of trying to enforce an unpopular law among a dissatisfied population. Jefferson, like his British counterparts, was willing to use questionable means to accomplish the end, even to the point of violating the rights and liberties of the people.

While the Republican Congress spun a web of embargo enforcement legislation, opponents of the embargo developed a complicated and at times effective pattern of resistance. Opposition to the Embargo and Supplementary Acts may be divided into two categories—legal and illegal.

Legal opposition took various forms, among which were newspaper editorials, protest meetings, petitions, and state legislative resolutions. Editors in the middle states and New England criticized the embargo from the beginning to the bitter end. The attacks were serious, bitter, vitriolic, and rebellious. A New York paper contended in January 1808 "that the states had the same right to resist oppression as the colonies had enjoyed." With the passage of the Enforcement Act obituary notices on liberty, on the Constitution, and on the Union appeared in several New England sheets. Many editors used mock catechisms and clever catch phrases to demonstrate their opposition. Finally references to the decline of commerce and the sufferings of the sailors filled the newspapers in the affected regions.[35]

Meetings, both spontaneous and planned, protested the embargo. In January 1808 a group of discontented sailors marched to the city hall of Philadelphia to complain of their condition. Over a hundred sailors marched to the government house in Boston, demanding work or bread. The Governor rebuffed the group, telling them he could do nothing. Several meetings were more formally organized and passed resolutions, such as those approved by a general meeting of Federalist young men in November 1808.[36]

Petitions, a favorite constitutional method of protest, were much in evidence during the period. Originating from individuals, groups, wards, cities, and counties, they were sent to state legislatures, the Congress, and the President. Some asked for special exemption from a particular section of the embargo; others declared that the Embargo and Supplementary Acts should be repealed.

Finally, following passage of the Enforcement Act, opponents initiated state legislative protests. The Massachusetts legislature adopted a set of four resolutions which declared the Enforcement Act to be "unjust, unconstitutional, oppressive, and not legally binding on the citizens of the Commonwealth"; recommended a memorial to Congress; announced that Massachusetts was ready "to cooperate with any of the other States in all legal and constitutional measures for procuring such amendments to the Constitution of the United States as shall be judged necessary"; and instructed the President of the Senate and Speaker of the House to send the resolutions to sister states.[38]

The legal opposition was irritating, but tolerable. More difficult to contend with were the illegal activities designed to circumvent the embargo. Three general categories of illegal activity may be noted: collusion with administrative officials such as collectors, smuggling, and resistance through use of force.

In the maritime communities it would have been impossible to expect collectors not to sympathize with their constituents' opposition to the embargo.

Some of the Collectors at the southward have grown more liberal in the construction of the Embargo; others are more strict. At Baltimore, we are told, coasters in ballast have been allowed to sail without giving bonds; while in North Carolina, a coasting vessel with staves, it is said, has been refused any clearance at all. . . .

Several collectors resigned rather than try to enforce the unpopular law, and several others had to be removed for failing to carry out the law. Leonard White has concluded that the collectors generally enforced the law. White did find exceptions:

The collector at York was probably in collusion with smugglers. The collector at New Bedford was removed. The collector at Sacketts Harbor resigned, as Gallatin believed "from fear, or at least from a wish not to lose his popularity with the people." There was want of energy in the collectors on Lake Ontario, and Pease of Edgartown, on Martha's Vineyard, was characterized by Gallatin as "a bad collector."[39]

Smuggling was widespread. Gallatin rendered a report in November 1808 listing fifty-four places from Maine to Georgia where violations of the embargo had occurred. Perhaps the most widespread use of smuggling occurred on the northern border, in particular the Lake Champlain regions of Vermont and New York.[40]

Resistance through use of force was evident throughout the embargo period. Opponents frequently assaulted collectors in line of duty and attacked revenue cutters. Even troops were at times unable to quell the disturbances.[41] No other law, save prohibition, has been as widely opposed through both legal and illegal means as was the embargo.

Administration of the Embargo and Supplementary Acts proved to be a nightmare for the executive and judicial branches of government. Executive enforcement has been well portrayed in Leonard White's *The Jeffersonians*. White concluded that administration of the embargo reached "a substantial degree of success." The federal judiciary's role in enforcing the embargo is more difficult to assess.[42]

The involvement of the judiciary was complex—from the district attorneys who had to cooperate with the collectors to enforce the legislation—to the Supreme Court which eventually had to interpret various sections of the acts. The courts also had to deal with the illegal resistance and the attempts of state courts to harass federal officials, in particular the collectors.

New England Federalists contended from the outset that the embargo was an unconstitutional act. To the dismay of the Republicans the constitutional question was first raised in the Massachusetts district court in the case of the *United States* v. *The Brigantine William*. John Davis, the district judge, was a stanch Federalist appointed to the bench in 1801 by John Adams. Joseph

Story and Francis Blake assisted district attorney George Blake. William Prescott and Samuel Dexter defended the brigantine *William*. Judge Davis rendered his decision on October 3, 1808, declaring that the law was constitutional under the power to regulate commerce, the necessary and proper clause, and the war power as a preparation for war. Instead of appealing the decision, which might have led to a definitive decision from the Supreme Court, Federalists chose to isolate the opinion as that of a single district judge and not a binding decision on the question.[43]

Although the constitutionality had been decided in the affirmative, at least in Massachusetts, convincing juries to convict under the Embargo and Supplementary Acts was another question. John Quincy Adams early in 1809 reported that notwithstanding the decision of the district judge on the constitutionality of the existing law the district court "after sitting seven or eight weeks and trying upwards of forty cases, has at length adjourned. Not one instance has occurred of a conviction by jury; and finally one of the jurymen is said to have declared that he never would agree to convict any person under these Laws, *whatever might* be the facts."[44]

Obtaining a conviction in North Carolina was equally difficult. In June 1809 the district attorney charged John Clarke and libeled his ship for a violation of the Enforcement Act. Clarke contended that the law was unconstitutional and "that this case did not come under the operation of the law, in as much as the greater part of the cargo was put on board when there was no law punishing the mere intention of violating the Embargo Act." The jury acquitted Clarke without leaving the jury box.[45] Juries acquitted Thomas Smead, Hanson Kelly, and Daniel M'Neill in 1811 for violating the embargo; but they convicted John Mitchell and others, securities upon an embargo bond for six times the value of the vessel and cargo. In the latter case the court did not permit the defendants to enter evidence by deposition because of Section 7 of the Enforcement Act which required that all witnesses, if alive, should be present and give evidence in person.[46]

District judges dismissed a variety of libels for violating the embargo. The Maine district court dismissed the libel of the *United States* v. *the ship Huntress* and ruled that the Enforcement Act made no provision for a prosecution by libel. In North Carolina Judge Henry Potter dismissed a libel against the Swedish ship *Slip*, charged with taking in a cargo without a permit, because foreign vessels were not within the meaning of the Enforcement Act.[47] The Georgia circuit court entertained an appeal on a libel against the brig *Charles* in May 1809. The question raised was whether the seizure was made on the high seas or within the waters of Spain. The vessel in proceeding up the St. Mary's River had crossed to the Georgia side, and custom officials seized it. The court ruled that the rule was too rigid, "that crossing to the Georgia side of the channel in navigating the river, and then recrossing shall amount to a violation of the embargo laws." The court reversed the condemnation of the district court and ordered the vessel restored to the owner.[48]

Even where district courts condemned a vessel or assessed a penalty, the circuit court frequently reversed the decisions. In Massachusetts the circuit court dismissed seventeen embargo cases, involving penalites ranging from $826 to $8,544.

Perhaps the supreme irony of the embargo controversy was the action of a Republican appointee to the Supreme Court, William Johnson. In order to implement the Supplementary Act of April 25, 1808, which permitted detention of all vessels bound coast-wise with cargoes exciting a suspicion of an intention to evade the law, Jefferson suggested to Gallatin in a letter of May 6 that the power of detention should be used freely so "that we may, by a fair experiment, know the power of this great weapon, the embargo." He further desired that his sentiments be communicated to the collectors. Gallatin dispatched a circular that same day. The circular warned the collectors to carefully watch shipments of certain commodities, such as flour, and indicated that the President recommended "that every shipment of the above articles for a place where they cannot be wanted for consumption, should be detained."[49]

Simeon Theus, collector at Charleston, immediately implemented the instruction by refusing to grant clearance papers for ships laden with cotton and rice. The merchants and shipowners appealed to the United States circuit court in Charleston for a *mandamus* to compel the collector to issue the clearances. In the case of *ex parte Gilchrist*, Judge Johnson on May 28 announced his decision which granted the *mandamus* and held Jefferson's instructions to the collector "to have been illegal and void, as unwarranted by the statute." He concluded with a warning,

The officers of our government, from the highest to the lowest, are equally subjected to legal restraint; and it is confidently believed that all of them feel themselves equally incapable, as well from law as inclination, to attempt an unsanctioned encroachment upon individual liberty.[50]

Johnson's opinion shocked Jefferson. From a Federalist such a rebuke could be tolerated, but from one of his own appointees it came close to treason. Jefferson wrote Governor Charles Pinckney of South Carolina, indicating that he had seen the proceedings of the court and was concerned "because of the quarter from whence they came, and where they could not be ascribed to any political waywardness." Jefferson included in his letter a copy of Attorney General Caesar A. Rodney's response to the opinion, which Jefferson indicated had been communicated to the "collectors and marshals for their future government." Rodney's opinion of July 15 attacked the right of the circuit court to issue a *mandamus* and warned of the dangers of judicial interference in administrative affairs.[51]

In a most unusual procedure Johnson replied to Rodney, completing his rejoinder in August and issuing it to the press in October. The well-oiled Republican political machine countered when Johnson appeared before the

Georgia circuit court in December. The grand jury rebuked the judge. After expressing support of the embargo, the grand jury stated,

We cannot pass unnoticed the attempt of the judiciary to defeat the intentions and salutary measures of our government by issuing a *mandamus* and compelling an officer of the revenue to violate those measures. Sophistical and logical deductions made in justification of such conduct are not satisfactory. We hope and trust such daring preciptancy will never in the future be exercised by any of the judges of the courts of the United States.

Johnson responded in almost eloquent terms.

If you are prepared gentlemen to waive the government of the laws and submit without repining to every error or encroachment of the several departments of government, avow it to your fellow citizen and prevail on them to abolish the constitution or get into office a feeble and submissive judiciary.[52]

Although the Johnson *mandamus* was an irritant, collectors, attorneys, and marshals continued to follow their instructions without any significant attention being paid to the opinion.

Where the government's suit survived the district and circuit court hurdles, two additional recourses were open to defendants: one, an appeal to the Supreme Court or two, a petition to Congress for relief. The Supreme Court heard thirteen cases involving the Embargo and Supplementary Acts, the first in 1810 and the last in 1817. The Court did not rule on the constitutional issue, but as Charles Warren has concluded, "Fourteen years later . . . the question had become so settled by general acceptance that Marshall in *Gibbons* v. *Ogden* was able to speak of the universal acknowledged power of the government to impose embargoes."[53] The opinions rendered before 1814 were instructive to the lower courts in interpreting the embargoes of 1812 and 1814. The petitions were of two types—one for remission of penalty, the second for release from imprisonment for debt because of the inability to pay the penalty. Only one petition of the former has been found, that of Anthony Buck, dated March 29, 1810. Buck was the security on the bond to reland a cargo. When the cargo was not relanded, Buck was assessed the penalty. Although the Committee of Commerce and Manufactures recommended that the penalty should be remitted and the House agreed, the session ended before a bill could be introduced and approved. Congress considered six petitions involving release from imprisonment, and it approved five of the six, negating only the petition of Phineas Carney.[54]

Opponents of the embargo found one additional civil remedy for frustrating the embargo laws—suing the collector or other officers of the government in the state courts. Although the extent of the practice has not been determined, the Supreme Court heard four cases on appeal. The opinion in *Slocum* v. *Mayberry et al.* (1817) clearly stated the Court's position. Varnum Slocum, surveyor of the customs for the port of Newport, Rhode Island, had seized the *Venus* under directions from the collector. The defendants brought a writ of reprieve in the state court for the restoration of the cargo. Speaking for the Court, Chief Justice Marshall held that the courts of the United States have exclusive jurisdiction of all seizures made on land or water for a breach of the laws of the United States and that any intervention of a state authority which might obstruct the exercise of this jurisdiction is unlawful. If the seizure should eventually be adjudged wrongful and without probable cause, the party may proceed by a suit at common law for damages for the illegal act. The common law remedy would have to be sought in the state court, the courts of the United States having no jurisdiction to decide on the conduct of their officers in the execution of their laws until the case shall have passed through the state courts. Feeling in this specific case that the procedure outlined above had been followed, the Court affirmed the state court's decision with costs.[55]

Though legal opposition through the courts could be countered, opposition through violence was much more difficult to control. Violence reached its zenith in the Lake Champlain region of New York and Vermont in the spring and summer of 1808. Smugglers loaded their products, particularly potash, on rafts, moved to the head of Lake Champlain, then sold it to Canadian conspirators. Jefferson issued a proclamation on April 19 declaring the region to be in a state of insurrection and calling upon the insurgents to cease and desist. Violence, however, was reported at Middlebury, Vermont, in June, where 150 men from Canada attacked and rescued a raft seized by the government and guarded by twelve men. In July thirty men fought twelve soldiers at St. Albans in order to rescue twelve barrels of potash and succeeded. The worst eruption occurred in August when Lt. Farrington seized a batteau supposed to be used in smuggling potash. The revenue cutter was fired upon, killing one man. Lt. Farrington ordered his men ashore to dislodge the snipers. Two persons—a soldier and a private citizen—who had come to assist the troops lost their lives in the ensuing battle. Newspapers reported that the military captured eight men, but four escaped. The federal marshal reported that the troops captured seven insurgents and committed them for trial in the state courts. Cyrus Dean, one of the seven indicted for murder, was convicted and executed. A Vermont newspaper reported his execution as follows: "He appeared perfectly composed and hardened, denied his crime, kicked his hat into his grave, spit upon his coffin; and pulled the cap over his eyes himself. No person prayed with him at the gallows." The captain of the vessel was also taken, indicted, convicted, and executed.[56]

The marshal also reported that the collector had seized seven or eight more of the insurgents. Since the Embargo and Supplementary Acts passed up to that time did not contain provisions for criminal violations, Attorney General Rodney recommended proceeding against the men on a charge of treason. At the October term of the Vermont Circuit Court, before Associate Justice Brockholst Livingston and District Judge Elijah Paine, the district attorney charged six men—John Taylor, Ezekiel Taylor, Job Hoxie, Joseph Tinkham, John Hoxie, and Frederic Hoxie—with treason. The grand jury did not indict the two Taylors, but it indicted the other four men. The indictment of Frederic Hoxie accused him of trying to prevent the execution of the embargo on June 30, 1808, at Alburgh. Further the indictment alleged that Hoxie, with sixty persons unnamed, levied war on the United States by resisting the collector of the revenue in the execution of his duty, shooting upon troops guarding a raft the collector had in his custody, rescuing the raft, and taking it to Canada. Hoxie pleaded not guilty to the charge on October 28. The trial commenced on the 31st. Judge Livingston directed the jury to acquit Hoxie, stating,

If the person . . . was hired for the purpose of evading the embargo laws, only in this instance, and for his own private emolument, although it may have been part of the plan to use violence, and force were actually employed against the collector or his agents to accomplish this object, but that this formed no link in a conspiracy to resist or impede the operation of these Laws within the district generally as far as their means enabled them . . . then the prisoner is not guilty of the crime of levying war. . . . It is the intention with which resistance to the law is made, not the opposition itself, that forms the criterion; otherwise every willfull opposition of a statute would necessarily be a levying of war.

The jury at 11:00 returned a verdict of not guilty. The district attorney dropped the prosecution against Job Hoxie. The marshal returned Joseph Tinkham's warrant *non est.* on October 27, 1808.[57]

At the November term of the Virginia circuit court the grand jury returned four indictments containing eleven names for violating the embargo. The bills accused each group of taking a vessel to a foreign port after clearing for a port within the United States. The trial was delayed until the May term when the court, presided over by Chief Justice John Marshall, ruled "that the offense charged in the indictment being created by statute and a penalty being prescribed for the commission of the act the penalty alone is recoverable and the act is not indictable," therefore the court quashed the indictments.[58]

Although violating the embargo was not an indictable offence until the Enforcement Act of 1809, obstructing process, assaulting officials, and rescuing goods were indictable offences. The first cases appeared in Maine where the grand jury indicted three men for resisting the collector. Juries convicted no one. In December the grand jury indicted Edward Thompson for assaulting Thomas Burnham, a deputy marshal, and Elijah Elder, an assistant to the deputy. The petit jury acquitted Thompson.[59]

A year later, at the December 1810 term, the grand jury indicted Pearle Spafford and Samuel G. Town for assaulting a deputy inspector and deputy collector and rescuing a boat David Angell had seized. The jury found Spafford guilty of rescue but not of assault, and the court fined him $20. The jury acquitted Town of both charges.[60]

The Pennyslvania circuit court grand jury indicted nine men for obstructing the marshal in the execution of a writ of arrest. Eight were convicted; the court fined one $300 and imprisoned him three months; the court imprisoned seven others for one month and fined each man $50; the petit jury acquitted the ninth person.[61]

Finally the Massachusetts grand jury returned four indictments against ten men for resisting an assistant collector and inspector and for rescuing goods. The district attorney dropped the first indictment involving four men. The jury acquitted the four men accused in the second indictment and a single person involved in the third indictment. Luke Thorndike, involved in the fourth indictment, was convicted and fined $50 plus costs.[62]

Enforcement was a difficult task. The small number of federal officials—surveyors, collectors, and marshals—could not cope with the widespread opposition and enforce the law in the manner the administration in Washington, D.C. desired. Realizing that the small number of federal officials could not effectively enforce the law, Jefferson determined to rely upon state officials, particularly the Governors. The Enforcement Act permitted the President or his designee to use militia to prevent a vessel from departing in violation of the law. Jefferson designated the Governors on January 17, 1809, through a circular letter issued by the Secretary of War, to use militia in enforcing the law. Alexander McIntire, the collector of the port of York, requested Charles Bean, captain of a militia company in Massachusetts, in accordance with the Enforcement Act, to board the brig *Betsey* and detain her, which Bean promptly did. William Boyd, reputed owner of the vessel shortly thereafter came on board and ordered the militia to leave, which they refused to do until the tide had ebbed so much that it was impossible for the vessel to leave. On February 28, Bean and his soldiers were arrested for a riot for entering the vessel and were carried before Jacob Fisher in Kennebunk, twenty miles from York. Justice Fisher declared the embargo laws unconstitutional. Bean and the soldiers were recognized in the sum of $50 to appear at the Supreme Court in York. The court discharged them when the grand jury did not return an indictment. Bean petitioned Congress for reimbursement of expenses amounting to $219.44. Although the Committee of Claims approved the petition and introduced a bill, no record of the passage has been found.[63] In the midst of the struggle over the embargo the Non-Importation Act again went into effect. Except for New York, where custom officials seized sixty consignments, the acts appear to have been ignored.[64]

The twin policies did not have their desired effect upon Britain or France. Neither repealed their trade restrictions. Jefferson finally relented to the repeal of the embargo on March 1, three days before he left office. Not willing to give up the general policy of economic pressure, Congress enacted a non-intercourse bill, prohibiting commercial intercourse with both Britain and France. The act provided penalties and forfeitures for violations and in addition stipulated that if a citizen should have "intercourse with, or to afford any aid or supplies to any public ship or vessel of Great Britain or France" he was liable to a prison term of not less than one month nor more than one year and a fine of not less than $100 and not more than $10,000. The Non-Intercourse Act was amended in May and again in June 1809.[65]

Seizures under the act quickly appeared in the dockets of the federal courts. In 1809 Maine reported twenty-two, and two each were reported in Louisiana and Pennsylvania. In 1810 there were three additional seizures in Maine and one each in Vermont, Massachusetts, South Carolina, and Louisiana.

The long interrupted negotiations resumed with the arrival of David M. Erskine in the United States. Erskine concluded an agreement with the Madison administration which included an end to non-intercourse against Great Britain. Unfortunately George Canning repudiated Erskine's agreement, and the negotiations again broke down. Madison, believing the agreement would be honored, had permitted a fleet of commercial vessels to sail for Great Britain, thus undermining the non-intercourse policy.[66]

The Congress which convened in the fall of 1810 replaced non-intercourse with an act popularly known as Macon's Bill Number 2, which opened trade with the world but stipulated that if either Britain or France should rescind their systems, we would revive non-intercourse with the other nation. Public vessels of Britain and France were still excluded, although the act reduced the criminal penalties for assisting such vessels to a forfeiture of $2,000, returnable either by indictment or information.[67]

France quickly took advantage of the act through the Cadore letter. Madison permitted Great Britain the three months required by the act; and when the time had elapsed and Britain had not rescinded her Orders in Council, he accordingly revived nine sections of the old non-intercourse law against Britain.[68]

Within a month Congress passed a Supplementary Act requiring American courts to accept Madison's proclamation as conclusive evidence of the French repeal and permitting entry of cargoes embarked from Britain before February. By the end of 1811 not only were merchants protesting the inability to bring their property back from Britain, but evasions of the law had stimulated Congress to request information from Gallatin. Gallatin responded on December 3, claiming that evasions of non-importation had arisen from three quarters: (1) "vessels have arrived from ports not belonging to Great Britain, with merchandise of British growth or manufacture of other countries"; (2) "coasting vessels, chiefly from the Northern ports, have brought large quantities of plaster of paris, commonly taken on board in the waters of Passamaquoddy Bay; and it is suggested that they had also occasionally received there, or from vessels at sea, other species of British merchandise"; and (3) "merchandise has been illegally imported by land from Canada, and as it is believed, principally through the State of Vermont." Gallatin's analysis appeared similar to the problems encountered in enforcing the embargo. Gallatin proposed several measures to promote more effective enforcement. He concluded that an evil of great magnitude arose from the inability of the district judge to perform the duties of office. He indicated that the only provision in force was to transfer suits to the circuit court, which "in a State where the court is already overburdened with business, is altogether inefficient." Gallatin also pointed out the need for a district court along the northern frontier of New York. That area contained seven collection districts, but the only district court in the state was at New York City. Not only was the district court the busiest in the United States, but the distance from the frontier to New York City, Gallatin asserted, was "one of the greatest obstacles to the execution of the revenue laws." Congress took no action on the corrections Gallatin proposed.[69]

The number of cases brought under the non-intercourse and non-importation laws was large. After a slow start in 1811 when the courts reported only fourteen cases, the number increased to thirty-five in 1812, forty-three in 1813, 106 in 1814, and then declined sharply to sixty-seven in 1815. From 1816 to 1820, when the last case appeared on a docket, the courts tried forty-five additional cases.

The last of the acts interdicting trade prior to the declaration of war was the Embargo of 1812. Madison requested a sixty-day embargo from Congress as a means of saving American shipping from capture when it declared war. Congress instead passed a ninety-day embargo on April 4. The act forbade all vessels in the ports under the jurisdiction of the United States bound to any foreign port to clear except with permission of the President. The law permitted foreign vessels to depart either in ballast or with whatever goods were on board. Coasting vessels could depart after posting bond equal to twice the value of the vessel and cargo. The legislation gave the President full authority to instruct the officers of the revenue, the navy, and the revenue cutters "as shall appear best adopted for carrying the same into full effect." The penalties provided were similar to those in the previous acts.[70]

The number of seizures was small—seventeen in Massachusetts and one in South Carolina in 1812, and two in Massachusetts in 1813. Before the ninety days ended, Madison requested and received a declaration of war. Not unlike the opposition to the embargo, the Supreme Court heard a number of appeals, and Congress received a variety of petitions. The Supreme Court rendered eighteen opinions from 1812 to 1818 concerning the non-intercourse and non-importation laws.[71] Congress received twenty-two petitions for direct relief.[72]

Violent opposition to the post-embargo laws was limited. Only three cases appeared in the courts, all in Massachusetts. Juries returned verdicts of not guilty in two cases but found four men guilty in the third case. The court assessed fines ranging from $100 to $300 against the men.[73]

The various acts interdicting trade proved as difficult to enforce as the Volstead Act would be a little more than a century later. It has become almost axiomatic in American legal history that an unpopular law cannot be forced upon an unwilling public. Madison would soon discover that the declaration of war would not alter the nature or scope of the opposition.

NOTES

1. Bradford Perkins, *The First Rapprochement: England and the United States, 1795-1805* (Berkeley and Los Angeles, 1967), 177; *Annals of Congress*, XIV:700-705, 746-776, 1178-1180, 1222-1223; 2 *U. S. Statutes at Large*, 339-342.

2. *Annals of Congress*, XV:207, 232, 412-413, 449-451, 537-729, 841-842, 851-878.

3. 2 *U. S. Statutes at Large*, 379-381.

4. James Maury to James Monroe, November 26, 1806, cited in Herbert Heaton, "Non-importation, 1806-1812," *Journal of Economic History*, 1 (November, 1941), 180.

5. Several of the early seizures appear to have been ludicrous. The collector at Baltimore seized two pairs of British shoes and the ship in which they had arrived. Another collector asked Gallatin "whether he should confiscate salt which came in sacks made of a prohibited material, flax." Heaton, "Non-Importation, 1806-1812," 180.

6. *Annals of Congress*, XVI:16, 17-20, 114-126, 150, 153-158; 2 *U. S. Statutes at Large*, 411.

7. The British believed two deserters had enlisted aboard the U. S. S. *Chesapeake*. Shortly after the *Chesapeake* left Norfolk she was hailed by the H. M. S. *Leopard*. When the *Chesapeake* refused to permit a search, the *Leopard* opened fire, killing three and injuring eighteen seamen. The British seized four sailors. Jefferson immediately closed all American ports to the British navy. See Bradford Perkins, *Prologue to War: England and the United States, 1805-1812* (Berkeley and Los Angeles, 1963), 140-146.

8. For an extensive portrayal of the negotiations see Perkins, *Prologue to War*, 1-139. A briefer summary may be found in Patrick C. T. White, *A Nation on Trial: America and the War of 1812* (New York and London, 1965), 33-45.

9. *Annals of Congress*, XVII:1064.

10. Heaton, "Non-importation, 1806-1812," 183.

11. 2 *U. S. Statutes at Large*, 469; Heaton, "Non-importation, 1806-1812," 183.

12. *Annals of Congress*, XVII:50-52, 1216-1223. For an interesting assessment of

Jefferson's motivation, see Burton Spivak, *Jefferson's English Crisis: Commerce, Embargo, and the Republican Revolution* (Charlottesville, 1979).

13. 2 *U. S. Statutes at Large*, 451-453.

14. *Annals of Congress*, XVII:1240.

15. Ibid., 1244-1257, 1269-1271.

16. 2 *U. S. Statutes at Large*, 453-454.

17. *Annals of Congress*, XVIII:153, 158, 160-161. 1599, 1649-1658, 1666-1675, 1679, 1694-1695, 1698-1713, 1744. During the debate, Representative Barent Gardenier of New York questioned the motive of the people supporting the embargo. Various members called him to order and requested the Speaker to stop him. The Republicans not only replied to the charges, but George W. Campbell of Tennessee challenged Gardenier to a duel. The two met at Bladensburg where Campbell severely wounded Gardenier. John B. McMaster, *A History of the People of the United States from the Revolution to the Civil War* (8 vols., New York, 1893-1913), III:295-296; Louis M. Sears, *Jefferson and the Embargo* (Durham, N. C., 1927), 202.

18. 2 *U. S. Statutes at Large*, 473-475. Section 7 created considerable embarrassment for Jefferson. Gallatin sought to restrict the permission to the West Indies, and this became the general rule. At Jefferson's request Congress terminated the authority in 1809. White, *The Jeffersonians*, 429-430.

19. *Annals of Congress*, XVIII:2083-2172, 2188-2189, 2198-2245; 2 *U. S. Statutes at Large*, 490.

20. Representative D. R. Williams related the following example to the House on April 22.

Application had also been lately to the custom-house officer of a Southern port for clearance to New Orleans for a ship, said to be laden with 500 hogshead New England rum. The collector, being surprised at so large a cargo of such an article, sent an inspector to examine it, and, on inspection, it was found to be 500 hogshead of rice instead of rum. Nothing would have been easier than for the vessel to have slipped into New Providence or Havana, landed its cargo, and reloaded with rum which could be carried into New Orleans, thus committing a double fraud—violating the embargo law and defrauding the revenue of the duty on the rum thus imported.

Annals of Congress, XVIII:2259-2260.

21. *Annals of Congress*, XVII:361-364, 369-370, 372, 378-379; XVIII:2245-2246, 2252, 2259-2269; 2 *U. S. Statutes at Large*, 499-502.

22. Jefferson to Governor Charles Pinckney, July 18, 1808, Jefferson, *Writings*, XII:102-103.

23. Gallatin to Jefferson, July 29, 1808, Gallatin, *Writings*, I:398-399.

24. Jefferson to Gallatin, August 11, 1808, Jefferson, *Works*, XI:41.

25. Gallatin to Jefferson, November 15, 1808, Gallatin, *Writings*, I:428.

26. Gallatin to William B. Giles, November 24, 1808, ibid., 428-435; *Annals of Congress*, XIX:232; 2 *U. S. Statutes at Large*, 506-511.

27. *Annals of Congress*, XIX:296, 931-932.

28. Ibid., 246, 100.

29. Ibid., 246, 985.

30. Ibid., 290.

31. Ibid., 999.

32. Ibid., 257-267.

33. McMaster, *History of the People*, III:326.

34. Charles Warren, *The Supreme Court in the United States History* (rev. ed., 2 vols., Boston, 1926), I:360; Levy, *Jefferson and Civil Liberties*, 139.

35. Walter W. Jennings, *The American Embargo, 1807-1809* (Iowa City, 1921), 91-95, 97-99, 103-104; McMaster, *History of the People*, III:290-292, 326-327; Sears, *Jefferson and the Embargo*, 148-151, 204-207.

36. Jennings, *The American Embargo*, 92-95; McMaster, *History of the People*, III:289-290, 323-325.

37. Jennings, *The American Embargo*, 102-107; McMaster, *History of the People*, III:327-329, 332-333; Sears, *Jefferson and the Embargo*, 152-153, 198.

38. Perkins, *Prologue to War*, 179; McMaster, *History of the People*, III:329-331; Sears, *Jefferson and the Embargo*, 186-187.

39. Jennings, *The American Embargo*, 116-117; Sears, *Jefferson and the Embargo*, 92-94; White, *The Jeffersonians*, 453-455.

40. Jennings, *The American Embargo*, 112-114; McMaster, *History of the People*, III:294-297; Sears, *Jefferson and the Embargo*, 89-91; White, *The Jeffersonians*, 443-450.

41. Jennings, *The American Embargo*, 114-116; McMaster, *History of the People*, III:304-307; Sears, *Jefferson and the Embargo*, 167-170; White, *The Jeffersonians*, 450-451.

42. White, *The Jeffersonians*, 472.

43. Warren, *The Supreme Court in United States History*, I:341-351; Homer Cummings and Carl McFarland, *Federal Justice: Chapters in the History of Justice and the Federal Executive* (New York, 1937), 68; Henry Adams, ed., *Documents Relating to New England Federalism, 1800-1815* (Boston, 1877), 223-224; *Federal Cases, 1789-1879* (30 vols., St. Paul, 1894-1897), 28, case number 16, 700.

44. John Q. Adams to William B. Giles, January 16, 1809, cited in Jennings, *The American Embargo*, 125.

45. Charleston *Courier*, June 26, 1809.

46. Charleston *Courier*, February 18, 1811.

47. Charleston *Courier*, April 14, and June 17, 1809.

48. Georgia circuit court, Minute Book, 1806-1816, pp. 157-159.

49. Jefferson to Gallatin, May 6, 1808, Jefferson, *Writings*, XII:52-53; Donald G. Morgan, *Justice William Johnson: The First Dissenter* (Columbia, 1954), 58.

50. Morgan, *Justice William Johnson*, 58-60; Charleston *Courier*, May 30, 1808; South Carolina circuit court, Minute Book, 1790-1809, p. 343.

51. Jefferson to Pinckney, July 18, 1808; Jefferson *Writings*, XII:102-103; Morgan, *Justice William Johnson*, 60-62; Charleston *Courier*, August 22, 1808.

52. Morgan, *Justice William Johnson*, 62-65; Georgia circuit court, Minute Book, 1806-1816, pp. 140-142.

53. Warren, *The Supreme Court in United States History*, I:351. See *U. S.* v. *Hall and Worth* (1810), Cranch, *Reports*, VI:171-176; *Durousseau and others* v. *the United States* (1810), Cranch, *Reports*, VI:307-324; *The Schooner Juliana* v. *the United States* and *the Ship Alligator* v. *The United States* (1810), Cranch, *Reports*, VI:327-329; *Brig James Wells* v. *The United States* (1812), Cranch, *Reports*, VII:22-26; *Schooner Paulina's Cargo* v. *The United States* (1812), Cranch, *Reports*, VII:52-68; *The Sloop Active* v. *The United States* (1812), Cranch, *Reports*, VII:100-107;

Hawthorne, Claimant of the Brig Clarissa Claiborne v. *The United States* (1812), Cranch, *Reports*, VII:107-108; *The United States* v. *The Brig Eliza* (1812), Cranch, *Reports*, VII:113-115; *The United States* v. *Gordon, and Others* (1813) Cranch, *Reports*, VII:287-290; *The Schooner Good Catherine* v. *United States* (1813), Cranch, *Reports*, VII:349; *The Brig Short Staple and Cargo* v. *The United States* (1815), Cranch, *Reports*, IX:55-64; *The William King* (1817), Wheaton, *Reports*, II:148-160; *Patterson* v. *The United States* (1817), Wheaton, *Reports*, II:221-226.

54. *Annals of Congress*, XIX:330, 1077, 1080; XX:36, 268, 556, 625, 644, 650, 1406, 1584, 1617-1618, 1818; XXVIII:120, 124, 996.

55. The four cases were *Crowell and Others* v. *M'Fadon* (1814), Cranch, *Reports*, VIII:94-98; *Otis* v. *Walter* (1817) and (1821), Wheaton, *Reports*, II:18-24, Wheaton, *Reports*, VI:583-592; *Slocum* v. *Mayberry et al.* (1817), Wheaton, *Reports*, II:1-13; and *Gelston et al.* v. *Hoyt* (1818), Wheaton, *Reports*, III:246-336. The owner of the *American Eagle* sued David Gelston and Peter A. Schenck in the New York courts for damages resulting from the seizure of his vessel. The court awarded Hoyt, the alleged owner, $107,369.43. Gelston petitioned Congress for relief in 1816, but Congress refused. After the United States Supreme Court upheld the state court's award, Gelston petitioned again, and Congress rejected him a second time. *Annals of Congress*, XXIX:1278, 1412; XXXI:1380, 1551.

56. James D. Richardson, ed., *A Compilation of the Messages and Papers of the Presidents* (10 vols., New York, 1897), I:438-439; White, *The Jeffersonians,* 450-451; McMaster, *History of the People*, III:304-307; Jennings, *The American Embargo*, 114-116; letter from John Willard to James Madison, August 14, 1808, (Microcopy M 179), reel 22; J. D. Lawson, ed., *American State Trials* (17 vols., St. Louis, 1914-1936), III:542-557.

57. Vermont circuit court, Docket, 1808-1809, (Federal Record Center, Waltham, Mass.), October term 1808, Special Session October 28, 1808; Vermont circuit court, Case Files; James Willard Hurst, *The Law of Treason in the United States* (Westport, Conn., 1971) 196-197.

58. Virginia circuit court, Order Book #7, 1808-1809, pp. 143, 206-207, 265-266, 268; Charleston *Courier*, June 9, 1809. In South Carolina the grand jury indicted John Stevens and Varnum Slocum in May 1809 for violating the embargo. After the district attorney learned of the ruling in Virginia, he dropped the prosecution. South Carolina circuit court, Minute Book, 1790-1809, p. 362.

59. Maine district court, Record Book, 1803-1812 (Federal Records Center, Waltham, Mass.), December term 1808.

60. Ibid., December term 1809 and March term 1810.

61. Pennsylvania circuit court, Minute Book, 1801-1811, pp. 28, 55, 77-81.

62. Massachusetts circuit court, Record Book #2, 1806-1811, pp. 410-414.

63. Jefferson, *Writings*, IX:202; *Annals of Congress*, XX:1764-1765.

64. Heaton, "Non-importation, 1806-1812, p. 185.

65. 2 *U. S. Statutes at Large*, 528-533, 547, 550-551; *Annals of Congress*, XIX:345, 414-436, 451-452, 911, 970-971, 1426-1429, 1437-1493, 1503, 1507, 1511-1520, 1523-1536, 1539-1541. Chief Justice Marshall decided in an opinion rendered in the circuit court of North Carolina in 1812 that Madison's proclamation of August 9, 1809, was illegal. Charleston *Courier* June 6, 1812.

66. White, *A Nation on Trial*, 57-60; Perkins, *Prologue to War*, 210-219.

67. 2 *U. S. Statutes at Large*, 605-606; *Annals of Congress*, XX:549-550, 571, 579-

582, 590, 592, 599-601, 637, 666, 674, 678, 680, 729, 754-755, 1160-1196, 1201-1202, 1219-1224, 1226-1253, 1257-1273, 1275-1279; XXI:1279-1299, 1300-1330, 1332-1355, 1438-1442, 1446-1463, 1484-1485, 1493-1496, 1559-1659, 1665-1678, 1682-1692, 1701, 1763, 1772, 1887-1928, 1930-1931.

68. White, *A Nation on Trial*, 75-77; Perkins, *Prologue to War*, 246-260.

69. *Annals of Congress*, XXIII:2102-2104.

70. 2 *U. S. Statutes at Large*, 700-701.

71. See *Whelan* v. *The United States* (1812), *Brig Penobscot* v. *The United States* (1813), *The Cargo of the Brig Aurora, Burnside, Claimant* v. *The United States* (1813), *The Schooner Hoppet and Cargo* v. *The United States* (1813), *The Schooner Anne* v. *The United States* (1813), Cranch, *Reports*, VII:112, 356-358, 363-366, 382-395, 570-572; *Harford* v. *The United States* (1814), *The Rapid* (1814), *The United States* v. *1960 Bags of Coffee* (1814), *The United States* v. *The Brigantine Mars* (1814), Cranch, *Reports*, VIII:109-110, 155-168, 398-418; *Brig Struggle* v. *The United States* (1815), *The Ship Richmond* v. *The United States* (1815), *The United States* v. *The Cargo of the Ship Fanny* (1815), *The Brig Ann* (1815), Cranch, *Reports*, IX:71-76, 101-104, 181-183, 289-291; *The Samuel* (1816), *The Ship Octavia* (1816), Wheaton, *Reports*, I:9-23; *The New York* (1818), *The Aeolus* (1818), Wheaton, *Reports*, III:59-77, 392-409.

72. See petitions Boardman and Pope (1812), Thomas P. Cope (1812), Obadiah Rich (1812), *Annals of Congress*, XXIII:72, 105, 217; Talcott Walcott (1813), General Memorial on British goods (1813), ibid., XXV:20, 23, 25, 67, 92-93; Stephen Girard (1813), Daniel Macauley (1814), John S. Trott and Martin Blake (1814), Stephen Glover (1814), William Stothard and Josiah Starkey (1814), Darby Fishing Company (1814), John G. Quarenburg (1814), Theodore Barrell and Nathaniel Gilbert (1814), ibid., XXVI:22, 25, 32-34, 46, 48, 55, 134, 569, 616, 639, 662-663, 693, 1284; XXVII:1935, 2555; Justin Elias Lyman (1814), John Frothingham and Arthur Tappan (1815), ibid., XXVIII:249, 266, 270, 287, 640; XXIX:24, 136; Talcott Walcott (1816), ibid., XXIX:100, 302-304; Robert Kidd (1817), ibid., XXX:19, 64; William G. Ridgely (1818), John Haslett (1817), John Troup (1818), ibid., XXXI:62, 113, 161, 164, 219, 280, 352, John Troup (1818), John Haslett (1819), ibid., XXXIII:77, 88-89, 97, 100, 120, 163. Congress only approved the petitions of Stephen Girard, Daniel Macauley, and William Stothard and Josiah Starkey.

73. Massachusetts circuit court, Record Book #3, part I, 1812, 502-503, 558-564.

5

Alien Enemies and the War of 1812

James Madison actuated the Alien Enemies Act, enacted in 1798 as part of the infamous alien and sedition laws, on June 19, 1812, when he issued a proclamation declaring that a state of war existed between the United States and Great Britain.[1] The Alien and Sedition Acts, the protest resolutions of Virginia and Kentucky, and the Republican reaction in 1801 have received more fictional than truthful attention from historians. The Alien Enemies Act, James Morton Smith has pointed out, was a Republican measure and designed to be a permanent piece of legislation in contrast to the other three that were inspired by the Federalists. The Virginia and Kentucky resolutions protested against the Alien Friends Act and the Sedition Act, not the Alien Enemies Act. Contrary to popular historian legend, the Alien Enemies Act did not disappear with the inauguration of Jefferson as President in 1801; instead it lay dormant until the declaration of war in 1812.[2]

The first section of the act stipulated that after a declaration of war all natives[3] of the hostile government or nation residing within the United States and not naturalized were "liable to be apprehended, restrained, secured and removed as alien enemies." The act authorized the President to control the manner in which the enemies were treated including the degree of restraint to which they would be subjected, under what conditions they might be permitted to continue their residency, and to provide for the removal of those who, not being permitted to reside within the United States, should refuse to depart. The act permitted aliens a reasonable time,[4] "consistent with the public safety, and according to the dictates of humanity and national hospitality" for the recovery, disposal, and removal of their goods and effects.

The second section authorized judges of both state and federal courts, upon complaint against any alien, to have the person apprehended and "after a full examination and hearing" to order such alien out of the United States, or "to give sureties to their good behaviour, or to be otherwise restrained, conformably to the proclamation or regulations which shall . . . be established . . . and may imprison, or otherwise secure such alien . . .until such order . . . shall be performed."⁵

To expedite the voluntary removal of aliens, Section 6 of the "Act to Prohibit American Vessels from Proceeding to or Trading with the Enemies of the United States and for Other Purposes," passed by Congress on July 6, 1812, authorized the President to give "at any time within six months after the passage of this act, passports for the safe transportation of any ship, or other property, belonging to British subjects, and which is now within the limits of the United States."⁶

The Department of State implemented the acts through a series of public notices published in newspapers throughout the country and detailed instructions to the United States' marshals in each judicial district. The first notice, dated July 7, 1812, ordered all British subjects to report forthwith to the marshals or persons appointed by them and to give the marshals their name, age, the time they had been in the United States, the persons composing their families, the places of their residence, their occupations or pursuits, and whether, and at what time they had made application to the court to become naturalized. The instructions required the marshals to make returns of such British subjects to the State Departement.⁷

Four days later Secretary of State James Monroe issued specific instructions to the marshals indicating that it was presumed that

all British subjects will act with propriety, and obey the law . . . yet should any of them disappoint this reasonable expectation, it will be your duty to make an early and special report of the improper conduct of such person *to this Department, that the President may be enabled to discharge the duty imposed on him, under such circumstances.*⁸

Through the summer and into early fall the marshals went about gathering lists of names. On October 13, 1812, the Secretary of State cautioned them to take measures to ensure that newly arrived alien enemies "report themselves to you; and to designate for them particular places of residence, at least thirty miles distant from the tide-water, to the limits of which designation they are to be confined."⁹

In February 1813 the State Department issued two new notices. The first required alien enemies travelling from one port to another by land or by water to secure a special passport from the marshal or the collector of the customs and directed alien enemies traveling from one district to another to report to the marshal immediately.[10] The second ordered alien enemies residing within forty miles of tide-water to apply to the marshal for passports to "retire to such places, beyond that distance . . . as may be designated by the marshals." The marshal could grant permission for an alien not engaged in commerce to remain where they were on a month to month basis.[11]

The marshals received more specific instructions in March emphasizing that the notices issued in February "*are to be enforced* and the persons designated for removal are immediately to repair to the places assigned to them for residence." If the marshal discovered "peculiar and extraordinary cases of hardship" and where "the character and deportment of the parties entitled them to particular considerations," the question of indulgence could be referred to the State Department but in no case should "*the removal of the individual be delayed for an answer from Washington.*"[12]

Citizen complaints concerning alien enemies slowly reached the federal government. Secretary of State Monroe received one letter in 1812. Matthew Billyway, a sheriff, complained that a British half-pay officer by the name of James Barton resided in his territory. Barton had renounced his pay but would not file his intention of becoming a citizen nor would he give his name and residence to the marshal. The sheriff indicated that Barton daily maligned the friends of the present administration and wondered if Monroe would let him know if Barton could continue to reside "among us and enjoy the rights of abusing the government."[13] Monroe received an anonymous letter from Charleston, South Carolina, early in 1813, claiming that the

marshal in addition to his other undue conduct, pays no respect to any orders received from the Government respecting *alien enemies*, but permits them, as well as *Prisoners of War* and *spies* to go about the country, to *bribe*, *corrupt*, and *poison* the minds of the people against their government and to collect whatever information the enemy may require of our situation.

The writer closed by stating that he would have signed his name except for the "fear of my being assassinated in the dark, by the friends and hirelings of England (with which the City at present abounds)."[14]

Monroe took no action in relation to Barton; however, the district judge, John Drayton, confirmed the South Carolina situation in May in a letter to Monroe in which he related that the marshal, Robert E. Cochran, had been arrested for several defalcations of office. Drayton indicated further that some confusion had occurred in the marshal's department respecting alien enemies. Drayton requested that the President appoint a new marshal as soon as possible.[15]

Peter Curtenius, marshal of New York, apparently delayed in

implementing the instructions from the department. On March 31, 1813, Monroe instructed Curtenius to direct all British subjects who had been ordered from New York City but had not yet done so to leave the city within twelve hours under a penalty "of a close confinement in jail, if they were found therein or within the interdicted limits afterwards, allowing them a reasonable time for traveling to the places which may be designated for their retirement." A week later Monroe again wrote asking clarification on the departure of several alien enemies for Lisbon, in particular whether they departed with the permission and/or knowledge of the marshal. The letter authorized Curtenius to arrest any aliens who failed to comply with the previous order unless the failure had arisen "from causes which appear to you entirely satisfactorily." Monroe finally instructed the marshal to make a report to the State Department of those who were removed and of those he had to arrest.[16]

The second letter stirred Curtenius into action. The New York *Spectator* of April 10 ran an order from the marshal, dated April 7, instructing keepers of boarding houses in the city to report the names of any alien enemies that might be in their houses, particularly transitory ones. No British subjects, the notice warned, were "permitted to remain in this city without a passport, and boarding house keepers are cautioned at their peril against secreting, aiding, and protecting them."[17]

Just as the system began to function, Monroe announced a major administrative shift on April 15, 1813. The Secretary of State informed the marshals that John Mason had been appointed "Commissary General for Prisoners of War, including the superintendancy of Alien Enemies." The instructions requested the marshals to address all future correspondence to Mason and obey all orders from him.[18]

Mason issued a circular on May 31, 1813, announcing a slight relaxation in the policy of removing aliens from the tide-water. The new policy permitted aliens who had declared their intention to become citizens of the United States at least six months before the declaration of war and were married to native owners of real property and those engaged in internal commerce to remain or, if removed, to return to their usual places of residence "provided such residence be not at or in the immediate vicinity of a town or port on navigable water; where military works are maintained, or a body of troops are stationed."[19]

The new Commissary General of Prisoners received a few complaints. For example Thomas Cochran, collector of Wilmington, North Carolina, in a letter of June 19, 1813, reported that alien enemies or itinerates had an intimate connection with commerce particularly in vessels under neutral flags "by which means . . . the Enemy get both information as to our situation as also supplies."[20]

In mid-August 1813 Mason issued instructions to all marshals that when an alien abused "the indulgence and hospitality of the country, in time of war with his nation," you will after "first taking care to establish the facts, place him immediately in close confinement."[21]

Close confinement for thousands of alien enemies was an impossibility, but how were the marshals of keep track of the various aliens they had ordered into the interior? This difficulty was overcome on November 12, 1813, when Mason instructed the marshals to secure from each alien a parole of honor, by which the alien pledged to behave with due respect to the law and authority of the United States, would not carry on a correspondence with any of the enemies of the United States, or "receive, or write any letter or letters to or from any Alien Enemy whomsoever, but through the hands of the said Marshal, in order that they may be read and approved by him."[22]

Enforcement of the act and the various notices and instructions from the State Department and the Commissary General of Prisoners appears to have been erratic. The returns from the marshals contained in the War of 1812 Papers at the State Department list nearly 7,000 aliens as follows:[23]

Connecticut	113
Maine	287
Mississippi Territory	1
Missouri Territory	19
New Hampshire	4
New York	4,744
Pennsylvania	961
South Carolina	351
Tennessee (East)	1
Virginia	493
	6,974

It appears that most marshals tried to enforce the act to the best of their ability, considering the lack of assistance, the communications problems of that era, the opposition to the war on the part of native citizens in several parts of the country, and the complicated instructions and notices that the State Department or Commissary General of Prisoners issued.

Alien enemies pursued a variety of courses to seek redress from the iniquities of the law. The various notices and instructions permitted petitions, initially to the Secretary of State and later to the Commissary General of Prisoners. Nearly one hundred petitions have been preserved at the State Department. A typical petition was that of John McNish of Savannah, Georgia, dated April 7, 1813:

The petition of John McNish respectfully sheweth that your petitioner is a subject of Great Britain but has resided for eleven years last past in the United States. That he has pursued the business of a merchant and factor but has never been concerned in importing goods from Europe, or in any foreign commerce. That your petitioner applied to become a citizen of the United States some time previous to the declaration of war by the United States against Britain, but owing to his not having reported himself to the clerk of the District Court in the manner prescribed by an act of Congress passed in the year eighteen hundred and two, he could not be admitted.

That your petitioner has always since he resided in the United States demeaned himself as a good and honest citizen well disposed toward the country he has voluntarily chosen for his residence and the government from which he derived protection. That for proof of his character and general conduct, he begs to offer the certification annexed to his petition.

That in consequence of instructions received from your honor by the marshal of the district your petitioner has been obliged to remove from Savannah. That this removal has caused him much inconvenience and if he is obliged to remain absent will materially injure his business.

He therefore prays that permission may be granted him to return back & remain in Savannah.[24]

Unfortunately no records have been found that indicate the number of petitions the State Department approved. Congress became involved with the issue in 1814 when it received two petitions: the first from Thomas Owen, praying to be naturalized by a special act in order to be exempted from the provisions of the act; the second from "sundry Aliens" formerly of New York City now residing at Fishkill, requesting permission to return to New York City to pursue their usual vocations "under such restrictions as Congress may think proper to prescribe." The House committee which considered Owen's petition reported that they felt Owen was a man "of fair and unsuspected character," yet the committee recommended that it would be "impolitic and inexpedient to exempt him from the provisions of the act. . . ." The Senate referred the petition of the sundry aliens to a committee where it died.[25]

In addition to petitions several aliens applied to the courts for redress. The first case appeared in the federal courts in July 1813 when William Bold petitioned the South Carolina district court to be discharged from the custody of the marshal. Bold claimed that he was a citizen since his father had been naturalized on May 26, 1786. The court ordered the petitioner discharged.[26]

The fullest judicial treatment of the Alien Enemies Act occurred in Pennsylvania where Charles Lockington petitioned the state Supreme Court for a writ of *habeas corpus*. Chief Justice William Tilghman allowed the writ on November 12, 1813, and set a hearing for the following day. At the hearing, John Smith, marshal of Pennsylvania who had committed Lockington to the Debtor's Apartment in the prison for the city and county of Philadelphia, defended his action by reciting the original act, the various public notices issued by the Secretary of State and the Commissary General of Prisoners, and the specific instructions issued to the marshals. Lockington, Smith maintained, had been treated appropriately within the act and the instructions. Lockington was an alien enemy, engaged in commerce, who reported voluntarily to the marshal on July 18, 1812, and who, on March 13, 1813, applied to the marshal for a passport to retire to Lancaster. The marshal changed the request to Reading, a place forty miles beyond tidewater. On November 9, 1813, Smith found Lockington in Philadelphia and thereupon directed him to retire to Reading. When Lockington refused, the marshal took him into custody and placed him for safekeeping in the Debtor's Apartment of the prison.[27] Smith then claimed that the Pennsylvania court should not have jurisdiction in the case because (1) the Act of Congress did not authorize a state judge or justice to take cognizance of the case of an alien enemy but such jurisdictions were only vested "upon complaint against an alien enemy"; (2) the Act of Congress did not authorize any court to discharge an alien enemy from the custody of the marshal; (3) the Chief Justice cannot derive nor exercise a jurisdiction under the laws of the state if such jurisdiction is in any wise contrary to the Constitution and laws of the United States made in pursuance thereof; and (4) when the marshal's actions were under the authority of the Constitution and laws of the United States, they were "cognizable by the courts, judges, and justices, of the United States, and not by the courts, judges, and justices of the state of Pennsylvania." Smith concluded by stating that he was ready and desirous of removing Lockington to Reading or of releasing Lockington in order that he might go there voluntarily and prayed therefore that Lockington should be remanded into his custody.[28]

The attorney for Lockington, Mr. Hare, countered: (1) that alien enemies were under the protection of the law of nations "which had not, at any period of time, authorized their being treated as prisoners of war"; (2) that the Alien Act provided for the apprehension of aliens only for the purpose of removal from the United States; (3) that the various notices from the State Department were not public acts, were not under seal, and were not signed by the President, nor was the authority of the President mentioned in them; (4) that the marshal's actions under the act were unconstitutional since Lockington had not been committed by a court, or judge, or justice, after a complaint, warrant, and full examination and hearing; and (5) that the Chief Justice had complete jurisdiction to issue a writ of *habeas corpus* and to discharge the prisoner "from an unlawful or irregular imprisonment, even under colour of authority from the United States."[29]

Alexander J. Dallas, district attorney of Pennsylvania, responded to Mr. Hare for the United States. Dallas agreed that alien enemies under international law had the right to withdraw from the enemy's country within a reasonable time. Under provisions of the act of July 6, 1812, the President was authorized to "give, at any time within six months after the passage of the act, passports, *for the safe transportation of any ship, or other property*, belonging to British subjects, and which is now within the limits of the United States." The President, Dallas contended, had permitted resident aliens freely to withdraw from the country for a period considerably exceeding six months. From the declaration of war of June 18, 1812, until the issuing of the public notice of February 23, 1813, requiring aliens to retire to a distance of forty miles from tide-water, "resident alien enemies were subjected to no other restraints, than that of reporting their names to the Marshal," or if travelling from one city or town to another, of securing a passport from the marshal. If an alien does not depart within a reasonable time, the alien enemies "cannot, by implication, from a tacit permission to remain within the United States, acquire, or enjoy, any right, inconsistent with what Congress, and the president, have ordained upon the subject."[30]

Moving to the specifics of the Act of 1798, Dallas maintained: (1) that the President of the United States was "authorized to cause alien enemies, residing in the United States, to be apprehended, restrained, secured, and removed, without resorting to the judicial power"; (2) that the President's authority had been exercised, "in due form of law"; and (3) "that from the return of the writ of *habeas corpus*, and the evidence exhibited by the marshal of the district of *Pennsylvania*," was sufficient "to prevent the Chief Justice, from taking further cognizance of the case."[31]

Chief Justice Tilghman rendered his opinion on November 22, concentrating on three points: the issue of *habeas corpus*, whether an alien enemy was a prisoner of war, and the Alien Enemies Act of 1798. Tilghman maintained that the authority of state judges in cases of *habeas corpus* emanated from the several states and not from the United States. "In order to destroy their jurisdiction," Tilghman reasoned, it was "necessary to shew, not that the United States have given them jurisdiction; but that Congress possess, and have exercised, the power of taking away that jurisdiction, which the States have vested in their own Judges." Even if the United States might assume an exclusive jurisdiction, it must have assumed it, which in this case, Tilghman pointed out, "would be intolerably grievous, without a great increase of Courts and Judges." If the jurisdiction were concurrent, the authority of the United States could still be preserved through an appeal. Tilghman warned, however, that "it seems to be the general opinion, that from a decision on a *habeas corpus*, no appeal, or writ of Error, lies; and, thus, points of vital importance to the *United States*, may be determined by State Judges, without an opportunity of revision." This could be overcome, Tilghman pointed out, by an act of Congress permitting appeals from such decisions. Tilghman felt that Congress had not made the jurisdiction exclusive and thus state judges had jurisdiction. He concluded that when he considered

the situation of a Pennsylvanian, imprisoned unlawfully, by colour or pretended authority from the United States, on the banks of the Ohio, or the shore of Lake Erie, with only one Federal Judge to whom he can apply, and that Judge in the city of Philadelphia, I feel as little inclination as I have *right*, to surrender the authority of the Commonwealth.[32]

Tilghman rejected outright the contention that alien enemies were prisoners of war and thus not entitled to a writ of *habeas corpus*. Instead the Act of 1798, which was the law of the land in this instance, controlled alien enemies. Tilghman rejected Lockington's counsel's contention that the apprehending, restraining, and securing of Section 1 were intended only for the purpose of removal out of the United States. Instead the section was a provision "for the public safety; which may require, that the Alien should *not* be *removed*, but kept in the country under proper restraints."[33]

Tilghman agreed with Dallas on the interpretation of the general thrust of the act to grant to the President extensive powers. The first section gave the President

a most extensive influence, which is subject to great abuse: but *that* was a matter for the consideration of those who made the law, and must have no weight, with the Judge, who expounds it. The truth is, that, among the many evils of war, it is not the least, to a people, who wish to preserve their freedom, that, from necessity, the hands of the Executive power, must be made strong, or the safety of the nation will be endangered.

Tilghman also agreed with Dallas's interpretation of the role of the judiciary in the second section of the act.[34]

Tilghman questioned the legality of the first order issued from the Department of State since it was not signed by the secretary, nor was the name of the President mentioned. But the order issued from the Commissary General of Prisoners, Tilghman thought, put "the matter out of doubt; for, the regulations there established which refer to, and adopt the former orders from the Department of State, are expressly declared to be the act of the president, although they are not signed by him, but the Commissary."[35]

Thus being of the opinion that the marshal had a right to take Lockington into custody and place him in the Debtor's Apartment for safekeeping until he "could conveniently be removed to *Reading*," Tilghman ordered the prisoner "remanded to the custody of the keeper of the Debtor's Apartment."[36]

The constitutionality of the Act of 1798 came before the Virginia circuit court with John Marshall presiding in December 1813. Mr. Hurt petitioned the court for a writ of *habeas corpus* to bring up the body of Thomas Williams, confined in the jail of Richmond on charges of being an alien enemy. Hurt argued that the law gave too much power into the hands of "ministerial officers" where adequate judicial power existed. Marshall avoided the constitutional issue by ruling that Williams should be discharged since the marshal had not assigned a specific place to which Williams should be removed.[37]

At the close of the war the Office of the Commissary General of Prisoners issued a circular to the marshals indicating that in consequence of the peace between the United States and Britain "British subjects, resident in this country cease to be Alien Enemies." The circular instructed the marshals to "consider all restrictions heretofore imposed on persons of that description" at an end and requested the marshals "to take immediate measures to discharge all such persons" within their districts "from any and every restraint imposed on that account."[38]

The United States' first experiment with the Alien Enemies Act had ended. The act had been applied fairly and judiciously, without major protest, and seemingly without widespread abuse. The act would not be implemented again for over a century. President Woodrow Wilson's proclamation of April 6, 1917, which declared that war existed between the United States and Germany, once again put the act into effect. The final use of the act occurred in World War II when President Franklin Roosevelt's proclamations of December 7 and 8, 1941, effectuated the act.[39]

NOTES

1. Richardson, ed., *Messages and Papers of the Presidents*, II:497-498.

2. Smith, *Freedom's Fetters*, 35-49; Henry Steele Commager, ed., *Documents of American History*, 9th ed. (2 vols., New York, 1973), I:178-184. The following examples demonstrate the extent to which historians have accepted the myth of Republican repeal of the Alien and Sedition Acts. "The new administration soon erased the despised Alien and Sedition Acts." Michael Kraus, *The United States to 1865* (Ann Arbor, 1959), 301. "Jefferson pardoned those imprisoned under the Alien and Sedition Acts—both of which had expired—and Congress rescinded the Naturalization law." Harry J. Carman and Harold C. Syrett, *A History of the American People* (New York, 1956), 274. "The Alien and Sedition Acts, anathema to the Republicans, had fixed dates of expiration, and the Republicans allowed them to die unlamented." Richard B. Morris, William Greenleaf, and Robert H. Ferrell, *America: A History of the People* (Chicago, 1971), 171.

3. The act defined "natives" as males of the age of fourteen years and upward.

4. The act permitted the full time specified in any treaty between the United States and the hostile government. On July 6, 1812, Congress hastily amended this section to exclude any treaty which had expired. 2 *U. S. Statutes at Large*, 781.

5. 2 *U. S. Statutes at Large*, 577-578.

6. 2 *U. S. Statutes at Large*, 778-781.

7. *The Case of Alien Enemies, Considered and Decided upon a Writ of Habeas Corpus Allowed on the Petition of Charles Lockington, an Alien Enemy by the Hon. William Tilghman, Chief Justice of the Supreme Court of Pennsylvania, The 22nd Day of November, 1813, reported by Richard Bache* (Philadelphia, 1813), appendix, iii-iv. Most of the marshals simply reported the date on aliens, although a few added notations. For example, the return of the marshal of Virginia for September 1, 1812, identified two persons for special consideration: one labeled as "a man of bad character"; the other, "of immoral habits." The marshal of Connecticut provided the following remark concerning John Grey, a printer from Danbury:

"Born in Halifax of tory parents who went there from Massachusetts, moved to Boston 1790, says he was admitted to vote there and in this state, claims not to be a British subject—a tool of the federal party to print libels on the government U. S." War of 1812 Papers (7 reels, National Archives, Record Group 59, Microcopy M 588), reel 3.

8. *The Case of Alien Enemies*, appendix, vi.

9. Ibid.

10. Ibid., appendix, v, dated February 6, 1813, notice published in "The Democratic Press," of February 11, 1813.

11. Ibid., dated February 23, 1813, notice published in "The Democratic Press," of March 3, 1813.

12. Ibid., appendix, vii, dated March 12, 1813.

13. Mathew Billyway to James Monroe, August 15, 1812 (Microcopy M 179), reel 26.

14. Anonymous to James Monroe, March 20, 1813, ibid., reel 27.

15. John Drayton to James Monroe, May 13, 1813, ibid.

16. Monroe to Peter Curtenius, March 31, and April 6, 1813 (Microcopy M 40), reel 14, pp. 209, 213.

17. New York *Spectator*, April 10, 1813.

18. *The Case of Alien Enemies*, appendix, vii.

19. Ibid., appendix, v-vi.

20. Thomas Cochran to John Mason, June 19, 1813 (Microcopy M588), reel 1.

21. *The Case of Alien Enemies*, appendix, vii-viii.

22. Ibid., appendix, viii.

23. (Microcopy M 588), reels 2-3. The last return of the marshal of Pennsylvania for September 16-30, 1814, listed Alien Enemies numbered 2093-2142. Although the returns that have survived list only 961 names, probably 1181 other aliens voluntarily reported. The files also contain several letters from the marshal of New Jersey, indicating that reports were attached, but no reports were found. A letter from James Burr of Louisiana indicated that a few aliens had been identified in New Orleans, but no specific report conforming to the State Department's guidelines has been found. It is quite probable that the marshals identified over 10,000 alien enemies.

24. (Microcopy M 179), reel 27.

25. *Annals of Congress*, XXVI:391, 1929.

26. South Carolina district court, Admiralty Journal, 1806-1814, p. 12.

27. *The Case of Alien Enemies*, 5-10.

28. Ibid., 10-12.

29. Ibid., 13-16.

30. Ibid., 17-21.

31. Ibid., 21-33.

32. Ibid., 33-38.

33. Ibid., 38-41.

34. Ibid., 41-44.

35. Ibid., 44-45.

36. Ibid., 45. After an unsuccessful attempt to secure a writ of *hapeas corpus*, Lockington sued the marshal in the Federal circuit court for assault and battery and false imprisonment. The circuit court agreed with Tilghman's opinion on the major

issues and rebuffed Lockington once again at the October term of 1817, *Federal Cases*, XV:758-763, case number 8, 448.

37. Virginia circuit court, Order Book #9, 1811-1816, pp. 263-264; Charleston *Courier*, December 21, 1813.

38. Charleston *Courier*, February 28, 1815.

39. The act is presently part of the United States Code, Title 50. Sections 21-24.

6
The War of 1812 and the Courts

The Madison administration not only had to deal with the problem of alien enemies but also citizen opposition to the war, particularly in the Northeast. The opposition took many forms—from circulating petitions to trading with the enemy. Once again the government tested the law of treason. The New York circuit court grand jury issued the first indictment for treason in September 1812. The district attorney charged William Shaw, also indicted for a misdemeanor in accepting a license to a British port, with sending "certain letters of dispatches addressed to the 'Right Honorable Lord Castlereagh, one of the principal Secretaries of States' of Great Britain" containing information and intelligence that it was desirable that a British squadron should appear "in the waters of the United States." Shaw also informed Castlereagh that the frigate *Constellation* would be ready for sea in less than two months. Shaw pleaded not guilty to both charges, and the petit jury acquitted him of the misdemeanor. When the district attorney did not offer to bring Shaw to trial on the treason charge, the court suggested that there was no probability of the district attorney being better prepared for the trial of the said indictment at the next term than he might have been at the present term. Since the Constitution of the United States "declared that in all criminal prosecutions the accused shall enjoy the right to a speedy and public trial," the court ordered the defendant discharged "from any further prosecution of the offense laid in the indictment."[1]

In the fall of 1813 the Pennsylvania district attorney charged William Pryor and Jesse Appleton with treason. Both were accused of taking provisions to the blockading British fleet. The grand jury indicted Pryor but not Appleton. At the trial, which commenced on April 22, 1814, Pryor pleaded not guilty. During the process of jury selection he challenged twenty-five jurors. The trial revealed that Pryor was a British prisoner who "sought to ransom himself and his fellows by going ashore with a British party under a flag of truce to help them purchase provisions." The prosecution contended that the intention of the prisoner was "to procure provisions for the enemy, by uniting with him in acts of hostility against the United States or its citizens." The defense contended that since the activity occurred under a flag of truce no "act of hostility was attempted, nor is there the slightest reason to believe that any was meditated by the prisoner, or by any of the party." Justice Bushrod Washington instructed the jury that "the act of going ashore under a flag of truce was not a sufficient overt act, because, though it evidenced intent, it was not sufficiently far advanced in the execution of that intent." The jury acquitted Pryor.[2]

Early in 1814 Representative Robert Wright of Maryland introduced a resolution in the House proposing that a committee of the whole House "be instructed to inquire into the expediency of extending the 2d section of the act for the establishment of rules and articles for the government of the armies of the United States, relative to spies, to the citizens of the United States." Representative Richard Stockton of New Jersey found the resolution unworthy of a hearing, contending that the law of treason was adequate and that the resolution would "subvert every principle of civil liberty, to place the citizens under the ban of martial law, to prostrate courts of justice and the trial by jury, which is guaranteed by the Constitution. . . ." The House on January 14 referred the topic to the Committee on the Judiciary which never reported on the resolution.[3]

Later in 1814 the New York district attorney charged two men with treason. The court ordered Nathan Ford discharged when the grand jury did not present him.[4] The grand jury indicted John Baxter. His counsel moved to quash the indictment on the grounds that the trial was not being conducted where the crime was committed. The court upheld the indictment on April 11 but ordered the trial moved to Jefferson County. No record of the trial has been found. However, in making a report to the Secretary of State the clerk of the court in 1825 reported that the court acquitted Baxter.[5] The Maryland grand jury in May 1815 indicted John Hodges and his brother for treason for specifically giving aid and comfort to the enemy. During the British retreat from Washington, D. C., in the summer of 1814, some of the people of Upper Marlborough took four stragglers and a deserter prisoner. Once they were missed, the British commander demanded that they be released or he would destroy the town. A committee of towns-people decided to release the prisoners and save the town and appointed John Hodges and his brother to take the prisoners from the guard and turn them over to the British, which they did. For this act the grand jury indicted

Hodges and his brother. Following the testimony of several witnesses for both the prosecution and the defense, Elias Glenn, the district attorney, "prayed the court to direct the jury that the mere act of delivering up prisoners or deserters is an overt act of high treason." Associate Justice Gabriel Duvall, who presided over the trial, eventually rendered his opinion on the law stating,

The overt act laid consists in the delivery of certain prisoners, and I am of opinion that he is guilty. When the act itself amounts to treason, it involved the intention, and such was the character of this act. No threat of destruction of property will excuse or justify such an act. Nothing but a threat of life, and that likely to be put into execution will justify.

The jury nonetheless "without hesitating a moment" acquitted the defendants.[6]

The indictments and trials continued in 1815. The New York grand jury indicted Mark Lynch, Aspinwall Cornwall, and John Hegeman for supplying the enemy with provisions, including fifty barrels of beef. The jury acquitted the defendants. In Pennsylvania the grand jury indicted John Fisher for serving as a pilot on board a vessel of war called the *Majestic*, "sailing and hovering on the coasts and shores of the . . . United States . . . with design to commit hostilities . . . and blockading the harbors, capturing vessels—the *Peggy* (unmanned) and the *George Washington* (manned) making prisoners of the crew. . . ." The jury acquitted Fisher on April 17.[7]

Finally, the Georgia grand jury returned a true bill against Joel L. Felt and William Seals for high treason. Mr. Cuyler, attorney for the defendants, moved for their discharge when the district attorney did not commence a prosecution. The court duly ordered the prisoners freed.[8] It would appear that the federal courts generally adopted a very narrow interpretation of treason. Where a case reached a jury, the jurors proved extremely reluctant to find a person guilty of that particular crime.

The use of treason to limit trade with the enemy would have been difficult if not impossible. Among the acts passed during the summer of 1812 was the "Act to Prohibit American Vessels from Proceeding to, or Trading With, the Enemies of the United States." Introduced on June 27 and approved by the President on July 6, the act required ships owned by citizens of the United States to post bond equal to the value of the ship and cargo before clearing, that they would not proceed to or trade with, the enemies of the United States. If a vessel should depart without giving bond, the ship and cargo would be forfeited; and the owner or owners, freighter, factor, or agent, master, or commander would "severally forfeit and pay a sum equal to the value of the . . . vessel and cargo; and the said master or commander, if privy thereto, and being thereof convicted," would be liable to a fine not exceeding $1,000 and imprisonment for a term not exceeding twelve months according to the discretion of the court.[9]

Section 2, reflecting the experience of trade with Canada during the embargo, contained a prohibition similar to that above but applied to transporting military stores, arms, munitions, and provisions into Canada in a wagon, cart, sleigh, boat, or otherwise. The act imposed penalties, including forfeiture equal to the value of the vehicle or provisions, a fine not exceeding $500, and imprisonment for a term not exceeding six months at the discretion of the court.

The final provision of the act forbade citizens to receive, accept, or obtain a license from Great Britain "for leave to carry any merchandise, or send any armed vessel into any port or place within the dominions of Great Britain, or to trade with any port or place." The act subjected violators to forfeiture of a sum equal to twice the value of the ship and cargo, imprisonment for a term not exceeding twelve months and a fine not exceeding $1,000. Thus early in the war federal officials could prosecute both for trading with the enemy and for using a license of the enemy. The government limited the use of the act during the remainder of 1812. There was one prosecution in Georgia for supplying the British with provisions, with no conviction, and one indictment in Maine where the jury was hung, and whereupon the district attorney agreed not to further prosecute.[10]

No prosecutions occurred for illegal use of licenses. The British, faced with the pragmatic problem of trying to supply food to its army and navy in Europe and the populace and military forces in Canada, had commenced at least by August to issue licenses to American shippers.

A typical license was one issued by Vice-Admiral Herbert Sawyer:

Whereas, Mr. Andrew Allen, his Majesty's consul at Boston, has recommended to me Mr. Robert Elwell, a merchant of that place AND WELL INCLINED TOWARDS THE BRITISH INTEREST, who is desirous of sending provisions to Spain and Portugal, for the use of the allied armies in Peninsula; and whereas I think it fit and necessary that encouragement and protection should be afforded him in so doing.

There are, therefore, to require and direct all captains and commanders of his Majesty's ships and vessels of war, which may fall in with any American or other vessel bearing a neutral flag, laden with flour, bread, corn and peas, or any other species of dried provisions, bound from America to Spain and Portugal, and having this protection on board, to suffer her to proceed without unnecessary obstruction or detention in her voyage; *Provided*, she shall appear to be steering a due course for those countries, and it being understood this is only to be in force for one voyage and within six months from the date thereof.

Given under my hand and seal, on board his Majesty's ship Centurion, at Halifax, this fourth day of August, 1812.

Herbert Sawyer
Vice-Admiral[11]

Later in the year the British circular of November 9, 1812, authorized its Governor in the West Indies to issue licenses for the importation of essential commodities. The circular stipulated,

Whatever importations are proposed to be made, under the order, from the United States of America, should be your licenses confined to the ports in the Eastern States exclusively, unless you have reason to suppose that the object of the order would not be fulfilled if licenses are not also granted for the importations from the other ports in the United States.[12]

A copy of the circular along with related orders fell into Madison's hands early in 1813. In February Madison laid the information before Congress and recommended that Congress consider an effectual prohibition

of any trade whatever by citizens . . . of the United States under special licenses, whether relating to persons or ports, and in aid thereof prohibition of all exportations from the United States in foreign bottoms, few of which are actually employed, whilst multiplying counterfeits of their flags and papers are covering and encouraging the navigation of the enemy.

The second session of the twelfth Congress did not take up the matter. The thirteenth Congress, however, which opened in May, soon discussed a bill to prohibit the use of licenses or passes granted by the British and approved such a measure on July 9. The act expanded the definition of licenses to include a pass or other instrument granted by Great Britain included within the penalties any person who "shall be either directly or indirectly concerned or assisting in obtaining, using, granting, or selling any such" paper and retained the provision for a forfeiture of a sum equal to twice the value of the vessel and merchandise while increasing the fine to a maximum of $5,000. The act also stipulated that any vessels using such papers were declared to be British ships and liable to search and seizure by public armed vessels, with the forfeiture in court accruing to the crew of the capturing vessel.[13]

Even with new legislation, prosecutions were few in 1813. The Rhode Island grand jury indicted three people for furnishing the enemy, but the district attorney dropped the prosecutions. The government brought three informations in Massachusetts for trading with the enemy, but the court condemned only the brig *Marstrand* for using a British license. The North Carolina district court dismissed a libel against the schooner *Matilda* for having on board a British license on the grounds that the crew was considered in a state of mutiny and the capture was unlawful.[14]

By 1814 the trade had grown to remarkable proportions. British General George Prevost wrote to Earl Bathurst, Secretary for War and Colonies, in August 1814 that "two thirds of the army in Canada are at this moment eating beef provided by American contractors, drawn principally from the

State of Vermont and New York." American General George Izard reported that on the Vermont side of Lake Champlain the highways were too narrow and too few to accommodate the herds of cattle that were pouring into Canada. "Like herds of buffaloes they press through the forests, making paths for themselves. Were it not for these supplies, the British forces in Canada would soon be suffering from famine, or their Government be subject to enormous expense for their maintenance."[15]

The number of criminal indictments in 1814 was again small. The Massachusetts district attorney charged George Rogers, Jr., and William Briggs with obtaining and using a British license or pass but later dropped the prosecutions. In Maine the grand jury indicted William Hume and others for transporting tar and flour from Eastport to New Brunswick for the supply of the enemy. They pleaded not guilty in May. The district attorney, finding that "the state of the country where the witnesses live, is such as renders it impossible to procure their attendance on the part of the government, is under the necessity of saying that he will not further prosecute this indictment." The court, therefore, dismissed the indictment.[16]

Only in Vermont were a number of people charged with trading with the enemy. The grand jury returnd a true bill against Joe L. Barber for violating the Act of 1812. He contended that "fat cattle" were neither provisions nor munitions of war within the true intent and meaning of the act. The judges divided in their opinion, thus permitting the question to be certified to the Supreme Court. In 1815 the Supreme Court ruled that fat cattle were provisions or munitions of war within the true intent and meaning of the act. The Vermont circuit court thereupon fined Barber $500 and imprisoned him for one week.[17]

George Sheldon, also indicted under the Act of 1812, came to trial in 1815. The jury told the judge that they were "ignorant if driving various cattle into Canada was a violation of the act, if the driving was transporting, and if the cattle were provisions of war." The judges being divided, they certified the issue to the Supreme Court. In 1817 the Court again ruled that fat cattle were munitions of war but surprisingly ruled that driving living fat oxen on foot is not a transportation thereof within the true meaning and intent of the act. The Court ordered the defendant acquitted.[18]

Juries acquitted several of the others indicted in 1814 during the term; the court continued the other cases. In 1816 a jury convicted Jeremiah Clapp, and the court fined him $150 and costs; likewise, the court fined Francis Ducloz $50 and imprisoned him one fortnight and fined Levi Hooker $2,658 plus costs. By 1817 either the others had been tried and acquitted, or the district attorney had dropped the prosecution.[19]

Libels and informations increased dramatically in 1814. The government libeled twelve vessels in Rhode Island, and the court condemned them for supplying the enemy and libeled three vessels for using a license. In Massachusetts the government libeled one vessel for trading with the enemy, one for using a British license, and one for both trading with the enemy and using a license. In Vermont the number of libels was extremely large. The government entered eighty-one at the May term and 113 at the October term. The May libels included over 1,700 pounds of pork plus seven barrels, forty-six head of cattle plus five yokes of oxen; and among the October libels were 631 head of cattle, one yoke of oxen, and three horses.[20]

The lower courts quickly decided several of the cases. In 1814 the Supreme Court heard several of these cases on appeal and added additional impetus to the government's efforts to suppress trade with the enemy and the use of licenses. In three different instances the Court dealt with the use of licenses. In the case of the *Julia*, a vessel which had been condemned by the Massachusetts district court, the Court upheld the forfeiture stating that sailing on a voyage under the license and passport of protection of the enemy, in furtherance of his views or interests, constitutes such an act of illegality as subjects the ship and cargo to confiscation as a prize of war. Thus the condemnation was not based upon the Act of 1812 but upon prize law. The case of the *Aurora*, which had been condemned by the Rhode Island district court, differed slightly from the case of the *Julia* in that the voyage had been to a neutral port. The Court ruled, however, that acceptance and use of any enemy's license on a voyage to a neutral port, prosecuted in furtherance of the enemy's avowed objects was illegal and subjected the vessel and cargo to confiscation. Finally in the case of the *Hiram*, which had been freed by the Massachusetts court upon a claim that the License Act of 1813 had exempted the vessel, the Supreme Court ruled that the vessel was still subject to condemnation under prize law since the act of sailing upon a voyage under the license and passport of protection of the enemy constituted an illegal act.[21]

The Court made similar rulings in a series of cases concerned with illegal trade. In the case of the *Rapid* the Court ruled that after a declaration of war an American citizen cannot lawfully send a vessel to the enemy's country to bring away his property. The Court ruled even more forcefully in the case of the *Sally* that property engaged in an illicit intercourse with the enemy was to be condemned to the captors, not to the United States. In the third case the Court ruled that a vessel sailing to any enemy's country after knowledge of the war and bringing from that country a cargo consisting chiefly of enemy goods is liable to confiscation as a prize of war.[22]

Congress became involved with the issue of illegal trading in the fall of 1814 when it received two resolutions requesting additional legislation. The Committee of Ways and Means, which undertook consideration of the matter, requested Secretary of the Treasury Alexander J. Dallas to furnish information, not concerning the extent of the problems but suggestions for correcting the evils. Dallas indicated that a general revision of the revenue laws at this time was impossible. He identified the causes of the problem in Vermont as follows:

1. That smuggling is extensively prosecuted, on the Northern frontier, by citizens of the United States, sometimes with, and sometimes without, the cover of a neutral character; in the course of which the enemy obtains important intelligence; he is furnished with cattle, and other essential supplies; and he is enabled to introduce his merchandise surreptitiously into our markets.

2. That the powers of the revenue officers are inadequate to the detection and prosecution of these offenses, because the right of search is not extended to every vehicle that may be employed; because the prohibitory laws do not sufficiently define and enumerate the subjects of an illicit trade; because no efficient act of prevention is authorized to be performed, even upon the strongest ground of suspicion; and because there is no force, civil or military, provided to aid the revenue officers in the execution of their duty, when cases of violent opposition occur.

3. That, limited as the general powers of the revenue officers appear to be, they are rendered still more inadequate by the terror which the officers now feel, of being exposed to suits for damages, under the authority of recent decisions in the courts of law; for it has been adjudged in Vermont, that the inspectors of the customs are not authorized, in any case, to make seizures, and that actions may be against them, to recover the whole value of the property seized, even when the property itself has been duly condemned, as forfeited by law.[23]

Dallas next explored the legal power and privileges of inspectors and other officers of the customs, summarized briefly the existing auxiliary means to execute the revenue laws and the laws prohibiting trade and intercourse with the enemy, and finally suggested several modes of amending the defects and correcting the evils which existed. The Committee of Ways and Means incorporated most of Dallas's suggestions into the bill presented to Congress in December 1814. The bill slowly worked its way through Congress, which approved it on February 4.[24]

The act resembled closely the Enforcement Act of 1809. Section 1 permitted federal revenue officers to stop and search persons or things suspected of transporting illegal goods. If the officers suspected that goods were concealed in a building, store, or dwelling-house, they would on application "to any judge or justice of the peace, be entitled to search and examine whether there are any such goods . . . which are subject to duty, or have been unlawfully imported." Under either procedure if goods were found they could be seized and secured for trial.

Sections 3 and 4 contained similar provisions to prevent the exportations of military stores, arms, provisions, money, or supplies of any kind to the enemy. If an officer believed a person was intending to violate the act, he could bring the person before any judge or justice to have them held to

security in a sufficient sum, with sufficient bail for his or their good behavior. For a violation of trading with the enemy, the owners of the goods
or the means of transporting them would be considered guilty of
misdemeanor and liable to be fined not exceeding $1,000 and imprisoned
for a term not exceeding three years.

To provide protection to officers from state suits, Section 8 stipulated
that if a suit should be commenced in any state court against any officer or
any person aiding or assisting an officer in accordance with the act, the defendant could, at the time of entering his appearance in such court, file a
petition for the removal of the cause for trial at the next circuit court of the
United States to be held in the district where the suit was pending and offer
good and sufficient surety for his entering bail in such court. The section required the state court to accept the surety and proceed no further in the
cause. For a cause already in progress, the section provided that the officer,
after final judgment for either party, could appeal such judgment to the
next circuit court. The circuit court then could try the cause and determine
the facts and the law "in the same manner as if the same had been there
originally commenced; the judgment in the case notwithstanding."
Excluded from the act was any prosecution for an offence involving corporal
punishment. The act included three additional provisos: one, providing that
no such appeal should be allowed in "any criminal action or prosecution,
where final judgment shall have been rendered in favor of the defendant, or
respondent, by the state court"; a second, giving the defendant the right to
plead the general issue and give "this act and any special matter in
evidence"; and three, permitting the defendant to recover double costs if
the plaintiff was nonsuited or the judgment passed against him.

Section 10 severely restricted mobility of Americans living in the border
regions. To cross into Canada and in any way hold any intercourse with the
enemy, a citizen had to obtain a passport "from the Secretary of State, the
Secretary of War, or other officer, civil or military, authorized by the
President . . . to grant the same, or from the Governor of a State or
Territory." Anyone voluntarily violating the prohibitions would be
considered guilty of a misdemeanor and liable to be fined up to $1,000 and
to be imprisoned for a term not exceeding three years. Likewise the statute
obliged any person coming from the enemy's territory under pain of the
same penalties "to report himself, forthwith, or as soon as practicable
thereafter, to the military commander, or to the collector, or other chief
officer of the customs of the district."

For persons found merely hovering upon the frontier or travelling
towards the border "at a distance from his or their usual place of
abode . . . and without any lawful business . . . and without a passport,"
Section 11 provided they should be held to security for good behavior "as a
person or persons suspected, upon probable cause, of being engaged in unlawful trade or intercourse with the enemy." A proviso was added that

"nothing contained in any part of this act shall be construed to alter, in any respect, the law of treason."

If using citizens within ten miles or the posse of the marshal were not sufficient to enforce the law, Section 12 authorized the President or his designee, in the case of resistance, to employ the land and naval forces of the United States or the militia "for the purpose of aiding and cooperating with the officers of the customs, and all other civil magistrates, in seizing and securing persons engaged, or suspected . . . to be engaged in unlawful trade or intercourse with the enemy. . . ."

The final section provided that the act would continue in force only during the continuance of the present war between the United States and Great Britain. Unbeknownst to the Congressmen who passed the act, the final draft treaty had been signed on December 24 and would shortly arrive in the United States. Madison sent the treaty to the Senate which approved it on February 16. Madison gave his approval the following day.[25] Thus the act was applicable for less than two weeks. Like the Enforcement Act which preceded it in 1809, it demonstrated that the Republican Congress and President were willing to use any means necessary to accomplish their ends, including massive violations of due process and the Bill of Rights.

The difficulties of obtaining convictions continued in 1815. The Massachusetts circuit court indicted and convicted George Rogers, Jr., of obtaining and using a license and fined him $100 plus costs. Rogers's attorney moved that the sentence be stayed, claiming that the President had pardoned his client. The court stayed the sentence and discharged the defendant. The Massachusetts grand jury indicted Samuel F. Coolidge for putting on board the *Miranda* fifty barrels of superfine type flour to sail from Boston to Halifax. Coolidge moved that the indictment be quashed because the grand jury, without having been sworn in, examined William R. Lee, a material witness for the United States. The court quashed the indictment and discharged Coolidge. In Georgia the grand jury returned two indictments for attempting to send provisions to the enemy, but the district attorney failed to prosecute. The grand jury in Virginia returned a true bill against one person for supplying the British with provisions. The petit jury convicted him, but the court suspended judgment.[26]

Forfeitures declined sharply as the war came to a close. The government libeled eight vessels for trading with the enemy and thirteen for license violations in Rhode Island, but the courts condemned only fifteen. In Massachusetts the government libeled one vessel for trading with the enemy and one for using a license. Vermont tried a large number of cases—164—however, this represented a decline from the 201 cases tried in 1814.[27]

The court continued a few cases into the post-war period. The Rhode Island court heard one license case and one trading with the enemy case in 1816, and the Massachusetts district court heard one trading with the enemy case in 1817. Only the Massachusetts case resulted in a condemnation.[28] In addition the Supreme Court heard several cases on appeal. It rendered its last decisions in trade and license cases in 1819.[29]

The end of the war did not end the interest or activity of a number of Americans engaged in commerce. Former privateers quickly shifted their allegiance after the war to the newly formed countries in South America and presented the government with a new challenge to the Neutrality Act of 1794.

NOTES

1. New York circuit court, Minute Book, 1813-1819, pp. 16, 23-24, 26; New York circuit court, Case Files, Box 4; (Microcopy M 40), reel 14, p. 206.

2. Pennsylvania circuit court, Minute Book, 1811-1815, pp. 181, 185-187, 191, 196-198; Pennsylvania circuit court, Case Files, Box 5, 1806-1814.

3. *Annals of Congress*, XXVI:881, 888, 936, 1123-1128.

4. On the word of two British deserters the government arrested Ford, a judge in Ogdenship, brought him 400 miles to New York City, and charged him with treason according to the New York *Evening Post*. Charleston *Courier*, February 13, 1814, citing the New York *Evening Post* of January 31; New York circuit court, Minute Book, 1813-1819, pp. 31, 34.

5. New York circuit court, Minute Book, 1813-1819, pp. 32, 44-46; *A Statement of Convictions, Executions, and Pardons*, U. S. 20th Congress, 2nd sessions, House Document 146 (1829), 94.

6. Lawson, ed., *American State Trials*, X:163-181.

7. New York circuit court, Minute Book, 1813-1819, pp. 88, 100; New York circuit court, Case Files, Box 2; Pennsylvania circuit court, Minute Book, 1811-1815, pp. 223, 226-229.

8. Georgia circuit court, Minute Book, 1806-1816, p. 491. Two other possible treason cases have been found. Two people in Boston were reported to have been charged with treason for supplying British ships off Cape Harbor with cattle. Charleston *Courier*, January 13, 1814. A second case occurred in Connecticut. Hezekiah Huntington, the district attorney, wrote Monroe on September 12, 1815, requesting "compensation" for witnesses to appear in the trial of Marsh Ely, charged with treason committed in December 1813. (Microcopy M 179), reel 32.

9. 2 *U. S. Statutes at Large*, 778-781; *Annals of Congress*, XXIII:314, 316, 319, 1560, 1571-1572, 1574.

10. Maine district court, Minute Book, 1812-1815, Dec. term 1812; *A Statement of Convictions, Executions, and Pardons*, U. S. 20th Congress, 2nd session, House Document 146 (1829), 150a.

11. J. Mackay Hitsman, *The Incredible War of 1812* (Toronto, 1965), 49-50.

12. Ibid., 99-100. Channing reported that Lord Sidmouth, the First Lord of the Admiralty, issued about 600 licenses. These were bought and sold openly in New York, and probably also at Philadelphia and Boston. Edward Channing, *A History of the United States* (6 vols., New York, 1905-1925), IV:531. Augustus J. Foster, the British Minister to the United States, issued additional licenses before he left the

country. Bradford Perkins, *Castlereagh and Adams: England and the United States, 1812-1823* (Berkeley and Los Angeles, 1964), 9.

13. Brant, *James Madison*, VI:145; 3 *U. S. Statutes at Large*, 84-86; *Annals of Congress*, XXVI:38, 45, 47, 52, 55, 446, 484.

14. *A Statement of Convictions, Executions, and Pardons*, U. S. 20th Congress, 2nd session, House Document 146 (1829), 49; Charleston *Courier*, May 14, 1813.

15. Hitsman, *The Incredible War of 1812*, 109; Brant, *James Madison*, VI:340.

16. Massachusetts circuit court, Minute Book, vol. VII, 1814-1815, pp. 474-477; Maine district court, Minute Book, vol. III, 1812-1815, Dec. term 1814.

17. Vermont circuit court, Minute Book, 1814-1816, Oct. term 1814; Cranch, *Reports*, IX:243-244.

18. Vermont circuit court, Minute Book, 1814-1816, Oct. term 1814; Wheaton, *Reports*, II:119-122.

19. Vermont circuit court, Minute Book, 1814-1816, Oct. term 1814.

20. Vermont circuit court, Minute Book, 1814-1816, Oct. term 1814; *A Statement of Convictions, Executions, and Pardons*, U. S. 20th Congress, 2nd session, House Document 146 (1829), 58-59, 83-87.

21. Cranch, *Reports*, VIII:181-203, 203-221, 444-451.

22. Ibid., 155-168, 382-384, 434-444.

23. *Annals of Congress*, XXVIII:757-761.

24. 3 *U. S. Statutes at Large*, 195-200; *Annals of Congress*, XXVIII:164, 181-185, 188, 305, 591, 757, 1033-1039, 1061, 1115.

25. See Brant, *James Madison*, VI:363-380; Perkins, *Castlereagh and Adams*, 39-127.

26. Massachusetts circuit court, Record Book, vol. VII, 1814-1815, pp. 338-340, 474-477; *A Statement of Convictions, Executions, and Pardons*, U. S. 20th Congress, 2nd session, House Document 146 (1829), 142, 150b.

27. Ibid., 53, 58-60, 87-91; Vermont circuit court, Minute Book, May and Oct. term 1815.

28. *U.S.* v. *Boat Rainbow*, Massachusetts district court, Record Book, vol. 9, 1816-1817, (Federal Records Center, Waltham, Mass.), 578-584, Rhode Island district court, Record Book, vol. 4, 1814-1816.

29. *The Hiram* (1816), Wheaton, *Reports*, I:440-447; *The Ariadne* (1817), Wheaton, *Reports*, II:143-148; *The Caledonian* (1819), Wheaton, *Reports*, IV:100-103; *The Langdon Cheves* (1819), Wheaton, *Reports*, IV:103-104. Nathaniel Goddard and other owners of *The Ariadne* and cargo appealed the Supreme Court's decision to Congress through a petition in 1818. The Committee of Ways and Means recommended approval, but Congress did not act. *Annals of Congress*, XXXI:871.

7

The Courts and the Independence of Latin America: Neutrality and Piracy

With the return of peace in 1815 the federal courts completed processing the various war related cases and in addition began to confront a growing problem of violations of the United States' neutrality law. Although neutrality violations had been pushed to the background after the Miranda and Burr trials, a steady stream of cases had been tried in the lower courts between 1808 and 1815. In the Massachusetts circuit court in 1808 John Crawford and Martin Blake pleaded guilty to augmenting the force of the *Minerva*, an armed ship of Great Britain. The court fined each man $40.[1]

Secretary of State Robert Smith issued a circular to the district attorneys of New Orleans, Maryland, New York, Pennsylvania, South Carolina, and Georgia on May 4, 1810, indicating that there was reason to believe that several vessels recently had been fitted out and armed or had their force augumented within the waters of the United States in violation of the Neutrality Act of 1794. Smith urged the district attorneys "to use every means" in their power "to ensure a rigid Execution of that Law, by endeavoring to bring to Punishment as well those who have already violated it, as those who may hereafter do so."[2]

The circular may have temporarily accomplished its purpose. The district attorney of Pennsylvania filed an information in August 1810 against the *Romona* for being unlawfully fitted out and armed, and in Georgia the grand jury issued an indictment against Michael Brouard for fitting or arming or increasing the force of a schooner called the *Amirable* or *Montebello*. Neither case ended with a conviction.[3] A year later the Pennsylvania grand jury indicted Alexis Grassin for unlawfully augmenting the force of a French armed vessel. The Grassin case resulted in two hung juries and eventual dismissal.[4]

While these miscellaneous cases were before the courts, a full-fledged expedition against Spain in Mexico unfolded in the Southwest.[5] José Bernardo Gutiérrez, commissioned evidently by Miguel Hidalgo, went to the United States in March 1811 ostensibly to solicit aid for the Mexican patriots. Not being received in Washington, D.C., he returned to Natchitoches, Louisiana, where he enlisted the assistance of Lieutenant August W. Magee,[6] a former army officer who had commanded a small force of United States troops policing the "neutral ground" between the Sabine River and the Arroyo Hondo. The leaders openly sought recruits for the expedition in Louisiana; and although the activity violated the Neutrality Act of 1794, the expedition left Natchitoches in the summer of 1812 without governmental interference. Among the Americans who joined the expedition were Colonel Samuel Kemper, Reuben Ross, Winfrey Lockett, Henry Perry, and Dr. John Hamilton Robinson. The force of some 500 encountered initial success, defeating a royalist group at Salado Creek and entering San Antonio de Bexar on April 1, 1813. When Gutiérrez ordered the massacre of seventeen royalist officers, several of the Americans, including Kemper, Ross, Lockett, and others, returned to the United States. Shortly thereafter José Alvarez de Toledo replaced Kemper and Gutiérrez as commander of the expedition, only to be soundly defeated by a new royalist force. Toledo and a few followers escaped across the Sabine in October 1813.[7] Secretary of State Monroe informed Pennsylvania district attorney Alexander James Dallas in December 1813 that Dr. John H. Robinson and General Irenee Amelot de Lacroix were lately at Pittsburgh and engaged in the unlawful business of exciting citizens of the United States to the invasion of the Spanish provinces. Monroe sent additional letters in February 1814 to the Governors of Louisiana and the Mississippi territory and to Tully Robinson, the district attorney of Louisiana. A letter of February 1814 to Robinson and Governor William C. C. Claiborne of Louisiana associated General Toledo with General Jean Humbert and Dr. Robinson.[8] The Pennsylvania circuit court indicted Lacroix in April.[9] The government arrested Toledo in New Orleans in the autumn of 1814, but John Dick, who replaced Robinson as district attorney, released him after six months because "no testimony whatever" appeared against him.[10]

The government received rumors of a new expedition in 1815. Madison issued a proclamation on September 1, commanding all persons "engaged or concerned in the same, to cease all further proceedings therein as they will answer to the contrary at their peril. . . ."[11]

Not only did the expeditions create problems for the government in the Southwest, but a number of persons holding commissions from various South American revolutionary governments used the United States as a base from which to prey upon Spanish and British commerce in the Gulf of

Mexico. The first group of this nature to attract attention in the South was the Lafittes, led by Jean Lafitte.

The Lafittes established an operation on the island of Grande Terre in Barataria Bay. The men were allegedly privateers, having operated under French licenses out of the island of Guadeloupe until the British seized that island. The group secured new licenses from the revolutionary republic of Cartagena, commenced operating in the Gulf, bringing the vessels and cargoes to Grande Terre, and selling the goods and vessels to Louisiana citizens without paying import duties.[12] Madison brought the matter to the attention of Congress in his third annual message when he said:

To secure greater respect to our mercantile flag, and to the honest interests which it covers, it is expedient . . . that it be made punishable of our citizens to accept licenses from foreign governments for a trade unlawfully interdicted by them to other American citizens, or to trade under false colors or papers of any sort.[13]

Governor Claiborne of Louisiana was equally upset, sufficiently so that he secured indictments against the Lafittes—Jean, Pierre, Dominique You (an alias for the elder Lafitte), and others. When Pierre Lafitte defied the Governor by appearing publicly in New Orleans, the Governor had him arrested. With the indictments pending and Pierre Lafitte in jail, Commodore Daniel T. Patterson, commander of the naval station at New Orleans, launched an expedition against Grande Terre in September 1814 with several ships and the schooner *Carolina*. The night the expedition left, Pierre Lafitte mysteriously escaped from jail. The expedition arrived at Grande Terre on September 16, captured a quantity of supplies and munitions, burned several buildings, and imprisoned a number of people, but none of the Lafittes.[14] Shortly thereafter, General Jackson accepted an offer by the Lafittes to assist in the defense of New Orleans. The saga of the Lafittes seemingly ended on February 6, 1815, when Madison issued a proclamation granting them a full pardon for all deeds committed prior to January 8, 1815.[15]

Late in December 1815 the United States government received the Spanish Minister Don Luis de Onís. Onís immediately protested the violations of United States neutrality laws. During the War of 1812 the United States was practically powerless to do anything about the numerous violations. In the post-war period new challenges arose. Obviously many of the violations had at least some support from the government or particular government officials and fairly substantial support from the citizens of the United States. Only when the privateers began to interfere with United States commerce was the favor withdrawn and the efforts to suppress the activity made sufficient to accomplish the task.

Commencing late in 1815 various agents representing Buenos Aires, Artigas, Mexico, New Granada, and Venezuela distributed and sold commissions as privateers in various seaport cities of the United States, particularly Baltimore and New Orleans. The number of commissions issued has not been and perhaps cannot be ascertained. Estimates of the number of Buenos Aires privateers ranges from thirty-three to forty-five; the Venezuelan fleet fluctuated in size from ten to seventeen; the Mexican colors were flown over ten to eighteen vessels. Baltimore was supposedly the origin of twelve of the vessels; and New Orleans, of fourteen. Charles S. Griffin identified twenty-one as a minimum number commissioned at Baltimore—this being the number which were formally in legal proceedings.[16]

The United States government quickly recognized Baltimore as a center of Spanish American patriot activity. Secretary of State Monroe wrote to the Maryland district attorney Elias Glenn on January 3, 1816, warning Glenn that the schooner *Mangoré* which arrived at Baltimore on December 28, "was originally fited [sic] out" at Baltimore. Monroe requested Glenn to "institute prosecutions against all parties now to be found, who may have had any concern in such object, so manifestly in contravention of the laws of the United States." Over the next three years Glenn received numerous letters from the State Department concerning ships, captains, and owners of privateers.[17]

The first success against the privateers occurred in Virginia, where the district attorney libeled the *Romp* and charged such of the crew that could be captured with piracy. In the course of preparing the case against the *Romp*, the Virginia district attorney discovered that the alleged owner of the *Romp* was Thomas Taylor of Baltimore. The Virginia district attorney asked the State Department to submit to him all papers relative to Taylor. Attorney General William Wirt felt Taylor could probably be prosecuted but felt it would be extremely difficult to do so in Maryland where Taylor was located. In September a justice of the peace arrested Taylor but later released him. The court then issued a second warrant for his arrest. The preparation for the trial continued with William Wirt assisting with the prosecution. Wirt requested Richard Rush to send the officers of the customs at Baltimore as witnesses for the trial. On December 16, 1816, Wirt reported to Monroe that the trial of two crewman had occurred before the witnesses arrived. William Hitching and John J. Mitchell admitted that they were Americans who had sailed from Baltimore and that the *Romp* cleared under American registry, but they insisted "that she sailed with a commission from the government of Rio de la Plata on board." They testified that at sea the captain read the commission and declared the vessel to be a Buenos Aires man of war under the name of *Santa Fesino*. Wirt reported:

[The] pretended Commission to the vessel was decided by the Court to be without any legal evidence of its genuineness, and as being a Commission accepted by

Thomas Taylor, who had sworn, in obtaining his American Register, that he was an American citizen and the schooner an American vessel. It was also shown that so far from constituting a protection to the crew, the acceptance of the Commission would itself have been an act of piracy under our treaty with Spain.

Wirt stated that the defense's main contention had been to emphasize the commonness and publicity of the practice in Baltimore "and from the openness, the notoriety, and impunity, with which it was done so near the seat of government, it was inferred that the government purposedly connived at it." The juries acquitted the two seamen, and Wirt refused to prosecute the others. John Marshall, the presiding judge, chided the men saying that they owned their clemency to the juries and not to the law "for that the act which had been proven upon them was, unquestionably, piracy."[18]

Onís continued his representations, identifying for the government the American privateer *True Blooded Yankee* being fitted out in New York to cruise under the flag of Buenos Aires. Monroe notified Jonathan Fisk, district attorney in New York, of the charge and requested him to take proper measures to frustrate the plan of the adventurers if the "information is found to be correct." Fisk reported in July that the Collector and Surveyor of the Port were watching the vessel and if her movement "should appear to be in violation of the laws of the United States, a prosecution will be instantly commenced against the offenders."[19]

The acquittal at Richmond probably inspired President Madison to request Congress on December 26 for additional legislation to "prevent violations of the obligations of the United States." Specifically Madison proposed such further legislative provisions

as may be requisite for detaining vessels actually equipped, or in a course of equipment, with a warlike force within the jurisdiction of the United States, or, as the case may be, for obtaining from the owners or commanders of such vessels adequate securities against the abuse of their armaments. . . .

The House quickly drew up a bill. The debates centered on Section 3, which authorized collectors to seize vessels suspected of violating previous sections until a decision of the President could be obtained or until the owners entered into bond and sureties to the United States double the amount of the value of the vessel and the cargo. Representative Erastus Root of New York not only doubted the constitutionality of the section but disliked the United States being asked to adopt a preventative measure purely to satisfy Spain. The House, nevertheless, approved on the 19th. The Senate delayed consideration for a month then quickly passed it on March 3. The act, limited to two years, provided a fine of $10,000 and imprisonment for not more than ten years for any person fitting out or attempting to fit out and arm, or procuring to be fitted out and armed, any ship or vessel with intent that such ship or vessel should be employed in the service of any foreign prince to cruise or commit hostilities or to aid or cooperate in any warlike measure whatever against the subject of a nation with whom the United States were at peace. The vessel in such a case would be forfeited. The act required owners of all armed ships to post bond, double the value of the ship and cargo, that the said ship would not violate the act.

Section 3 remained in the bill. Section 4 provided a fine of not over $1,000 or imprisonment of not more than one year for any person increasing or augmenting the force of a ship of war or other vessel in the service of a foreign prince or state.[20]

While the new legislation was under consideration by Congress, the State Department continued to pressure the Maryland district attorney and collector to take action against vessels and captains at Baltimore. Glenn reported to Monroe on January 15 that he had taken action against the schooner *Mangoré's* commander James Barnes, charging him with piracy for having taken a commission from a foreign nation to cruise against the king of Spain. Glenn indicted that Barnes had not been arrested and that the information supplied by the collector identified as owner a person who was currently in France. Glenn added that he had asked the Spanish consul to prosecute various owners, but the consul would not supply an affidavit. In February Monroe supplied Glenn with several letters from Onís on the subject of alleged violations. In March the new Secretary of State, Richard Rush, tried to pin the district attorney down with a long letter requesting specific information in regard to the *Potosí*, the *Mangoré*, the *Orb*, and the *Romp*.[21]

A week later Rush asked the collector, James H. McCulloch, to investigate the *Orb* and a Captain James Chaytor. The same day Rush ordered the collector at Norfolk, Charles K. Mallory, to investigate the *Independence of the South* and the *Altavela*, two armed vessels docked at Norfolk, and sent a similar letter to William Wirt, district attorney of Virginia. In April the State Department requested Thomas Rutter, marshal of Maryland, to arrest Captain Barnes and Captain Chase for injuries committed on the high seas against Spanish subjects.[22]

Difficulties in Maryland multiplied late in April. A justice of the peace arrested Don Joseph Almeida on a charge of piracy under the Spanish treaty. Judge Bland of the Baltimore county court issued a writ of *habeas corpus*. Judges Bland and Hanson heard the case. Among the objections on the part of the prisoner was a charge that Congress had not power under the Constitution to invest any judge or justice of the peace with any judicial authority, which is confined by the Constitution to the Supreme Court and such inferior tribunals as Congress shall from time to time ordain. Both judges concurred in this objection and ordered the prisoner discharged. The Baltimore *Federal Gazette* concluded that the decision in effect declared "that no state Judge or Justice of the Peace has power to arrest or commit any person for a violation of the laws of the United States."[23]

The pressure from the State Department and the investigations by the district attorneys and collectors began to show fruit in the fall of 1817. The district attorney of Pennsylvania filed an information in October against the brig *Ellen* for an illegal outfit. The President agreed to release the *Ellen*, provided the owner discharged the munitions and gave sufficient sureties that her future destination should be conformable with the law.[24]

At the October term of the circuit court in Massachusetts, the grand jury charged John Palmer and Thomas Wilson, mariners, and Barney Callaghan of the privateer *Congresso* with assaulting certain mariners, subjects of the King of Spain, piratically and feloniously setting upon, boarding, breaking, and entering a vessel called a *Spanish Hugger*, and stealing the vessel valued at $10,000 and twenty bags of cocoa valued at $400. The defendants pleaded not guilty. The court assigned James T. Austin and Harrison G. Otis as counsel. The jury acquitted the men. The report of the indictment in the Boston *Independent Chronicle* and Boston *Patriot* revealed the feeling of many Americans toward the activities against Spain.

To the surprise of almost everyone, the three men belonging to the crew of the South American privateer *Congresso*, have been indicted on the high charge of piracy and it is expected their trial will commence this day. We cannot believe that any jury of this humane metropolis will construe their offense in the heinous light in which it is placed by the indictment. However irregular may have been their proceedings, it is believed they were not of sufficient enormity to deserve the dreadful punishment of Death.[25]

The day the article appeared the court ordered the two editors, Davis C. Ballard and Edmund Wright, Jr., to appear in court and show cause why an attachment should not be issued against the paper for a contempt. The editors filed an answer on November 4, claiming that the article

was not intended as an improper interference with the judicial proceedings of this court, in the equity and impartiality of which these despondents have the utmost confidence, or with a view of having any influence on the event of the trial spoken of, or on the public opinion in relation to that event, but the design of said publication was merely to give the public what was thought innocent intelligence relative to a subject of general interest, nor were these despondents aware that such publication was in any point of view improper or disrespectful of this Court, the least suggestion or idea of which would altogether have prevented its insertion and that since these despondents have been convinced as they now are of the impropriety of the said paragraph they respectfully regret the insertion of it.

The court accepted the apology and discharged the editors from the process.[26]

The American people almost universally held the attitude expressed by the editors. The grand jury of the Pennsylvania circuit court in October refused to indict Richard Beebe and Robert H. Howard for piracy but preferred the lesser charge of consulting with pirates. The petit jury acquitted the two men at their trial in April 1818. In December the grand jury refused to indict John D. Needham and nine others for enlisting in the service of a foreign state as soldiers, specifically for booking transportation on the *Ellen*, charged previously with an illegal outfit.[27] The Maryland grand jury indicted Joseph Almeida and John Chase, whom the petit jury acquitted of a charge of piracy. Additional arrests, but no convictions, occurred in South Carolina and Georgia.

A few successes occurred in 1817. In September the brig *B*, an American registered vessel with some armament and thirteen men, cleared for the West Indies. Shortly afterwards she was found hovering on the coast and augmenting her force. The collector of Newport, Rhode Island, William Ellery, ordered her seized. In November Ellery libeled the brig *B* and preferred an indictment against Thomas Jones, the owner and master of the said schooner. The court ordered the vessel forfeited to the United States. On the request of John Quincy Adams, Asher Robbins, the district attorney, entered a *nolle prosequi* in the case against Jones. Evidently the move surprised Justice Story. Adams wrote to Ellery in July,

If the facts stated by the "DA & collector" are not correct, the President certainly was deceived; and the suggestion of Justice Story is of such a nature, that I must particularly request you to give me such information respecting the case as you may possess, and which may fully disclose its real character.[28]

In the second case James Barnes, on behalf of the owners and crew of the privately armed Buenos Airean vessel the *Pueyrredón*, libeled the brig *Bello Corunnes*. The court ordered the *Corunnes* restored to the Vice Consul of Spain, Bernardo Malagamba, stating,

It does not appear to me that the Province of Buenos Ayres [*sic*] is a free sovereign and independent state and in alliance and union with four other free sovereign and independent states, by the name & confederacy of the United and independent Provinces of South America, and as such, have the right to levy war, make peace . . . issue commissions of reprisal & letters of marque. . . .[29]

While attention on the Atlantic seaboard focused on Buenos Aires privateers, Onís protested in January 1816 "that 1,000 men from Kentucky and 300 from Tennessee intended to invade Mexico and asked that such exploits be prevented as well as the exportation of munitions to the Mexican revolutionists." James Miller informed Monroe in July that a new expedition was being formed under the command of Henry Perry. Miller enclosed a copy of a circular that appeared in the New Orleans press claiming that Perry already had 1,000 men engaged and could count on additional aid from Tennessee and Kentucky.[30] Madison quickly issued a proclamation on September 1, 1816, calling upon "all faithful citizens who have been led, without due knowledge or consideration, to participate in the said unlawful enterprises, and to withdraw from the same without delay. . . "[31]

Dick, with assistance from Commodore Daniel T. Patterson, investigated the rumor. Dick reported that Patterson's naval force seized a large quantity of arms supposedly intended for the group on the river but that Patterson had not discovered any persons and thus neither arrested nor prosecuted anyone. Dick reported almost a year later that Perry, General Humbert, and their followers had "passed separately through Attakapas, and assembled about two leagues west of the Sabine. Thence they embarked for some place on the coast of Mexico, were wrecked, dispersed, and their plans, whatever they were, totally defeated."[32] The latter part of Dick's report was not accurate. Perry had not gone to Mexico but to Galveston Island where he joined forces with a larger expedition.

In the fall of 1816 José Manuel de Hererra commissioned Luis de Aury, a Frenchman, commander of the fleet of the Mexican Republic. A few days later Hererra and Aury created a government at Galveston. Colonel Perry with a force of one-hundred and Francisco Javier Mina with 200 men augmented Aury's group, making a total force of from 400 to 800 and a naval fleet of from twelve to eighteen vessels. In April 1817 Mina commenced an expedition into Mexico. At Sota la Marina Aury deserted, returning to Matagorda. Perry also left, marching overland to La Bahía. The Royalists defeated the weakened Mina force in October at San Luis Potosí where they captured some seventy-five Americans and imprisoned them in Mexico or sent them to Spain. Only four of the prisoners were reported to have survived.[33]

After the expedition left Galveston Jean Lafitte occupied the island with a fleet of eighteen to twenty vessels flying the Venezuelan flag. On finding Galveston occupied by Lafitte, Aury sailed for Amelia Island in Florida.[34]

Amelia Island had been occupied in June 1817 by Gregor McGregor, an Englishman, with a small force of men obtained principally at Baltimore, Charleston, and Savannah. McGregor claimed commissions from the Republics of Mexico, Buenos Aires, New Granada, and Venezuela to conquer Florida. McGregor left in early September to seek supplies. Shortly after his departure Aury appeared with two large privateers bearing the title "of Captain-General of the Navy of the Independent States of Mexico and New Granada, Political and Military Chief of the Island of Amelia, and General-in-chief of the sea and Land Forces destined to expel the Authorities of the King of Spain from the Provinces of Florida." Aury assisted the remains of McGregor's force in repelling an attack by the royalists; but the groups, one labelled the American faction headed first by Ruggles Hubbard and after his death in October by Jared Irwin and the other the French party led by Aury, quickly became embroiled with internal bickering.[35]

In his first annual message to Congress on December 18, James Monroe outlined what he knew of the situation on Amelia Island and Galveston and indicated,

To obtain correct information . . . to inspire just sentiments in all persons in authority, on either side, of our friendly disposition . . . and to secure proper respect to our commerce in every port and from every flat, it has been thought proper to send a ship of war with three distinguished citizens along the southern coast with instructions to touch at such ports as they may find most expedient for these purposes.

Shortly before issuing the annual message, Monroe started the necessary preparations to take Amelia Island. Late in December the government force took the island. Monroe reported the capture to Congress via a special message on January 13, 1818.[36]

Monroe's annual message stimulated Congress again to become involved in the neutrality question. Speaker Henry Clay offered the following addition to a traditional resolution, referring the appropriate portion of the President's message to a select committee:

That the committee be instructed to inquire whether any, and if any what, provisions of law are necessary to insure to the American colonies of Spain a just observance of the duties incident to the neutral relation in which the United States stand, in the existing war between them and Spain.

In explaining the reason for the addition, Clay commented on the case of the *Ellen* and the ten men indicted at Philadelphia. The men, he said, were British disbanded officers who had united "themselves with the Spanish patriots in the contest existing between them and Spain." In route to South America they had touched at the port of Philadelphia, later taking passage on a vessel bound to some port in South America. "At the instigation of some agent of the Spanish government," Clay continued, "a prosecution was commenced against these officers. . . ." If these facts were correct, Clay argued, then "it becomes an imperious duty in the House to institute the inquiry contemplated by the amendment which I have proposed." The House approved the amendment and on January 5 the House received a bill aimed at consolidating all neutrality legislation into a single act. Debate commenced on March 17 and lasted until March 25, when the House approved the bill without a division. The Senate concurred on April 13, and the President signed the bill on April 20, 1818.[37]

The act, containing twelve sections, repealed the Acts of 1794, 1797, 1800, and 1817. The statute made accepting a commission to serve a foreign prince, state, colony, district or people in war against a prince, people, etc., with whom the United States are at peace; enlisting or procuring others to enlist in the service of a foreign state; fitting out or procuring to fit out a vessel; increasing or augmenting the force of a vessel; and setting on foot within the United States a military expedition against a friendly power, high misdemeanors with the following fines and imprisonments:

	Fine Max. (in dollars)	Imprisonment Max.
Accepting a commission	2,000	3 yrs.
Enlisting	1,000	3 yrs.
Fitting out, within the U. S.	10,000	3 yrs.
Fitting out, without the U. S.	10,000	10 yrs.
Augmenting	1,000	1 yr.
Military expedition	10,000	3 yrs.

The most severe penalty was assigned to any citizen or citizens who would fit out a vessel without the United States or command, serve abroad, or purchase "any interest" in such a vessel. The act specified that the offender would be tried in the district where the person was apprehended or first brought into the United States.

Section 7 authorized the district courts to "take cognizance of complaints, by whomsoever instituted, in cases of captures made within the waters of the United States, or within a marine league of the coasts or shores thereof." Section 8 empowered the President to employ the land or naval forces and the militia to execute the prohibitions and penalties of the act. Section 9 permitted the President to compel any foreign ship or vessel to depart the United States "in all cases in which, by the laws of nations or the treaties of the United States, they ought not to remain within the United States."

The new law retained the bonding provisions of the Act of 1817. The act instructed collectors to detain vessels built for warlike purposes and about to depart, when circumstances render it probable that they are intended to commit hostilities against a friendly power.[38] The consolidation of previous legislation into a single act certainly was beneficial to those responsible for enforcing the law. Clay partially won his point by having the wording include colonies. The greatest benefactor, however, was Spain. While Spain conceivably could have purchased munitions and warships from the United States, she had not; whereas the rebellious colonies were heavily dependent upon the United States for such materials.

The number of cases brought to trial in the federal courts increased dramatically in 1818. Indictments for piracy occurred in most of the seacoast states. The Louisiana district court convicted William Wyatt of murder and piracy on board the American schooner *Fox Island*. At the October term of the circuit court in Massachusetts, the district attorney charged John Williams, John P. Rog, Francis Frederick, Nile Peterson, and Nathaniel White with murder and piracy. The men, members of the crew of the *Plattsburg*, had been arrested in Copenhagen and returned to the United States for trial. The jury found the first four guilty but acquitted White. The court adjudged the guilty men to be pirates and felons and ordered "each of them to be hanged by the neck until they and each of them be dead." After the execution the court ordered the marshal to deliver the bodies to "such Surgeon . . . as the court shall direct . . . for the purpose of dissection. . . ." In February 1819 the executions were carried out in Boston.[39] The judge's order for dissection, permitted under the Crimes Act of 1790, was the only such order found for the entire period. The order illustrates the growing reprehension of piracy and murder on the high seas.

The Massachusetts grand jury indicted a second group of men—William Holmes, Edward Rosewaine, and Thomas Warrington—at the October term for the crimes of piracy and murder. After conviction by the jury, the counsel for the men moved for a new trial, claiming that the court had misdirected the jury concerning the points of law raised at the trial. The defense counsel questioned the jurisdiction of the circuit court on three counts: whether the vessel on board of which the offence was committed was owned by a citizen or citizens of the United States, whether the prisoners were citizens of the United States, and whether the offence was committed on board a vessel not sailing under the flag of any nation. The defense counsel also questioned whether the burden of proof of the nationality of vessel was on the United States or on the prisoners. The judges divided in opinion on the motion and immediately certified the case to the Supreme Court for an opinion. The Supreme Court in 1820 certified, in an opinion written by Justice Washington, that the circuit court had jurisdiction although the vessel was not owned by a citizen or citizens of the United States and that the vessel had no real national character, even if the prisoners or any of them were not citizens of the United States. On the other point, the court said the burden of proof was on the prisoners. At the May 1820 session of the Massachusetts court the opinion was read, and the motion for a new trial denied. The court sentenced the men to be hanged on June 15, 1820, on which date the sentence was carried out.[40]

The Maryland district attorney charged thirteen men with piracy and fifteen with a misdemeanor. After Justice Gabriel Duvall charged the grand jury, District Judge James Houston revealed that a copy of the *National Intelligencer* containing an essay signed by Franklin respecting the South American privateers, had been enclosed in a blank cover and sent to him.

Houston indicated that the essay contained a paragraph which "might be construed into a threat, and might have been, and probably was intended as a threat." The gist of the paragraph was that anyone "who should condemn persons for engaging in the holy cause of assisting the Patriots of South America, could not long expect to live either as a judge or a man." Houston asserted that the "threat" would not deter him from the faithful discharge of his duty.[41]

Prior to the meeting of the court, Glenn requested the opinion of the attorney general on how he should go about the prosecution. Wirt recommended that the captain and crew of the privateer *Fourth of July* be indicted under the original 1790 act of Congress defining piracy. He indicated that the crew would counter with their commission but that should be objected to since it was issued by a sovereign not recognized by our government. Wirt pointed out that the Virginia district court had issued a ruling in the case of the *Romp* the previous year. The owners, Wirt contended, should be indicted as accessories to piracy. Wirt concluded that as a safeguard all also should be indicted under the Act of 1817. The misdemeanor charges would be predicated upon the Neutrality Act of 1794.[42]

When the trials commenced late in November, Wirt journeyed to Baltimore to assist Glenn with the prosecution. The court tried and acquitted Thomas Taylor of piracy. In the misdemeanor trail of Joseph Karrick for violating the Act of 1794, the court ruled that the act prohibited the fitting out and arming of a vessel to be employed in the service of another foreign province or state but that the counts founded upon that section could not be maintained since the United States government had not acknowledged the independence of the South American provinces and thus they were not foreign states within the meaning of the acts of Congress. The court ruled likewise that the Act of 1817, except for adding the words colony, district, or people, retained basically the same wording. The case was then sent to the jury which, after an absence of about an hour, returned a verdict of guilty. The defense filed a motion to arrest the judgment. The following day the court arrested the judgment, ruling that two counts of the indictment were insufficient. Karrick and the others against whom indictments had been found were bound over to appear before the court the next term.[43] The district attorney on May 5, 1824, entered a *nolle prosequi*.

The largest number of piracy cases occurred in Georgia where the grand jury indicted sixteen persons for piracy in 1818. The indictment also charged five of the sixteen with a misdemeanor for serving on board a foreign armed vessel in violation of the Act of 1818. Ralph Clintock, William Taylor, and Robert Vestals were convicted of the misdemeanor, but the court stayed their sentencing pending the outcome of their trial for piracy. The petit jury acquitted William Ramsay of the misdemeanor. The piracy trials were carried over to the next term of the court.[44]

In New York in August, Associate Justice Brockholst Livingston issued warrants against Captain Skinner, Don Manuel H. Aguirre, and a Mr. Delano for "knowingly being concerned in furnishing, fitting out or arming, in the port of New York, two ships, called the *Curiazo* and *Horatio*, with the intent that they should be employed in the service of some foreign prince or people, to cruise . . . in violation of the Neutrality Act of 1818." The defendants claimed that the ships had not been armed but only fitted out. The attorney for the prisoners quickly requested that they be charged before the circuit court or the charges be dropped. Aguirre, alleged Minister from the government of Buenos Aires, in addition claimed immunity from prosecution as a Foreign Minister. The judge rejected Aguirre's contention, stating that the United States had not recognized the independence of Buenos Aires or accredited the Minister, and thus Aguirre was liable to prosecution. The judge, however, discharged the prisoners since the ships had not been armed.[45]

Aguirre's actions irritated President Monroe. In a letter to John Quincy Adams of August 17, Monroe agreed with Adams that Aguirre could not be protected against arrest. He added,

He ought to have known the fact, and not mentioned it, but in truth his whole proceeding here, has manifested his utter incapacity for his trust, or that, misguided by others, he had believed that he could, by taking advantage of the public feeling in favor of the colonies, force the government into measures forbidden by our laws, disgraceful to the character, and repugnant to the national interest.

Monroe felt that the law which allowed vessels to be built "provided they be not armed, or, if armed provided the intent is not made to appear that they are to be employed against a power with whom we are at peace" as favorable "to the Colonies as it can be to be consistent with our neutrality."[46]

The favorable press the patriots received from late 1816 to 1817 began to sour in 1818. The New Orleans *Gazette* lamented in September 1818 the injury inflicted on the commerce of New Orleans "by the numerous picaroons which swarm in the Gulf of Mexico, the West-Indian seas, and along the Atlantic Coast of Florida." The paper praised the activity of the naval officers at New Orleans but felt that "their means are inadequate to afford complete protection to the coast. To accomplish that object would require the naval force at present on this station to be more than doubled." In September 1818 the Charleston *Courier* reprinted an article from the St. Christopher's *Gazette* asking the government to do something. The paper maintained,

If some of our citizens are so unprincipled as to fit out, in our ports, vessels to cruise against the commerce of neutral and friendly nations, it is the duty of the government to prevent them. Such conduct not only exposes our vessels to vexations, searches, robbery and capture, and renders us odious to our commercial neighbors, but it may involve us in war. Such conduct is not only disgraceful to us, but injurious to the patriot cause. How can any cause prosper with so profligate a character as the patriot cause must have if its flag is only a cover for Buccaneers? . . . It is due to the honest merchants due to the honor of our flag, and to the peace and prosperity of the nation.[47]

The growing piratical nature of the privateers prompted Congress in February 1819 to pass an act to protect the commerce of the United States and to punish the crime of piracy. The act, approved on March 3, 1819, authorized the President to employ public armed vessels to protect merchant vessels and included instructions to the commander of public armed ships to take and send into any port any armed vessel which attempted or committed piratical aggression. The law permitted merchant vessels to defend themselves against aggression by any armed vessel other than a public armed vessel of a nation in amity with the United States. If the vessel which attempted a piratical aggression should be captured, it would be condemned to the captors. Finally the act stipulated that if any person or persons should commit the crime of piracy, as defined by the law of nations, and should afterward be brought into or be found in the United States, the offender or offenders upon conviction before a federal court should be punished with death. Congress phrased the section deliberately to overturn court rulings that only Americans who had committed piracy could be tried under the piracy provisions of the Crimes Act of 1790. The act was limited to the end of the next session of Congress.[48]

The new legislation, combined with increased efforts on the part of federal officials, brought a flood of indictments during 1819. In addition, the Supreme Court rendered opinions in three cases providing the first interpretation of the post-war neutrality legislation.

The district attorneys charged one hundred persons with piracy in 1819, including nineteen in Maryland, twenty in Virginia, two in Massachusetts, twenty-two in South Carolina, three in New York, thirty-three in Georgia, and one in North Carolina.

In January John Quincy Adams wrote to Elias Glenn urging Glenn to commence judicial proceedings against George Clark, who belonged to a vessel believed to have been fitted out in Baltimore and sailed under the flag of Artigas. Clark was alleged to be guilty of piracy and other atrocities. In April Adams again wrote to Glenn revealing that the State Department had received representations from the French, Spanish, and Portuguese Ministers concerning piratical depredations alleged to have been committed upon several vessels of the respective nations by vessels fitted out at Baltimore. Adams concluded:

[The] President considers the Honor, as well as the most important interests of the Country, deeply concerned in the repression of these piratical transactions, and he cannot but regret that while every other port of our Maritime Coast the means of repressing them have in a great Measure been successful, they have hitherto been found ineffectual at Baltimore.[49]

Glenn responded within a week indicating that where he had been able to secure sufficient evidence, indictments and libels had been preferred. He regretted the role that Baltimore had played in the violations but claimed that he had done all that was possible to observe the law. He attributed the difficulties to three things. First, he thought,

The subordinate officers of the revenue, are not sufficiently vigilant and careful in their Examinations of vessels, whose preparations, are of a warlike nature. By a diligent and attentive scrutiny of such things as must necessarily be found on board these vessels, I believe, for the Collector to interpose authority and detain such vessel, until the pleasure of the President should be known in the case, according to the Provisions of the now existing law. Or if the Inspectors of the Revenue would communicate to me, such facts as would Justify me in filing a libel, that would immediately be done.

Glenn warned, however, that such libels were attended with some degree of hazard "for it might happen, that a vessel loaded with arms and other military stores, may be intended solely for a mere commercial adventure, and for the purposes of trade. This is perfectly legal and not prohibited by any law." The second cause of difficulties was the lack of watchfulness in the commanders of the revenue cutters, whose duty, Glenn felt, should be to examine suspected vessels after they had left the port of Baltimore. Third, he complained of the difficulty in procuring testimony. Since owners, captains, and mariners were equally criminal under the law, it was difficult to find men who were acquainted with the facts and willing to give evidence since "you know they are not bound to give Evidence, when it may tend to criminate themselves. . . ." Glenn concluded that several times he had taken testimony from various people, but when they had to swear to it, they refused.[50]

Adams informed Glenn on May 1 of a complaint received from the Minister of Portugal concerning outrages committed on the coast of Brazil by the privateer *Irrestible*, commanded by John Daniels. The Minister alleged that the vessel had been fitted out and manned by Americans at Baltimore. Adams suggested that Daniels might be prosecuted on his return to the United States.[51]

Within a week Glenn replied that the grand jury was in the process of hearing the case of John D. Daniels, and Glenn expected that he would be indicted. Before the month ended Glenn was able to report that the grand jury had indicted John F. Ferguson, who acted as commander, and sixty-one crewmen of the *Irrestible* for piracy. Ferguson and twelve others were arrested. Glenn also requested a *nolle prosequi* for four people who testified against the others.[52]

During the summer the Baltimore press added its criticisms of the federal officials to that of the President and Secretary of State. In June and July the Baltimore *Morning Chronicle* and the Baltimore *Telegraph* editorially condemned the activity of the privateers. The *Chronicle* led off, stating that it was a

notorious fact that there has been much clandestine intercourse carried on by some of the citizens of Baltimore with the Patriots of South America, in defiance of a *positive law of Congress*, and in violation of *solemn existing treaties*. What reproach has been brought upon this city by this shameful and clandestine traffic it does not become us to say. Such, however, is the fact;—it has been written in characters of sunbeams—this shameful traffic must sooner or later be abandoned, unless our government is prepared at once to take up arms against his Catholic majesty.

A letter from a Baltimorean published in the *Telegraph* decried the violations against Spain and placed the blame in part on the President for failing to employ the navy, as authorized under the new legislation to suppress the piracy. The letter ended sarcastically:

I commend the object of the president's tour; but he may find hereafter, that it would be quite as popular to himself and beneficial to his country had he made some arrangements prior to his departure, for the faithful execution of the duties pointed out in that act. These arrangements made, it would much gratify our feelings to find some activity shews in putting them into effect.

An editorial in the *Chronicle* of July 8 blasted not only the President but the entire government, concluding:

But if our chief magistrate looks with unconcern on the piraticals committed by his countrymen—if all the cabinet participate in such apathy—if Congress is infected with the paralysis—if our courts of injustice are touched with this torpidity—if all the branches of the government, executive, legislative and judicial, are alike insensible to the stern and imperious mandates of honor, to the Deity alone can our supplications be made, can our wrongs be exposed for redress. Even in the last and awful case, we do not despair of the republic; our Maker can turn the hearts of his creatures—He can bring order out of chaos, and light out of darkness. We can, as a last resort, although of a sombre character, confide in our Creator and not despair of our republic.[53]

Before the year was out Glenn had preferred nineteen charges of piracy and eleven of misdemeanor. The court tried seventeen of the men—juries convicted seven and acquitted ten. The President pardoned five of the seven convicted men; the court sentenced the other two to be hanged. The district attorney entered *nolle prosequis* in fourteen cases, including one case that was carried over from the previous year.[54]

The twenty charged with piracy in Virginia were members of the crew of the *Irresistible*. In reporting their capture and transportation to Richmond for trial, the Norfolk *Herald* stated that it did not wish to prejudice their case,

But while we watched their countenances as they moved in grim procession from the prison to the wharf, we were forcibly reminded of a scene in the play of Robin Hood, where that merry wight yclept Little John takes the chair and wig of justice to try his prisoners, Scarlet: and we could not help asking ourselves, what chance these unfortunate wretches would have, if their *looks* were to be taken in evidence against them? After enumerating three other reasons why the prisoner ought to be hanged, our sagacious justice Little John, adds—"And, fourthly, you must be hanged you have a d_____d hanging look."[55]

Samuel Poole was the first of the twenty tried. After hearing the evidence, Chief Justice Marshall charged the jury and concluded that "it was impossible that 'the Act of Congress could apply to any case, if it did not to this' yet the standard referred to by the Act of Congress must be admitted to be so vague as to admit some doubt. The writers on the law of nations give us no definition of the crime of piracy." Marshall recommended that the jury return a special verdict "which might submit the law to the more deliberate consideration of the court." The jury in a few moments brought in the following verdict:

If the plunder of a Spanish vessel on the high seas in April, 1819, by the crew of a vessel sailing and cruising at the time under no commission whatever which crew had previously cruised in a private armed vessel commissioned by the Government of Buenos Aires, a Spanish Colony at war with Spain, and while on such cruise in the month of March, 1819, had mutinied, confined their officer, left that private armed vessel, and seized by violence the *Irrestible*, a vessel at that time cruising under the government of Artigas, then also at war with Spain, and the said vessel (the *Irrestible*) when so seized lying in the port of Margaritta; and while thus cruising in the *Irrestible* without any commission committed the robbery charged in the indictment, be piracy under an Act entitled "An Act to protect the commerce of the U. S. and punish the crime of piracy," then we find the prisoner, Samuel Poole, guilty of the piracy charged in the Indictment; if the plunder above stated be not piracy, under the said act of Congress, then we find him not guilty.[56]

The jury returned similar verdicts on sixteen of the others, and it acquitted three. When Marshall and St. George Tucker could not agree on a verdict, the court certified the causes to the Supreme Court, which in 1820 ruled that the Act of 1819 was a constitutional exercise of the power of Congress to define and punish the crime of piracy.[57]

The Georgia circuit court encountered more difficulties in 1819 than any other circuit court. Not only did the court have the trials of Ralph Clintock and others held over from 1818, but also the grand jury issued thirty-three new indictments for piracy. The trial jury convicted John Williams, alias Henry Williams, and others on December 20. The defendants' counsel moved that the prisoners should be discharged because the jury separated before the court received the verdict. The judge overruled the motion but ordered a new trial. The new trial on December 24 resulted in a verdict of not guilty. Meanwhile on December 21 the petit jury convicted Ralph Clintock of piracy; and the following day John Furlong, alias John Hobson, of two counts of piracy and two counts of murder. On the 23rd the jury convicted David Bowers and Henry Mathews of two counts of piracy and acquitted them on four counts, and the district attorney entered a *nolle prosequi* on three other counts. When the various prisoners who had been convicted were brought before the court for sentencing on December 31, the prisoners' counsels moved for arrest of judgment, raising a number of questions on which the judges divided in opinion, thus permitting the cases to be certified to the Supreme Court for an opinion.[58]

Clintock sailed as a first lieutenant on the vessel called the *Young Spartan*, owned without the United States and commissioned by Aury at Ferdandina, after the United States took possession of it. Clintock had been convicted of piracy, committed on the *Norberg*, a Danish vessel, in consequence of practicing the following fraud upon her:

The second officer of the privateer brought on board some Spanish papers, which he concealed in a locker, and then affected to have found them on board. The vessel was then taken possession of, the whole original ship's company left on an island on the coast of Cuba, and the second officer being out in command, took the name of the original captain, sailed for Savannah, and entered her there, personating the Danish captain and crew. The *Young Spartan* followed, and put into a port in the vicinity.

Clintock's counsel contended that the commission from Aury exempted the prisoner from the charge of piracy; the fraud practiced on the Dane did not support the charge of piracy, as an act piratically done, and not in the exercise of belligerent rights; the prisoner is not punishable under the provisions of the Section 8 of the Act of 1790; and the Act of 1790 does not extend to an American citizen entering on board of a foreign vessel, committing piracy upon a vessel exclusively owned by foreigners.

The Supreme Court rejected each of the contentions and certified that Aury's commission did not exempt the prisoner from the charge of piracy; that although the fraudulent practices of the Dane may not in itself support the charge of piracy, the whole transaction as stated in the indictment and in the facts inserted in the record, does amount to piracy; that the prisoner is punishable under the provisions of Section 8 of the Act of 1790; and that the act of the 30th of April 1790 does extend to all persons on board all vessels which throw off their national character by cruising piratically and committing piracy on other vessels.[59]

Counsel for John Furlong contended on both of the murder counts the judgment should be arrested because the indictment: did not charge the prisoner as a citizen of the United States; did not charge the act as committed on board of an American vessel; Section 8 of the Act of 1790 was virtually repealed by the Act of 1819. The motion to arrest on the two counts of piracy centered on the virtual repeal of the Act of 1790 by the Act of 1819. The Supreme Court certified that the Act of 1819 had not repealed the Act of 1790. Furthermore the Court ruled that it was not necessary that the indictment should charge the prisoner as a citizen of the United States nor that the crime was committed on board an American vessel, inasmuch as it charges it to have been committed from on board an American vessel by a mariner sailing on board an American vessel.[60]

The motion filed by the attorney of Bowers and Mathews was similar to that of Furlong, with the exception that on the conviction of piracy committed on the *Asia*, the counsel contended that it was not competent for the jury to find that the piracy was committed on the high seas when the evidence ascertained that the *Asia*, at the time she was boarded, was at anchor in an open roadstead at the Island of Bonavista. The court again rejected the contentions, finding that it was competent for the jury to find that the piracy was committed on the high seas, upon evidence that the *Asia* was at anchor in an open roadstead at the island of Bonavista.[61]

On receipt of the certificates from the Supreme Court, the Georgia circuit court on March 27 sentenced the four men to be hanged on April 28, 1820. The president ordered the sentences reprieved for a limited time, although in the case of Bowers and Mathews he directed the marshal not to reveal the reprieve until the day of execution. Adams received several letters containing pleas for clemency for Ralph Clintock.[62] On June 9 Monroe reprieved Clintock for an indefinite time and pardoned Bowers and Mathews. Clintock was still kept in chains, although his health had deteriorated because of the two years in prison. In July the court authorized the marshal, John H. Morel, to provide some relaxation from the rigors of his confinement including the removal of the chains.[63]

Grand juries in four states indicted forty-three individuals for piracy, three for murder, and two for corresponding with pirates. The trials resulted in twenty-five convictions for piracy and eventual sentences of death and two convictions for corresponding with pirates with sentences of three years in prison and $5 fines for both men. Juries acquitted three men charged with murder and eighteen men charged with piracy. The president pardoned twenty of the twenty-five, but five were executed.[64]

Not only did the government attempt to control the activities of the "pirates" through new legislation and the courts, but also the State Department pressured the rebel governments to suppress the piratical activities by recalling all the commissions which were not issued by the proper authorities and in a proper manner.[65]

The efforts of the government in 1819 seemed to be directed principally to the activities of privateers operating on the Atlantic Coast. In the spring of 1819 another expedition formed in the Southwest to invade Texas. General John Adair was chosen to lead the expedition; but when he declined, General James Long of Virginia took his place. Long went as far as to advertise in a New Orleans newspaper for recruits. In June his army left Natchez, "proceeded to Natchitoches and thence to the Sabine." Although United States officials including the army tried to stop the expedition, the army of 300 to 400 men moved to Nacogdoches, established a civil government, and chose Long as president. Long went to Galveston to secure the cooperation of Lafitte, but "the pirate refused him aid." Returning to Nacogdoches, Long found that most of his party had fled before an advancing royalist force. The Americans who escaped being killed or captured crossed the Sabine back into the United States. Long, however, was not finished. After matters quieted down in 1821, "he recrossed into Texas and collected his scattered forces . . . at Galveston with Lafitte. Leaving his men there he journeyed to New Orleans to obtain aid and food." Although the expedition failed, another violation of American neutrality had been cooly pulled off under the eyes of government officials in the Southwest.[66]

The Spanish Minister, in addition to his continual protests, instructed the Spanish consuls at various ports to adopt a new strategy of entering claims or libels against prizes of privateers brought into the United States. When the *Divina Pastora* arrived at New Bedford, Massachusetts, with a cargo of cocoa, cotton, indigo, hides, and horns, valued at $10,000, the Spanish Consul, Don Juan Stoughton, libeled the vessel, claiming that the vessel was originally the *Esperanza* bound on a voyage from Laguira to Cádiz and that she had been captured and brought into New Bedford contrary to the law of nations and in violation of the rights of Antonio Seris, a merchant of Cádiz who had been consigned the cargo. Don Daniel Utley, a citizen of the Provinces of the Rio de la Plata, answered the libel on behalf of himself and all concerned in the capture of the *Divina Pastora*. Utley claimed the Provinces of the Rio de la Plata were free and independent states and had the power to levy war and make peace and "that at the Fort of Buenos Aires, on the 15th day of October 1815, commissioned a certain schooner called the *Mangore* [sic] to cruise against the vessels and effects of the kingdom of Spain. . . " The *Mangoré* commenced a cruise on January 1, 1816, and on October 31, 1816, captured the *Divina Pastora*. Utley boarded the vessel as prize master and was given a copy of the commission of the *Mangoré* which commission Utley submitted to the court. The district court ordered the vessel restored to the libelant. Utley appealed the decision to the circuit court and from thence to the United States Supreme Court.

Marshall rendered the opinion of the Supreme Court in 1819. He referred to the *Palmer* decision of 1818, which he said "established the principle that the government of the United States, having recognized the existence of a civil war between Spain and her colonies, but remaining neutral," should consider as lawful

those acts which war authorizes, and which the new governments in South America may direct against their enemy. Unless the neutral right for the United States, as ascertained by the law of nations, the acts of Congress, and treaties with foreign powers, are violated by the cruisers sailing under commissions from those governments, captures by them are to be regarded by us as other captures, jure belli, [by the right or law of war] are regarded; the legality of which cannot be determined in the courts of a neutral country.

Marshall continued,

If it appeared in this case that the capture was made under a regular commission from the government at Buenos Aires by a vessel which had not committed any violation of our neutrality, the captured property must be restored to the possession of the captors. But if, on the other hand, it was shown that the capture was made in violation of our neutral rights and duties, restitution would be decreed to the original owners.

Since the Court could not pronounce a decree based on the former proceedings, it reversed the decision of the circuit court and remanded the cause for further proceedings.[67]

The *Estrella* presented the Court with a similar set of circumstances. The former Spanish owner libeled the *Estrella* with her cargo in the district court of Louisiana. The vessel sailed from Havana to the coast of Africa in April 1817. The privateer *Constitution*, flying Venezuelan colors, captured her on April 24 and forcibly brought her "within the jurisdiction of the United States, when she was recaptured by the United States ketch, *Surprise*, and conducted to New Orleans." The libel of the owner, Hernandez, claimed that the captors had no lawful commission, that if they had a commission it was issued or delivered within the waters and jurisdiction of the United States, and that the *Constitution*, previous to her cruising, had been fitted out and armed, increased or augmented in force, and manned by sundry citizens of the United States within the jurisdiction and waters of the United States in violation of the laws of the United States and the laws of nations.

J. F. Lamoureux, prize master of the *Estrella*, interposed a claim, which stated that the *Constitution* was duly commissioned by the republic of Venezuela, although the commission was lost when the *Constitution* sank in a storm. The district court ordered the claim of Lamoureux dismissed, and the vessel restored to the libelant. Lamoureux appealed the decision to the Supreme Court. There, Justice Livingston, speaking for the Court, acknowledged that it was satisfied that the *Constitution* had had a commission at the time of making the capture and that no evidence was offered that the commission was issued within the United States. Concerning the second allegation that United States' neutrality laws had been violated by augmenting the force and supplying the crew, Livingston stated,

Where restitution of captured property is claimed on this ground the burden of proving such enlistment is thrown upon the claimant; and that fact being proved by him, it is incumbent upon the captors to show, by proof, that the persons so enlisted were subjects or citizens of the prince or state under whose flag the cruiser sails, in order to bring the case within the proviso of the Neutrality Act of 1794 and the revision of 1818.

The Court admitted that the right of adjudicating on all captures and questions of prize exclusively belonged to the courts of the captors' country, except where the captured vessel was brought or voluntarily came, *infra praesidia* (within the protection), of a neutral power. The neutral power had a right to inquire whether its own neutrality had been violated by the cruiser which made the capture, and, if such violation had been committed, was duty bound to restore to the original owner the property captured by a cruiser illegally equipped in its ports. The court affirmed the sentence of restoration of the district court with costs.[68]

President Monroe commented on the successes of 1819 in his third annual message on December 7, 1819. He indicated, however, that it was

of the highest importance to our national character and indispensable to the morality of our citizens that all violations of our neutrality should be prevented. No door should be left open for the evasion of our laws, no opportunity afforded to any who may be disposed to take advantage of it to compromise the interest or the honor of the nation. It is submitted, therefore, to the consideration of Congress whether it may not be advisable to revise the laws with the view of this desirable result.[69]

Congress acted deliberately. The Senate received a bill in March and approved it in April. The House added its concurrence with amendments in May. The Senate accepted the House amendments and approved the final version on May 15. The law, entitled "An Act to continue in force, 'An Act to protect the commerce of the United States, and punish the crime of piracy,' " extended the Act of 1819 for two years. The act declared persons committing robbery on any ship or vessel, or ships' company, to be pirates. Any person engaged in any piratical cruise or being of the crew of any piratical ship who should land from such ship and on shore commit robbery would be adjudged a pirate. A proviso was added:

Nothing in this section contained shall be construed to deprive any particular state of its jurisdiction over such offenses, when committed within the body of a country, or authorize the court of the United States to try any such Offenders, after conviction or acquittance, for the same offense in a state court.[70]

Whether aided or not by the new legislation, the number of charges brought in 1820 remained high, totaling 130—seventy-eight in Georgia, twenty-nine in Louisiana, twelve in South Carolina, six in Virginia, three in Maryland, and one each in Pennsylvania and Rhode Island. No convictions resulted from the indictments and trials in Georgia, South Carolina, Virginia, Maryland, and Pennsylvania. The Maryland grand jury in February issued a strong presentment complaining of the activity of the privateers and also slave traders. The presentment concluded,

If there are not laws to punish privateering, and dealers in human flesh—if the general government, as is much feared is the case, will not, or does not take the necessary steps to prevent these practices, so disgraceful to society and humanity, *let all those concerned in either or both be, by universal consent, held and considered infamous.*[71]

The district attorney of Louisiana charged twenty-nine men with various crimes—nine with piracy, eighteen with illegally fitting out a vessel, and two illegally enlisting aboard a foreign vessel. Juries tried and convicted twenty-six of the men. The court sentenced the eighteen convicted for illegally fitting out a vessel to twelve months in prison and a fine of $20 each, the two for illegal enlisting to six weeks in prison and a fine of $100, and the six for piracy to be hanged. One of the six died before sentencing; Monroe pardoned four; and the disposition of one has not been found. Three of those charged with piracy had a *nolle prosequi* entered in their case.[72] The Rhode Island circuit court convicted William G. Cornell for piracy and ordered him to be hanged.[73]

The trials of 1819 and 1820 had revealed one of the major weaknesses of the federal criminal law—the inability of the President to commute a death sentence. Early in the second session of the sixteenth Congress, Senator James Barbour of Virginia introduced a resolution requesting the Judiciary Committee to inquire "into the propriety of so modifying the law punishing piracy as to authorize the president of the United States to commute capital punishment for confinement in penitentiary houses." Barbour supported his resolution on December 4 by defending the superiority of the penitentiary system of punishment over the old code, by contrasting the mildness and good effects of the one with the cruel yet ineffectual operation of the other, and by maintaining that the penitentiary system was not only humane but was superior because of its salutary effects on the subject of the punishment. The Senate agreed to the resolution without opposition.[74]

In February 1821 the Judiciary Committee reported that it was inexpedient to make the modification suggested. The committee indicated that the report of the grand jury of Philadelphia on the penitentiary in that city and the reports of the commissioners in New York and Massachusetts had influenced their decision. In addition the committee maintained that in the "catalogue of human offense, if there is any one supremely distinguished for its enormity over others, it is piracy." The committee felt that executive clemency "has more than sufficient range for its exercise, without the aid sought for by this resolution" and concluded that "capital punishment is the appropriate punishment for piracy, and that it would be inexpedient to commute it for confinement in penitentiary houses."[75]

It appeared that various Congressmen were concerned with the President's pardoning power which had been used frequently to free men convicted of piracy. Monroe defended his actions in his second inaugural address, delivered on March 5, 1821.

Many culprits within our limits have been condemned to suffer death, the punishment due to that atrocious crime. The decisions of upright and enlightened tribunals fall equally on all whose crimes subject them, by a fair interpretation of the law, to its censure. It belongs to the executive not to suffer the executions under these decisions to transcend the great purpose for which punishment is necessary. The full benefit of example being secured, policy as well as humanity equally forbids that they should be carried further. I have acted on this principle, pardoning those who appear to have been led astray by ignorance of the criminality of the acts they had committed, and suffering the law to take effect on those only in whose favor no extenuating circumstances could be urged.[76]

The activity of the courts in 1821 entered a period of decline. The district attorneys brought only fifteen charges of piracy and robbery—eight in Georgia, five in Louisiana, and two in Pennsylvania. Pennsylvania and Louisiana reported no convictions. The Georgia court charged eight men with robbery—as defined under the Act of 1820—on the *San Pedro*, the *Cosmopolite*, and a ship name unknown. The jury acquitted the men for robbing the *San Pedro* but found them guilty of robbery on the unknown ship. The district attorney entered a *nolle prosequi* on the charge of robbing the *Cosmopolite*. The court sentenced the eight to be hanged the first Wednesday of April 1822.[77]

Stymied by Congress, Monroe reprieved the death sentence for the eight men but did not grant a pardon. The marshal of Georgia, John H. Morel, reported to the circuit court in December 1822 that of the seven prisoners remaining (John Martin died) all were in "chains and shackles in the strongest room in the hall"; however, they had only one blanket each and would require more in cold weather. The court ordered the marshal to provide sufficient bedding and clothes for the prisoners. Again the following year the marshal made a similar report, and again the court ordered him to supply the needed winter clothes with utmost economy. In December 1823 the court suggested to the grand jury the propriety of examining the situation of the prisoners. The grand jury immediately appointed a committee to conduct an investigation. The committee reported on December 16th that the prisoners were as comfortably fed, clothed, and lodged as their condition allowed and also recommended the prisoners to the clemency of the President. Later in the year the grand jury recommended that two additional blankets and winter clothes be furnished to the prisoners. The court ordered the marshal to furnish the needed items. By 1824 the tide had shifted strongly in favor of the prisoners. The Committee of the Grand Jury in August 1824 reported that the prisoners had

suffered much from the long continuance of their being enchained and your Committee have viewed with pain the suffering that these poor creatures must have endured. The leg on which the irons have been placed has decreased a great deal in size and there can be but little doubt that in a short time in the same situation the use of their legs would be in danger of being lost.

The committee found that the treatment by the marshal and the sheriff of the jailed had been humane. The committee concluded by recommending that the irons should be taken off the prisoners forthwith. The full grand jury endorsed the report. Finally in 1825 the President pardoned the seven prisoners.[78]

The Supreme Court interpreted the Neutrality Act and international law nine times between 1821 and 1822. Rhode Island, Louisiana, South Carolina, and Virginia each supplied one case while five came from Maryland.[79] The most important of the nine—*Santissima Trinidad and the St. Ander*—was decided in 1822. The consul of Spain filed a libel in 1817 in the district court of Virginia against eighty-nine bales of cochineal, two bales of jalap, and one box of vanilla, originally constituting part of the cargoes of the Spanish ships *Santissima Trinidad* and *St. Ander* and alleged to have been unlawfully and piratically taken out of those vessels by the privateers the *Independencia del Sud* and the *Altrevida*, manned and commanded by persons assuming themselves to be citizens of the United Provinces of the Rio de la Plata. The district court ordered restitution to the original Spanish owners, which the circuit court confirmed.

The Supreme Court dealt with two major issues. First, the Court reaffirmed that if the *Independencia* was a public ship, the captures were legal since the United States had recognized the existence of a civil war between Spain and the colonies and had "avowed a determination to remain neutral between the parties . . . and to allow to each the same rights of asylum and hospitality and intercourse." Secondly, the Court indicated that if the neutrality of the United States had been violated, then the cargoes could be restored. Two grounds were advanced to prove that a violation of neutrality had occurred. First it was claimed that the *Independencia* and *Altrevida* were originally equipped, armed, and manned as vessels of war in our ports; and second, there was an illegal augmentation of the force of the *Independencia* within our ports. The Act of 1818 defined illegal augmentation as increasing the number or caliber of guns or adding equipment solely applicable to war. On the first question, the Court, speaking through Justice Story, decided against the libelants, accepting the evidence of the claimant that the vessel was originally sent to Buenos Aires as a commercial venture. Story contended that the ship was contraband and, if captured, would have been justifiably condemned. He countered,

But there is nothing in our laws, or in the law of nations, that forbids our citizens from sending armed vessels, as well as munitions of war, to foreign ports for sale. It is a commercial adventure which no nation is bound to prohibit; and which only exposes the persons engaged in it to the penalty of confiscation.

On the second point, Story agreed that an illegal augmentation had been conducted in the United States, specifically an increase in the crew of about thirty persons in the case of the *Independencia* and the mounting of weapons and an increase in the crew in the case of the *Altrevida.* Thus the decision of the lower courts, ordering restitution, was upheld.[80]

Although public interest in the problem of piracy appeared to wane after 1821, the problem continued with the focus shifted from the revolting Spanish colonies, whose independence the United States recognized, to Cuba, where Spanish authorities commissioned vessels to eliminate the pirates but who in turn commenced engaging in piracy. At the June 1822 session of the circuit court of South Carolina, the district attorney charged James Ross, Charles Owen, Juan Escandell, William Layfield, Manuel Pereyra, Francisco José (otherwise called Francisco Pere), José Rosa, and Antonio Tacares with piracy. The court acquitted Ross in June. The jury convicted Owen, and the court sentenced him to be hanged. The court continued the trial of the others until the next term.[81] During the summer the Spanish authorities entered the fray. In August 1822 John Quincy Adams submitted to the district attorney, John Gadsden, the translation of the letter from the Minister of Spain, relating to the case of Juan Escandell, requesting a postponement of the trial until evidence could be obtained from Havana and from Porto Cavello, that "they were regularly commissioned by the King of Spain."[82]

The trials held at the second session of the circuit court in November resulted in the acquittal of Escandell, José Rosa, and Antonio Tacares, but the juries convicted Manuel Pereyra and Francisco José of two counts of piracy. Pablo Baon contacted Justice Johnson shortly after the trial and requested a pardon for Pereyra. Johnson evidently indicated that Pereyra would have to declare the names of the crew of the piratical vessel on which he embarked if his plea for clemency was to be considered. Baon reported to Johnson in December that Pereyra could only identify three by name. Johnson wrote the President on December 11 proposing that the men should be returned to Cuba to see if the authorities were actually interested in the suppression of piracy. The President pardoned Pereyra on July 7, 1823.[83]

Monroe briefly mentioned the continuing problem of piracy, now centering in the West Indies, in his sixth annual message to Congress on December 3 and pointedly brought it home by a special message on December 9. Monroe reported that the continued outrages

seem to call for some prompt and decisive measures on the part of the government. All the public vessels adapted to that service which can be spared from other indispensable duties are already employed in it; but from the knowledge which has been acquired of the places from whence these outlaws issue and to which they escape from danger it appears that it will require a particular kind of force, capable of pursuing them into the shallow waters to which they retire, effectually to suppress them. I submit to the consideration of the Senate the propriety of organizing such force for that important object.[84]

The Congress hastily complied passing on December 22, 1822, an act providing for an additional force for the suppression of piracy. Late in January 1823 Congress also approved renewing the Act of 1820.[85]

Shortly after Congress approved the extension of the Act of 1820, it received embarrassing news from the President. Rumors of an expedition against Puerto Rico, fitted out in the United States, began circulating in December 1822. On December 11, Representative Cadwallader D. Colden of New York submitted a resolution asking the President to lay before the House any information he might have with regard to "any hostile expedition which may have been prepared in the United States . . . and to inform this House whether any measures have been taken to bring to condign punishment the persons who may have been concerned in such expedition, contrary to the laws of the United States." John Quincy Adams hastily asked the district attorneys of Pennsylvania and New York to check out the rumor and, if it proved to be true, "to ascertain how and why the expedition, if so armed and fitted out, so far eluded the notice of the public officers of the United States, as to have met with no obstruction, or to have been known to any of the Executive Department of this place." Ingersoll replied within a week that such an illegal expedition was fitted out in Philadephia and sailed in the month of August. He did not know why and how the expedition eluded the public officers. The collector, Jonathan Steele, reporting to William H. Crawford at the Treasury, was equally perplexed, contending that "no evidence or information whatever was received at this office either before the departure of the brig, or subsequent thereto . . . of her being unlawfully equipped, or engaged in any enterprise prohibited by the laws of the United States." Ingersoll surmised that the Minister of Spain was aware of the expedition "but refrained from complaint here, preferring to take measures for its destruction after its concentration in the West Indies."[86]

The President revealed this intelligence to Congress through a special message on February 4 and enclosed the reports from the district attorneys and collectors and the documents they had managed to assemble.[87] Congress seemed unconcerned and let the matter drop without any additional action. John Quincy Adams tried to insure a more accurate and quicker flow of information from the district attorneys. In May 1823 he issued a circular to the district attorneys in the maritime districts informing them that they were to obtain and forward to the State Department copies of all the proceedings in the district and circuit courts of the United States, "in cases of Foreign Vessels brought on suit into Port upon charges of Piracy, aggression upon vessels of the United States; or relating to the slave trade; and in cases of process against or trial of individual *Foreigners* for those offenses."[88]

Results from the naval activity in the West Indies became evident during the fall sessions of the circuit courts from New York to South Carolina.[89] At New York the district attorney separately charged William Gourley and Joseph Perez with piracy. The court tried Gourley on September 1 and found him guilty of murder; however, the judges differed over whether the court had jurisdiction or not and certified the case to the Supreme Court for an opinion.[90]

The Perez trial meanwhile occurred on September 9. The jury reported that they were evenly split and prayed to be discharged. The court directed the jury to retire for further deliberations. The jury returned again and indicated that they were still split, at which point the court ordered the jury discharged. Mr. Niven, counsel for Perez, moved on the 15th that Perez should be discharged on the grounds that the jury had been discharged illegally. The judges divided in opinion on the motion and thus certified the case to the Supreme Court for an opinion.[91]

Although the Supreme Court did not render a separate opinion in the Gourley case, in the case of Perez the Court certified that the trial court is invested with the discretionary authority of discharging the jury from giving any verdict in cases of this nature whenever, in their opinion, there is a manifest necessity for such an act or the ends of public justice would otherwise be defeated. "The prisoner Josef [*sic*] Perez is not entitled to be discharged from custody, and may again be put to trial, upon the indictment found against him, and pending in the said court." The court tried Perez again, convicted him, and sentenced him to be hanged. The President pardoned him on May 31.[92]

Monroe optimistically reported in his seventh annual message on December 2, 1823, that the augmentation of the naval force in the West Indies "has been eminently successful in the accomplishment of its object.

The piracies which our commerce in the neighborhood of the island of Cuba had been afflicted have been repressed and the confidence of our merchants in a great measure restored." He warned however that our exertions have "not been equally effectual to suppress to same crime, under other pretenses and colors, in the neighboring island of Puerto Rico. They have been committed there under the abusive issue of Spanish commissions." Monroe reported that a special agent had been sent to demonstrate but that the Governor answered only by referring him to the government of Spain. In turn the United States instructed our Minister to Spain to "urge the necessity of the immediate and effectual interposition of that government, directing restitution and indemnity for wrongs already committed and interdicting the repetition of them." The Minister was denied access to the Spanish government.[93]

In his eighth and last annual message to Congress, Monroe again mentioned the problem in the Caribbean and submitted to the consideration of Congress "whether those robbers should be pursued on the land, the local authorities be made responsible for these atrocities, or any other measure be resorted to to suppress them."[94] On December 21 and again on the 23rd, the Senate Committee on Foreign Relations requested from the President details on the extent of the injuries suffered, the measures taken to correct the evil, and whether, in the opinion of the executive, it would be necessary to adopt new measures and if so what other measures would be most advisable. The President responded to the first two queries on January 13, submitting to Congress reports from the Secretary of the Navy and the Secretary of State. Monroe indicated that in response to the last question, he felt three expedients were available: the pursuit of the offenders to the settled as well as the unsettled parts of the island from whence they came, reprisal on the property of the inhabitants, and a blockade of the ports of those islands. Monroe desired that a "power commensurate with either resource be granted to the Executive, to be exercised according to his discretion and as circumstances may imperiously require." Monroe concluded that it was his belief "that the Government of Spain and the governments of the islands, particularly Cuba . . . will faithfully cooperate in such measures as may be necessary for the accomplishment of this very important object."[95]

Three days before the Senate received the President's response it commenced considering a bill for the suppression of piracy in the West Indies. The lengthy bill would have increased the navy; authorized commander and crews of armed vessels, under instructions from the President, to pursue pirates on the island of Cuba or any other island of Spain in the West Indies; permitted a blockade of a port or city if the pirates should happen to escape the pursuing force and find refuge in said city or port; would permit the commander and crew of armed merchant vessels to recapture vessels captured by pirates; and would have dealt with salvage and judicial procedure.[96] The Senate approved the bill after striking the section permitting the blockade of a port or city. House consideration commenced on March 1.

The House proceeded to strike all of the bill except a section which authorized the building of ten new naval vessels. In this form Congress enacted the bill into law on March 3.[97]

Late in 1825 the government received information that vessels were being built in New York for warlike purposes. Secretary of State Henry Clay requested that Robert Tillotson, the district attorney, investigate and prosecute under the 1818 law if evidence could be secured. Tillotson reported on December 15 that he had discovered one armed vessel owned by an American which he felt was intended for some South American government. Tillotson asked whether the ship was subject to forfeiture "until her papers are changed." Tillotson entered no prosecution concerning the vessel.[98]

In his first annual message to Congress on December 6, 1826, John Quincy Adams optimistically reported that the suppression of piracy in the West Indies had

been accomplished more effectually than at any former period. . . . The irregular privateers have within the last year been in a great measure banished from those seas, and the pirates for months past appear to have been almost entirely swept away from the borders and the shores of the two Spanish islands in those regions.[99]

The following year Adams reported to Congress that "the piracies with which the West India seas were for several years infested have been totally suppressed. . . ."[100] Adams was not totally correct. Piracy had been almost, but not completely, eliminated. In 1826 the Massachusetts grand jury indicted John Duncan White and Sylvester Colson for murder (three counts) and piracy and murder (one count). The trial jury convicted White of murder on one count. White's counsel requested an arrest of judgment contending that the prisoners should be entitled to separate trials. The judges divided in opinion and thus certified the question to the Supreme Court. The jury meanwhile convicted Colson on the second count. The court delayed the trial on the third count of murder and the count of piracy and murder while awaiting the verdict of the Supreme Court. The Court issued its opinion in 1827 indicating that whether the persons were tried jointly or singly was to be determined by the court before whom the indictment was tried. In May 1827 the court sentenced the two to be hanged.[101]

The year 1827 brought the last trials under the Jeffersonian courts for violations of neutrality or piracy. The Virginia circuit court indicted Pepe (otherwise called José Helareo Casaras), Couroo (otherwise called Joseph Mirando), and Felix (otherwise called Felix Barberto) on four counts of murder and one of piracy. Marshall ordered the marshal to return a jury of six Virginia freeholders and six aliens. The Chief Justice gave no indication as to why he made this unique requirement for the make-up of the jury. The jury convicted the men on two counts of murder. The court sentenced the men to be hanged on August 20. The Georgia circuit court grand jury indicted Gabriel Gardner and thirteen crewmen of the schooner *Williams* for piracy. After the jury acquitted Gardner, the district attorney entered a *nolle prosequi* for the thirteen crewmen.[102]

The last reported violation occurred fittingly in Baltimore but did not result in a prosecution. John Nauts reported to collector James H. McCulloch that a vessel was being fitted out under the direction of Captain Cottrel although no armaments were on board. Clay ordered the collector to place the vessel under bond if a violation of the law had occurred. No violation was evidently detected since the vessel was not bonded, nor were any of the principals arrested and charged with a crime.[103]

The federal government's response to neutrality violations evolved in conjunction with foreign policy considerations and the economic impact of violations on American commerce. Violations against Spain from overland invasions in the Southwest to the capture of vessels initially received applause rather than condemnation from the public. Once the independence of most of the Spanish colonies had been assured, a treaty with Spain resolving the boundary between the United States and Spain in the West had been negotiated, and the privateers began seizing vessels of all nations, not just of Spain. The public demanded more effective enforcement of existing laws and the passage of new statutes.

Congress responded with new legislation aimed at increasing the ability of the navy to capture maritime violators and of the district attorneys to successfully prosecute the offenders. The executive branch supplied encouragement, instructions, and occasional assistance to the district attorneys. Finally the public demonstrated a greater willingness to serve as witnesses and when on juries to convict indicted persons.

NOTES

1. Massachusetts circuit court, Record Book #2, 1806-1811, pp. 308, 313-314.

2. (Microcopy M 40), reel 13, p. 427.

3. Pennsylvania district court, Information Dockets, 1808-1839, August 1810; Georgia circuit court, Minute Book, 1806-1816, p. 242.

4. Pennsylvania circuit court, Minute Book, 1811-1815, pp. 54, 88, 95; Pennsylvania circuit court, Case files, Box 5.

5. Captain José Menchaca may have launched an expedition in 1811. See Elizabeth H. West, ed., "Diary of José Bernardo Gutiérrez de Lara, 1811-1812," *American Historical Review*, 34 (October, January, 1928-1929), 57-58; Harris Gaylord Warren, *The Sword was their Passport: A History of American Filibustering in the Mexican Revolution* (Baton Rouge, 1943), 1-72; and J. Villasana

Haggard, "The Neutral Ground Between Louisiana and Texas, 1807-1821," *Louisiana Historical Quarterly*, 28 (October, 1945), 1053-1059.

6. Magee died in Texas in 1813.

7. Henry Stuart Foote, *Texas and the Texans* (2 vols., reprint, Austin, 1925), I:185-193; Charles C. Griffin, *The United States and Disruption of the Spanish Empire* (New York and London, 1937), 106-107; Elizabeth H. West, ed., "Diary of José Bernardo Gutiérrez de Lara, 1811-1812," 55-61; A. Curtis Wilgus, "Spanish American Patriot Activity Along the Gulf Coast of the United States, 1811-1822," *Louisiana Historical Quarterly*, 8 (April, 1925), 197-200.

8. Monroe to Dallas, December 15, 1813, Monroe to Governors of the Louisiana and Mississippi territories and Tully Robinson, February 14, 1814, and Monroe to Robinson and Governor Claiborne, February 17, 1814 (Microcopy M 40), reel 14, pp. 222-225, 230-231.

9. Pennsylvania circuit court, Minute Book, 1811-1815, p. 193; Pennsylvania circuit court case files, Box 5.

10. Dick to Secretary of State, March 1, 1816, *American State Papers, Foreign Relations*, IV:431; Warren, *The Sword was their Passport*, 77-95.

11. Richardson, ed., *Messages and Papers of the Presidents*, II:546-547.

12. John Spencer Bassett, *The Life of Andrew Jackson* (2 vols. in 1, reprint, Archon Books, 1967), 149-150.

13. Richardson, ed., *Messages and Papers of the Presidents*, II:480.

14. Louisiana district court, Minute Book, 1815-1819, pp. 4-6; Francois-Xavier Martin, *The History of Louisiana* (2 vols., New Orleans, 1827-1829), II:327-329; Alcée Fortier, *A History of Louisiana* (4 vols., New York, 1904), III:84-93; Charles Gayarré, "Historical Sketch of Pierre and Jean Lafitte," *Magazine of American History*, 10 (July, December, 1883), 286-298, 389-390; Charles B. Brooks, *The Siege of New Orleans* (Seattle, 1961), 32, 40-48.

15. Gayarré, "Historical Sketch of Pierre and Jean Lafitte," 395; Richardson, ed., *Messages and Papers of the Presidents*, II:543-545.

16. Charles C. Griffin, "Privateering from Baltimore during the Spanish American Wars of Independence," *Maryland Historical Magazine*, 35 (March, 1940), 7-9. The Charleston *Courier*, July 23, 1819, reprinting an account from the Baltimore *Morning Chronicle* of July 13, listed forty-five vessels fitted out, refitted, or received their supplies in the United States.

17. Monroe to Elias Glenn, January 3, 1816 (Microcopy M 40), reel 14, pp. 271-272.

18. Secretary of State to Attorney for the United States in Virginia, July 26, 1816 (Microcopy M 40), reel 14, p. 318; William Wirt to Secretary of State, August 2, 1816, ibid., 319; Wirt to Richard Rush, December 4, 1816 (Microcopy M 179) reel 35; Wirt to Rush, December 16, 1816, ibid; Providence *Gazette*, July 13, 1816.

19. Monroe to J. Fisk, July 20, 1816 (Microcopy M 40), reel 14, pp. 315-316; Fisk to Monroe, July 24, 1816 (Microcopy M 179), reel 34.

20. *Annals of Congress*, XXIX:40, 88, 199, 205, 715-756, 763-764; XXX:766-768, 770, 1067, 1079-1085; 3 *U. S. Statutes at Large*, 370-371.

21. Richard Rush to Elias Glenn, March 21, 1817 (Microcopy M 40), reel 15, pp. 4-5.

22. Richard Rush to James H. McCulloch, March 28, 1817 (Microcopy M 40), reel 15, pp. 8-9; Richard Rush to Charles K. Mallory, March 28, 1817, ibid., 7; Richard

Rush to William Wirt, March 28, 1817, ibid., 8; Richard Rush to Thomas Pulter, April 12, 1817, ibid., 14.

23. Charleston *Courier*, April 23, 1817, citing the Baltimore *Federal Gazette*, April 14, 1817. The grand jury also indicted the three defendants for piracy and robbery aboard the *Industria Raffaelli*. In the course of the trial the judges differed in opinion over whether "a robbery committed upon the high seas, although such robbery, if committed upon land, would not, by the laws of the United States, be punishable with death, is piracy" under Section 8 of the Act of 1790 and whether the circuit court had jurisdiction over the offence. The Supreme Court in 1818 certified that the court had jurisdiction, that the act was piracy under the Act of 1790, and that the crime of robbery "as mentioned in the said act of Congress, is the crime of robbery as recognized and defined at common law." Wheaton, *Reports*, III:610-644.

24. Pennsylvania district court, Information Dockets, 1808-1839, October 1817; John Quincy Adams to Charles J. Ingersoll, November 18, 1817 (Microcopy M 40), reel 15, p. 86.

25. Massachusetts circuit court, Record Book #10, 1817-1818, pp. 245, 390-391.

26. Ibid., 407-409.

27. Pennsylvania circuit court, Minute Book, 1816-1819, pp. 97, 103, 129; Pennsylvania circuit court, Criminal Case Files, Box 6, 1815-1824; Maryland circuit court, Minute Book, 1811-1821, May 3, 5, 8, and 9, 1817 (7 reels, National Archives, Record Group 21, Microcopy M 931), reel 1; Thomas Parker to John Quincy Adams, December 24, 1817 (Microcopy M 179), reel 39; Willie Davies to John Quincy Adams, January 2, 1818, (Microcopy M 179), reel 40.

28. Rhode Island district court, Minute Book, vol. 5, November 13, 1817; Asher Robbins to John Quincy Adams, December 23, 1817 (Microcopy M 179), reel 39; John Quincy Adams to Asher Robbins, February 28, 1818 (Microcopy M 40), reel 15, p. 171; John Quincy Adams to William Ellery, July 7, 1818, ibid., 185.

29. Rhode Island district court, Minute Book, vol. 5, pp. 320-331.

30. James Miller to James Monroe, July 28, 1815 (Microcopy M 179), reel 32.

31. Richardson, ed., *Messages and Papers of the President*, II:546-547.

32. Dick to Secretary of State, March 1, 1816, *American State Papers, Foreign Relations*, IV:431.

33. Wilgus, "Spanish American Patriot Activity Along the Gulf Coast of the United States, 1811-1822," pp. 204-206; Griffin, *The United States and the Disruption of the Spanish Empire*, 109-110; Warren, *The Sword was their Passport*, 146-172.

34. Wilgus, "Spanish American Patriot Activity Along the Gulf Coast of the United States, 1811-1822," p. 206.

35. Ibid., 207-208; A. Curtis Wilgus, "Some Notes on Spanish American Patriot Activity along the Atlantic Seaboard, 1816-1822," *North Carolina Historical Review*, 4 (April 1928), 174-175; Griffin, *The United States and the Disruption of the Spanish Empire*, 110-113.

36. Richardson, ed., *Messages and Papers of the Presidents*, II:582-583, 593-594.

37. *Annals of Congress*, XXXI:291, 360-361, 384-385, 542; XXXII:1403-1429, 1431-1439, 1452-1455, 1469, 1764-1765, 1785-1814, 1897-1943.

38. 3 *U. S. Statutes at Large*, 447-450.

39. Massachusetts circuit court, Record Book, vol. 12, 1818-1819, pp. 162-163,

189-194; John Quincy Adams to George Blake, November 1, 1817 (Microcopy M 40), reel 15, p. 77; Charleston *Courier*, March 2, 1819.

40. Massachusetts circuit court, Docket Book, vol. 4, 1812-1821, May 1820; Wheaton, *Reports*, V:412-420; Charleston *Courier*, June 27, 1820.

41. Charleston *Courier*, November 17, 1818.

42. Wirt to Elias Glenn, November 6, 1818, Letters Sent by the Attorney General's Office (2 reels, National Archives, Record Group 60, Microcopy T 411), reel 1, pp. 44-48.

43. Charleston *Courier*, December 24, 25, 1818; Glenn to John Quincy Adams, April 19, 1819, (Microcopy M 179), reel 44; Maryland circuit court, Minute Book, 1811-1821, Nov. 26, 1818, December 5, 15, 17, 1818, and May 5, 1824.

44. Georgia circuit court, Minute Book, 1816-1823, pp. 41-42, 46-47.

45. Charleston *Courier*, August 7, 1818.

46. Monroe, *Writings*, VI:64-65.

47. Charleston *Courier*, September 16, 20, 1818.

48. *Annals of Congress*, XXXIII:246-256; XXXIV:1403, 1417; 3 *U. S. Statutes at Large*, 510-514.

49. John Quincy Adams to Glenn, January 28, 1819, April 12, 1819 (Microcopy M 40), reel 15, pp. 248-249, 283-285.

50. Glenn to John Quincy Adams (Microcopy M 179), reel 44.

51. Adams to Glenn, May 1, 1819 (Microcopy M 40), reel 15, pp. 91-92.

52. Glenn to Adams, May 8, 28, 1819 (Microcopy M 179), reel 44.

53. Charleston *Courier*, June 24, 1819, reprinting an editorial from the Baltimore *Morning Chronicle* and a letter published in the Baltimore *Telegraph*; Charleston *Courier*, July 16, 1819, reprinting an article from the Baltimore *Morning Chronicle* of July 8.

54. Maryland circuit court, Minute Book, 1811-1821, May 6, 19, 21, 25, November 22, 25-27, 1819, March 2, 1820 (Microcopy M 931), reel 1.

55. Charleston *Courier*, July 10, 1819, reprinting article from the Norfolk *Herald*. Little John may have been a reference to Chief Justice John Marshall who presided over the circuit court.

56. Charleston *Courier*, August 3, 1819.

57. Wheaton, *Reports*, V:153-183; Charleston *Courier*, June 5, 1820.

58. Georgia circuit court, Minute Book, 1816-1823, pp. 56-57, 59, 63-69, 73, 83-90, 94-97, 104-114.

59. Wheaton, *Reports*, V:144-153.

60. Wheaton, *Reports*, V: 184-206.

61. Ibid.

62. Georgia circuit court, Minute Book, 1816-1823, pp. 103-114; John Quincy Adams to John H. Morel, April 5, 1820 (Microcopy M 40), reel 16, pp., 20-21; John Condit to John Quincy Adams, April 10, 1820, J. Meigs to John Quincy Adams, April 28, 1820 (Microcopy M 179), reel 48.

63. John Quincy Adams to John H. Morel, June 9, July 20, 1820 (Microcopy M 40), reel 16, pp., 72-73; Morel to John Quincy Adams, July 31, 1820 (Microcopy M 179), reel 48; Georgia circuit court, Minute Book, 1816-1823, p. 139; (Microcopy T 967), reel 1, vol. III: pp. 40-41, 50-53. No record of a pardon for Clintock has been found.

64. Massachusetts circuit court, Record Book, vol. 13, 1819-1821, pp. 150-157;

John Quincy Adams to Thomas Parker, May 14, 1819 (Microcopy M 40), reel 15, pp. 296-297; Parker to Adams, June 2, 1819, (Microcopy M 179), reel 44; Charleston *Courier*, March 22, and May 11, 1820; New York circuit court, Minute Book, 1819-1828, pp. 8, 10-11, 17-18, 27, 29, 34, 37, 39, 42-43; New York circuit court, Case Files, 1790-1853, Box 2; Louisiana district court, Minute Book, 1819-1825, pp. 1, 18, 20, 26, 33, 27; Docket Book, 1815-1820, pp. 182, 215, 222, 230, 392, 396; John Quincy Adams to Nicholson, April 3, 17, 1820 (Microcopy M 40), reel 16, pp. 18, 27.

65. Sketch of Instructions for agent for South America—Notes for Department of State, Monroe, *Writings*, VI:92-102.

66. Wilgus, "Spanish American Patriot Activity Along the Gulf Coast of the United States, 1811-1822," pp. 213-215; Warren, *The Sword was their Passport*, 233-254.

67. Wheaton, *Reports*, IV:52-65.

68. Wheaton, *Reports*, IV:298-311.

69. Richardson, ed., *Messages and Papers of the Presidents*, II:627-628.

70. *Annals of Congress*, XXXV:499, 641, 693-694; XXXVI:1588, 2053, 2207-2211, 2231, 2236; 3 *U. S. Statutes at Large*, 600-601.

71. Georgia circuit court, Minute Book, 1816-1823, pp. 122, 128, 142-144, 151-152, 160-163, 166-167, 171, 173-178; Charleston *Courier*, November 30, 1820; Parker to Adams, July 2, 1820 (Microcopy M 179), reel 48; Adams to Parker, July 29, 1820 (Microcopy M 40), reel 16, pp. 99-100; Virginia circuit court, Order Book #11, 1820-1824, pp. 1, 9-10; Pennsylvania circuit court, Minute Book, 1820-1828, p. 4; Charleston *Courier*, February 15, 1820. Although Glenn's successes were few, he received strong support for reappointment as district attorney from James McCulloch and William Winder. Monroe reappointed him to a four-year term in 1821 and in 1824 promoted him to district judge. McCulloch to General Samuel Smith, February 3, 1821, William Winder to President Monroe, February 6, 1821 (Microcopy M 439), reel 7.

72. Louisiana district court, Docket Book, 1815-1820, p. 238; Docket Book, 1820-1830, pp. 10-11, 15, 25-26; Minute Book, 1819-1825, pp. 63, 68, 70, 74-75, 79-85, 130-131. The cases strained Monroe's patience. Attached to the pardons of Raynor, Lacroix, Lebrequet, and Roneg was a statement from the President that the pardons were unconditional but that the men "should be prevailed on to quit New Orleans immediately, as it is apprehended, should they remain they will too easily relapse into associations of a vicious character." John Quincy Adams to John Nicholson, Marshal of Louisiana, October 21, 1820 (Microcopy M 40), reel 16, p. 165.

73. Rhode Island circuit court, Minute Book, 1817-1821, June 1820.

74. *Annals of Congress*, XXXVII:28, 31.

75. Ibid., 326-328.

76. Richardson, ed., *Messages and Papers of the Presidents*, II:658.

77. Georgia circuit court, Minute Book, 1816-1823, pp. 220, 223-224, 240, 245, 247, 253, 255-256.

78. Georgia circuit court, Minute Book, 1816-1823, p. 309; Minute Book, 1823-1824, pp. 4, 6-8, 13, 91-92, 108, 196-197; (Microcopy T 967), reel 1, vol. IV, pp. 114-115.

79. See *The Bello Corrunes* (1821), Wheaton, *Reports*, VI:152-176; *The Nueva Anna and Liebre* (1812), Wheaton, *Reports*, VI:193-194; *La Conception* (1821),

Wheaton, *Reports*, VI:235-239; *The Gran Para* (1822), Wheaton, *Reports*, VII:471-489; *The Santa Maria* ((1822), Wheaton, *Reports*, VII:490-495; *The Arrogante Barcelones* (1822), Wheaton, *Reports*, VII:496-519; *The Monte Allegre and the Rainha De Los Anjos* (1822), Wheaton, *Reports,* VII:520-522; *The Irrestible* (1822), Wheaton, *Reports*, VII:551-552; and *The Santissima Trinidad and the St. Ander* (1822), Wheaton, *Reports*, VII:283-355.

Reports, VII:283-355.

80. Ibid., 283, 355.

81. South Carolina circuit court, Minute Book, 1821-1836, pp. 42-46, 48-49.

82. Adams to Gadsden, August 19, 1822 (Microcopy M 40), reel 27, p. 382.

83. South Carolina circuit court, Minute Book, 1821-1836, pp. 57, 59; Johnson to Adams, December 2, 11, 1822 (Microcopy M 179), reel 55; (Microcopy T 967), reel 1, vol. IV, pp. 60, 80.

84. Richardson, ed., *Messages and Papers of the Presidents*, II:782; *Annals of Congress*, XL:24.

85. *Annals of Congress*, XL:29, 32-33, 35, 277-278, 287, 314, 331-332, 348-349, 369, 371, 384, 447, 449; 3 *U. S. Statutes at Large*, 721.

86. *Annals of Congress*, XL:354; John Quincy Adams to C. J. Ingersoll and J. Fisk, January 1, 1823 (Microcopy M 40), reel 18, p. 77.

87. *Annals of Congress*, XL:appendix, 1245-1271.

88. Circular to District Attorney (Microcopy M 40), reel 28, pp. 164-165.

89. The Virginia circuit court indicted and convicted Manuel Catcho for piracy, and Judges Marshall and Tucker sentenced him to be hanged. The Pennsylvania circuit court indicted and acquitted Joseph Haskell and Charles Franswan of a variety of crimes, among which were murder and piracy. The South Carolina circuit court indicted and acquitted Miguel Pessares of piracy. Virginia circuit court, Order Book #11, 1820-1824, pp. 360-363; Pennsylvania circuit court, Minute Book, 1820-1828, pp. 144-145, 147, 155; South Carolina circuit court, Minute Book, 1821-1836, pp. 104, 111.

90. New York circuit court, Minute Book, 1819-1828, pp. 202, 211, 254.

91. Ibid., 202, 205, 209-210, 217-218; New York *Post*, September 10, 16, 1823.

92. Wheaton, *Reports*, IX:579-581; New York circuit court, Minute Book, 1819-1828, pp. 243-249.

93. Richardson, ed., *Messages and Papers of the Presidents*, II:782.

94. Ibid., 826-827.

95. *Congressional Debates*, I:34, 198-199.

96. Ibid., 158-162.

97. Ibid., 461-463, 714-734; 4 *U. S. Statutes at Large*, 131.

98. Henry Clay to Tillotson, November 29, 1825 (Microcopy M 179), reel 63; Tillotson to Clay, December 15, 1825, ibid.

99. Richardson, ed., *Messages and Papers of the Presidents*, II:875-876.

100. Ibid., 929.

101. Massachusetts circuit court, Docket Book, vol. 5, 1822-1833, October 1826, May 1827.

102. Virginia circuit court, Order Book #12, 1825-1831, pp. 199, 201, 204-207; Georgia district court, Minute Book, 1813-1843, pp. 255-256.

103. John Nauts to James H. McCulloch, October 14, 1828, Nathaniel Williams to Henry Clay, October 18, 1825, (Microcopy M 179), reel 66.

8

The Courts and the Slave Trade

The Jeffersonian era saw increased activity with respect to the international slave trade. The Federalist Congresses had passed two acts pertaining to the trade: one in March 1794 which forbade the fitting out, building, equipping, or loading of a vessel intended for the slave trade; and a second in May 1800 which made it illegal for a citizen of the United States to have "any right or property" in a vessel carrying slaves "from one foreign country or place to another." The latter law authorized public vessels to seize violators, with the proceeds from the sale of the seized vessel to be divided as in the case of prizes. The federal courts tried at least nineteen slave trade cases between 1799 and 1801. The courts condemned fifteen vessels and ordered them sold and released two vessels; the disposition of two others has not been found.[1] During the same period, however, Newport, Rhode Island, alone recorded thirty-nine suspicious clearances, and other ports reported at least that many.[2]

The attempt to enforce the law under the Federalists quickly subsided under the Republicans. Three of the leading Rhode Island slave traders—Simeon Potter, Charles and James DeWolf—supported Jefferson in the election of 1800. They persuaded Jefferson after his victory to establish a revenue district for Bristol and Warren, thus undercutting the authority of William Ellery, collector at Newport and the man principally responsible for fourteen prosecutions and thirteen condemnations of slave trade vessels in 1799 and 1800. The collector of the new district was Charles Collins, captain of a convicted slaver and part owner of the slavers

Armstadt and *Minerva*. On the day the Senate confirmed Collins, the *Minerva* landed 150 slaves at Havana.[3] Ellery wrote to a friend:

The slave traders, as if determined to set Congress at naught, are driving on their trade Jehu-like. Not less than eight or ten vessels have sailed or are about to sail from Bristol to Africa. But forsooth most of them, like DeWolf's vessels, claim they go for elephant's teeth and gold dust. I expect that the houses of some of the Great Folks will be adorned with ivory, and their horses shod with gold. Some suspect and hope that the slave act will be repealed at the next session of Congress. I can see that this open defiance of law will be as likely to effect it as the late exploit of the Indians was to procure a collector of customs for the district of Bristol.[4]

Although slaves could be brought to the United States by noncitizens, all states had prohibited the trade.[5] Enforcement of the state laws was remiss. Representative Thomas Lowndes of South Carolina lamented the inability of the state to enforce its own laws. He concluded,

With navigable rivers running into the heart of it, it was impossible with our means, to prevent our Eastern brethren, who, in some parts of the Union, in defiance of the authority of the General Government, have been engaged in this trade, from introducing them into the country. The law was completely evaded, and, for the last year or two [1802-1803], Africans were introduced into the country in numbers little short, I believe, of what they would have been had the trade been a legal one.[6]

One of James DeWolf's captains, Charles Clark, verified Lowndes's report. He wrote on January 1, 1802, from Charleston:

I don't see that the Trade stops much, for they come in two or three hundred some nights. I believe there had been landed since New Years as much as 500 slaves. They land them outside the harbor and march them in at night. . . . The revenue cutter seized one brig bound from New Orleans to Charleston. She was cleared from New Orleans by calling them passengers. They clear out from there and go into Havana "in distress," and ship from there to the United States, or sell if the price is high.[7]

Several of the southern states thus tolerated if not countenanced the illegal importation of slaves. When a number of blacks recently emancipated by the French on the Island of Guadeloupe landed at Wilmington, North Carolina, however, the House of Representatives received a memorial requesting Congress to adopt a preventative measure.[8] The committee which received the memorial reported a bill on January 26. The House debated the proposal on the 7th and approved it with modifications on the 17th, 48 to 15. The fifteen negative votes all came from north of the Mason and Dixon line.[9] The Senate approved the bill without a division on February 25.[10]

The act prohibited the importation of any negro, mulatto, or other person of color, except a native, a citizen, or a regular seaman of the United

States or seamen of countries between the Cape of Good Hope into any state which by law has prohibited or shall prohibit such importation. A penalty of $1,000 could be assessed for each person imported in violation of the act, and the ship or vessel with its furniture and apparel would be forfeited.

Section 3 enjoined collectors and other officers:

Notice and be governed by the provisions of the laws now existing, of the several States prohibiting the admission or importation of any negro, mulatto, or other person or color, as aforesaid. And they are hereby enjoined vigilantly to carry into effect the said laws of the said States, conformably to the provisions of this act, any law of the United States to the contrary notwithstanding.[11]

Late in 1803 South Carolina, bowing to economic pressure and the difficulty of enforcing its law, converted the illicit traffic into a legal one by repealing the ban on slave trade. The action by South Carolina brought a quick response from Representative David Bard of Pennsylvania who exclaimed to the House on January 6, 1804, "Had I been informed that some formidable foreign power had invaded our country, I would not, I ought not, be more alarmed than on hearing that South Carolina had repealed her law prohibiting the importation of slaves." Bard proposed that a tax of ten dollars be imposed on each slave imported. When the Committee of the Whole on February 14 considered the resolution, Representative Lowndes answered for South Carolina, claiming that the difficulty of enforcing the prohibition was the principal reason for the repeal. Lowndes opposed the tax, claiming it was an unjust imposition on the people engaged in agriculture in South Carolina.[12]

Bard's reply not only condemned the slave trade but in a moving passage attacked slavery itself.

Americans boast of being the most enlightened people in the world. . . . They have denounced tyranny and oppression, they have declared their country to be an asylum for the oppressed of all nations, but will foreigners concede this high character to us, when they examine our census and find that we hold a million of men in the most degraded slavery? This nearly one-fifth of our whole population; in some of the States nearly half. Here, then, is a fact that must have weight to sink our national character, in spite of volumes to support it. It is a fact, from which foreigners will infer, that we possess the principles of tyranny, but want the power to carry them into operation, except against the untutored and defenseless African. If, then, we hold a consistency of national character in any estimation, we will give every discouragement in our power to the importation of slaves.[13]

Samuel L. Mitchell of New York regretted that the previous laws against the slave trade had been so little regarded. He indicated:

Some time ago he had seen a list of American vessels then known to be hovering on the coast of Guinea in quest of captive negroes. . . . In various parts of the nation outfits were made for slave-voyages, without secrecy, shame or apprehension. The construction of the ships, the shackles for confining the wretched passengers, and all the dismal apparatus of cruelty, were attended to with systematic coolness of an ordinary adventure.

He estimated that in the previous twelve months, 20,000 blacks had been transported from Guinea and smuggled into South Carolina and Georgia.[14] The following day Representative John B. Earle of South Carolina recommended that Congress postpone action on the tax, for he had information that the South Carolina legislature, scheduled to meet in April, would repeal the act. The House thus postponed the proposal until March.[15]

Three days after voting for postponement of the tax resolution the House received from the Senate a bill providing for the temporary government of the Louisiana territory. The introduction of slaves into Louisiana had become a concern shortly after the conclusion of the Purchase Treaty. Three sections of the bill pertained to the transportation of slaves: (1) the importation of slaves into the territory from outside the United States was prohibited; (2) it was unlawful to bring into the territory from the United States any slave which had been imported since May 1, 1798, or which might hereafter be imported into the United States; and (3) the only slaves to be imported into Louisiana would be by a citizen of the United States moving into the territory for actual settlement and at the time of such removal being the *bona fide* owner of such slave or slaves. The penalty for violating the first two clauses was a fine of $300; in each case the slave would be freed. Congress approved this stringent act for only one year.[16] Congress in March 1805 approved a bill which eliminated all restrictions upon the slave trade except that relating to foreign ports.[17]

The issue arose again in 1806 when Congress became concerned about the volume of the trade into the territories. The House appointed a committee which reported that numerous slaves recently imported into Charleston had been conveyed to the territory of Orleans and proposed that the practice should be prohibited. The committee introduced a bill on March 27 but dropped it later in the session.[18]

Late in 1805 the House again undertook consideration of the resolution proposing a tax on imported slaves. An explanation was offered that twice the South Carolina House had approved a repeal act, but each time the bill had failed in the Senate. The House received a tax bill in January 1806 but eventually dropped it.[19]

Enforcement of the legislation was erratic. During Jefferson's first three years, the Federal courts considered a total of twelve slave trade cases. Eleven of the cases were libels against ships, and one was a criminal prosecution. The courts condemned six ships in Rhode Island, four in

Georgia, and one in Massachusetts. Judge Thomas Bee of South Carolina dismissed the only libel he heard, claiming that the trade was legal under the Constitution until 1808. The lone criminal prosecution occurred in Maryland where the court found Stephen Vickeroy guilty for illegally carrying a slave, fined him ten dollars, and imprisoned him for twenty-four hours.[20]

With the reopening of the slave trade in South Carolina, prosecutions almost came to a halt. From 1804 to 1807 the number of prosecutions dropped significantly while the number of open violations increased. Only seven cases were recorded for the period; three involving libels of ships, three actions for debt, and one criminal prosecution. The South Carolina court condemned two vessels; the New York court, one. The South Carolina court dismissed three actions for debt, but the court declared that reasonable or probable cause had existed. One of these cases involved José Antonio de Mendoce. The court ordered the case discontinued when it was revealed that the slaves were intended for Savannah and not for Charleston. The Pennsylvania district attorney accused Thomas Browne of serving on board a vessel employed in carrying slaves from one foreign port to another. The grand jury refused to indict him.[21] During the same period, 1804-1807, the British navy managed to capture at least four slavers belonging to citizens of the United States—the *Ann* of Rhode Island and the *Tartar* of South Carolina in 1806 and the *Nancy* of South Carolina and the *Amedie* of South Carolina in 1807.[22]

South Carolina's opening of the slave trade brought a flood of vessels to Charleston. Senator William Smith of South Carolina reported in 1820 that, according to the Custom House records, 202 ships arrived at Charleston bringing 39,075 slaves. Elizabeth Donnan, after studying newspaper advertisements for the same years, suggested that many other ships bearing slaves also arrived. Donnan found 149 ships listed in advertisements, of which 114 also appeared on the Custom House lists, or a total of 237 from both sources. The Custom House records revealed that of the 202 ships it recorded, 128 were from the United States—sixty-one from Charleston, fifty-nine from Rhode Island, four from Baltimore, two from Norfolk, and one each from Boston and Connecticut. The consignees of the slave ships were Charleston, thirteen; Rhode Island eighty-eight; Great Britain, ninety-one; and France, ten. Unfortunately, the Acts of 1794 and 1800 prohibited citizens of the United States from carrying slaves from one foreign country or place to another, not from a foreign country to the United States.[23]

After 1805 the administration commenced some feeble efforts to enforce the existing statutes. Madison wrote to the district attorney of Maine in 1805 enclosing a certification from the consul at London that the brig *Harry and James*, said to belong to Portland, had been concerned in the slave trade and requested the district attorney to inquire into the matter and, if he could, secure sufficient evidence to institute a prosecution. Again in 1806 Madison sent similar requests to David Howell of Rhode Island to investigate the ships *Charles and Harriet, Israel,* and *Oneida*; to George Blake of Massachusetts, to investigate the ship *Juliana*; and to Nathan Sanford of New York, to investigate the ship *Asposia.* Benjamin Cowell reported to Madison in September 1806 that he had attempted to obtain a deposition from the crew of the ship *Charles and Harriet* but was threatened by a mob and left town without the depositions. No prosecutions resulted from these investigations.[24]

Attention after 1805 focused on Congress and necessity of implementing Article I, Section 9 of the Constitution which provided that "the migration or importation of such persons as any of the states now existing shall think proper to admit, shall not be prohibited by Congress prior to the year 1808. . . ." Jefferson submitted his second annual message to the second session of the ninth Congress on December 2, 1806, toward the end of which he congratulated the Congress on the

approach of the period at which you may interpose your authority, constitutionally, to withdraw the citizens of the United States from all further participation in those violations of human rights which have been so long continued on the unoffending in-habitants of Africa, and which the morality, reputation, and the best interests of our country have long been eager to proscribe.

The following day Senator Stephen R. Bradley of Vermont gave notice that he would introduce on the 8th a bill to prohibit the importation of slaves into the United States. Bradley introduced the bill, and the Senate referred it to a committee. The House referred the message to a select committee. Both committees were controlled by representatives from the slave states, 4 to 3 in the House and 4 to 1 in the Senate.[25] The House committee reported a bill on December 15, which was read twice and committed to a Committee of the Whole on the 17th. The Bradley bill would not emerge from committee until January 15, 1807.[26]

The House bill, which contained six sections, prohibited the importation with intent to sell, keep, or dispose of "any negro, mulatto, or other person of color"; forbade the building, equipping, fitting, or loading of any vessel for the purpose of bringing a prohibited person into the United States; provided for the forfeiture of any vessel found within the jurisdiction of the United States with a prohibited person on board; and stipulated that any prohibited person imported illegally would be forfeited and that the person concerned in buying or selling such prohibited person should be fined. Prohibited persons seized under the bill would be sold by the United States. The debates, extending over nearly three months, turned on two key issues: What should be the status of blacks who were forfeited to the government, and what should be the appropriate penalty for violating the act?

Early in the debates Representative John Smilie of Pennsylvania declared that he would never approve a bill which made the government a slave trader. He had no objection to funding the expense of sending the Africans back to their country. After Representative James Sloan of New Jersey moved to give the blacks their freedom, Representative Peter Early of Georgia retorted with an extended and incredible speech, revealing in depth the racist feeling of the early nineteenth century. Early stated that though slavery was an evil "regretted by every man in the country, to have among us in any considerable quantity persons of this description, is an evil far greater than slavery itself." Early felt that the law could not be executed. No one would inform "because to inform will be to lead to an evil which will be deemed greater than the offense for which information is given, because it will be opposed to the principle of self-preservation, and to the love of family. No, no man will be disposed to jeopardize his life, and the lives of his countrymen." Early then revealed that "whenever people of color are found in a state of freedom—I mean in the States where they are found in considerable numbers—they are considered as the instruments of murder, theft, and conflagration." Early then assured the House that if the law should be enforced and even a single cargo of blacks should be freed they would be killed. "Not one of them would be left alive in a year." He concluded by pleading with the House to seriously consider a measure "which will place us and the people of color in a situation in which we must determine our own lives and theirs."[27]

Supporters of the motion made a moving moral defense of freeing illegally imported blacks.

The moment they arrive in any harbor within the jurisdictional limits of the United States, they are met by this law which we are now passing. It finds them, by the laws of God and man, entitled to their freedom as clearly and absolutely as we are. They are not, by any law, human or divine, the slaves of any master. They are not the lawful property of any owner. They are no more the property of those who hold them in duress than the man who is robbed is the property of the highwayman while in his power. Their detention is a wrongful, false imprisonment. In this very bill we declare it to be high crime. By the same law we condemn the man-stealer and become the receiver of his stolen goods. We punish the criminal, and then step into his place, and complete the crime which we had only begun. We ourselves do that which we prevent him from doing that which he crossed and recrossed the Atlantic, at the hazard of his life and the sacrifice of his character and his conscience, to be unable to do. We sell his victims as slaves, receive the price of their slavery, and put it into the public treasury; and the vendee holds them and their children, from generation to generation, in perpetual slavery, by the title derived from our law. In short, we assume to ourselves, as a Government, the exclusive right of selling slaves imported into the United States.[28]

Later in the debates the Speaker, Nathaniel Macon, indicated that he considered the question a commercial one. "If this is not a commercial question," he said, "I would thank the gentleman to show what part of the constitution gives us any right to legislate on this subject. It is in vain to talk of turning these creatures loose to cut our throats."[29]

Representative John Smilie found the Speaker's contention somewhat novel and added that the question was connected with principles of a higher order than those merely commercial.

I beg leave on this occasion to refer to the principles of 1776, which have indeed been since laughed at, but which are now beginning, I hope, to be held in universal estimation. The Declaration of Independence contains this sentence: "We hold these principles to be self-evident, that all men are created equal, that they are endowed, by their Creator, with certain inalienable rights; that among these are life, liberty, and the pursuit of happiness." Will the honorable Speaker tell us how these rights are connected with commercial principles?

Joseph Clay of Pennsylvania replied that "it must appear to every man of common sense, that the question could be considered in a commercial point of view only. . . ." He added,

The Declaration of Independence is to be taken with great qualification. It declared those men have an inalienable right to life; yet we hang criminals—to liberty, yet we imprison—to the pursuit of happiness, yet he must not infringe on the rights of others. If the Declaration of Independence is taken in its fullest extent, it will warrant robbery and murder, for some may think even those crimes necessary to their happiness.[30]

The House defeated the Sloan motion 36-63. A later motion providing that "no person shall be sold as a slave by virtue of this act" was decided by the Speaker in the negative. Finally, the Senate bill provided for indenturing blacks illegally imported in a free state until the age of twenty-one. Early moved to strike the indenture section and substitute a provision that would leave it to the state to dispose of the blacks. The House incorporated Early's proposal into the final bill.[31]

Smilie introduced the second issue when he indicated surprise at finding no penalty attached "to one of the highest crimes man could commit." He believed there "was not a State in the Union that did not inflict the punishment of death on willful murder. A captain of a ship engaged in this traffic was guilty of murder."[32]

The opposition speeches were preverse yet tragic. Again they reveal the racial attitudes of the early nineteenth century. Benjamin Tallmadge of Connecticut felt that since Mosaic law provided the death penalty for a man stealer, the same penalty should be inflicted now. Ebenezer Elmer of New Jersey countered that if we believed the Mosaic law was now binding, he would support the death penalty; but he believed the punishment of death immoral "because the crime did not imply murder, and had no analogy to it. . . . The crime was committed merely out of a love of gain." Several

Southern representatives felt that the several gentlemen were connecting the slave trade with slavery. James Holland of North Carolina responded:

People of the South do not generally consider slavery as a moral offense. The importer might say to the informer that he had done no wrong, not even so bad as he. It is true that I have these slaves from Africa; but I have transported them from one master to another. I am not guilty of holding human beings in bondage. But you are.

Holland later disputed the fact that the trade was immoral by stating that it was a well-known fact that "the negroes imported are brought from a state of slavery. There is only a transfer from one master to another; and it is admitted that the condition of the slaves in the Southern states is much superior to that of those in Africa. Who, then will say that the trade is immoral?" Joseph Stanton, Jr., of Rhode Island added that he hoped the law would be strong enough to prevent the trade but could not believe "that a man ought to be hung for only stealing a negro."[33]

Theodore Dwight of Connecticut could not accept Holland's contention that the question did not involve morality. He asked,

Who empowered us to judge for them as to which is the worse and which the better state? Have these miserable beings ever been consulted on the question of this removal? Who can say that the state in which they are born, and to which they are habituated, is not more agreeable to them than one altogether untried, of which they have no knowledge, and about which they cannot even make any calculations?[34]

Committees twice inserted the death penalty into the House bill, and twice the full House removed it.[35] When the House took up the Senate bill on February 9, the Committee of the Whole struck imprisonment and substituted the death penalty. Again the full House substituted fine and imprisonment for the death penalty.[36]

Surprisingly, the amendment which necessitated the conference committee concerned the coastwise slave trade. The conference report limited the trade to vessels under forty tons. Early claimed that such a law would be evaded, and John Randolph of Roanoke claimed the provision "touched the right of private property." Randolph said he "had rather lose the bill, he had rather lose all the bills of the session, he had rather lose every bill passed since the establishment of the Government, than agree to the provision contained in this slave bill. It went to blow up the Constitution in ruins." He concluded by asserting that "if ever the time of disunion between the States should arrive, the line of severence would be between the slaveholding and the non-slaveholding states." The opposition notwithstanding the House approved the conference report 63 to 49—the slave states opposed the measure 39 to 12, while the free states supported it 52 to 11.[37] The approved bill, similar to revenue acts, contained ten sections. The criminal penalties were as follows:

	Fine	Imprisonment	Forfeiture
Building, fitting out, equipping vessel	$20,000*	None	Vessel
Transporting slaves to foreign country	$ 5,000*	None	Vessel
Transporting slave to United States	$ 1,000-$10,000	5-10 years	Vessel
Purchasing or selling illegally imported slave	$ 800*	None	Slave
Hovering off coast with intent to sell slave	None	None	Vessel
Captain, master or commander of vessel violating law, seized by public vessel	$10,000 max.**	2 years min.	Vessel & Slaves

*one moiety to United States, the other to the informer
**one moiety to the United States, one to officers and men who made the seizure.

The last sections of the act pertained to the coastwise trade, limited to vessels of forty tons or more, and provided various forfeitures and fines for violations. For example, if a captain failed to list every negro, mulatto, or person of color on the manifest, the vessel could be forfeited and the captain could be fined $1,000 for every negro, mulatto, or person of color so transported.[38]

Although Congress passed the Slave Trade Act long before the effective date, the shippers wanted a last minute exception. Late in 1807 Robert Marion of South Carolina presented the House a petition from several Charleston merchants stating "that many vessels had cleared" from Charleston "for the purpose of importing slaves, before the law was passed" and "some had cleared out after the passing of the law and had been detained by accidents beyond the time limited by law" and requesting that a relief act be passed. Marion moved that this petition be referred to the Committee of Commerce and Manufacturers. Josiah Masters of New York objected, asserting that "if there was any subject in favor of which a petition should not be referred it was the slave trade. These petitioners knew when the prohibitory law would go into operation, and they were not entitled to relief by the laws of God or man." The House defeated the motion to refer 39 to 37.[39]

Commencing late in 1807, several cases were brought before district courts for violations of the 1807 law, including two in South Carolina, one in Pennsylvania, and one in Georgia—none of which ended in a conviction or forfeiture. The South Carolina court tried the case of the *United States* v. *The Schooner Kitty.* Captain M'Neil of the revenue cutter *Gallatin* instituted the suit against the *Kitty*. The *Kitty* appeared to be the case referred to in the petition. The vessel sailed from Charleston on November 19, 1806, for Africa. She arrived off the coast of Africa on January 1 with a crew of eleven. By August, after three seamen had died, the steward had run away, and the captain had discharged the first mate "as an incorrigible drunkard." Only the captain and five of the crew remained.

In August, the ship's papers were seized by the governor, and detained for a fortnight. In September a report of war with Great Britain obliged the vessel to run up the river to avoid being captured. In October, only two of the crew were fit for duty, and the vessel was so leaky as to be three weeks under repair; provisions for their return could not be procured till November, on the 16th of that month she sailed, and on the 16th of January 1808, was seized . . . by the captain of the revenue cutter.[40]

Judge Bee ruled that "if ever there was a case of hardship, occasioned by no fault of the party, this is one." He ordered the suit dismissed but that the claimants should pay all costs. He recommended also that the district attorney enter a *nolle prosequi* on the prosecution instituted against the captain for the penalty, which was done accordingly.[41]

Historians of the slave trade have often criticized the federal government for the lack of an energetic program for the enforcement of the Slave Trade Act of 1807. These historians have missed the largest concerted evasion of the act which occurred between 1809 and 1810 when several thousand refugees from Cuba arrived with their slaves in various United States ports and were ultimately given legislative exemption from the provisions of the 1808 law.

Most of the refugees were French who had fled to Cuba from Haiti in the 1790s. After re-establishing themselves in Cuba, they were again forced to flee when the Spanish crown collapsed before Napoleon in 1808. Spain, heavily involved in the European conflict, left Cuba under the control of Captain-General Salvador de Muro, Marques Someruelos, who, distrusting the recent French settlers, ordered many of them expelled in 1808 and 1809.[42] The French fled with their slaves—some headed for various locations in the Caribbean; others, to the United States. Upon arrival in Charleston and New Orleans, the United States officials seized the vessels and slaves for violations of the 1807 law. The South Carolina circuit court took up four such cases between May 23 and 25, 1809; the Louisiana district court, eleven cases between June 17 and 20, 1809.[43]

Senator William Branch Giles of Virginia brought the problem to the attention of Congress on June 12, 1809, when he requested the formation of a committee to inquire whether a law should be passed for remitting the penalties and forfeitures incurred by the French emigrés.[44] The Senate formed the committee, and two days later it reported a bill. The Senate passed the bill on the 22nd. Opponents raised a few objections in the House, which took up the bill in the Committee of the Whole on the 28th. Representative John Ross of Pennsylvania objected to any relaxation of the law. Several southern representatives contended that the purpose was not to circumvent the law but further it by permitting the legal landing and re-exportation of the slaves. After adding a section for the relief of Andrew Foster and Jacob P. Giraud, who had petitioned on June 6 for relief from a seizure at New Orleans for their vessels for bringing two slaves from New York to Orleans, the House approved the bill. Madison added his approval the same day.[45]

The act authorized the President to remit any penalty or forfeiture incurred under the Act of 1807 by any person concerned in bringing any slave or slaves owned by any person or persons forcibly expelled from the island of Cuba with the proviso that the slaves and persons expelled would have arrived directly from Cuba on the same vessel. The act also permitted the President to make arrangements with the French Minister for transporting the exiles who should desire to depart from the United States to any port or place within the territories of France. Thus the act permitted the re-exportation of the refugees and their slaves but did not mandate it.[46]

Madison quickly commenced the process of remitting penalties and forfeitures. By September one vessel in Pennsylvania, one in Georgia, three in South Carolina, and forty-nine in Louisiana had obtained relief. The forty-nine vessels in Louisiana had brought into the United States 2,481 whites and 2,662 slaves. Only one vessel, the schooner *Sally* condemned in South Carolina, did not obtain relief.[47]

Governor William C. C. Claiborne of Louisiana warned the President in the summer of 1809 to expect immigrants to arrive from other Spanish colonies. Secretary of State Robert Smith informed Claiborne that, in the opinion of the President, immigrants from other than Cuba would subject themselves to the penalties of the general Slave Trade Act.[48] On October 4, 1809, customs officials seized the brig *Joseph Ricketson* at New Orleans after it arrived from Jamaica with five slaves belonging to French refugees, and they seized the *Victory* on November 2 after it arrived at New Orleans from Curaçao with six slaves who were property of French refugees.[49]

Harry Caldwell and Amasa Jackson, owners of the *Joseph Ricketson*, and Jeremiah Reynolds, owner of the *Victory*, hastily submitted two petitions to Congress in December 1809 and January 1810. The petitions claimed that they brought French families and their slaves who had been expelled from Cuba and had not been able to secure immediate passage to the United States. The families had resided temporarily in Jamaica and Curaçao respectively. Congress granted the petitioners a special relief act on January 30, 1810.[50]

The court records of Louisiana reveal that the President granted thirteen additional vessels relief—nine from Cuba, three from Jamaica, and one from Santo Domingo. New York recorded two cases of remission.[51] Thus the President granted seventy-one vessels, captains, or cargoes of vessels exemption in 1809 and 1810 from the provisions of the 1807 law.[52]

Although the Cuban problem prompted the government to grant certain exemptions from the law of 1807, when government officials learned of illegal activities concerning the trade directly with Africa, it reacted differently. In July 1810 Henry Dearborn wrote Albert Gallatin enclosing the testimony of Samuel Spencer, a seaman, detailing how the vessel *Mount Etna* cleared from Boston for Rio de Janeiro where the cargo was landed and all the seamen were discharged. The consul John B. Dabney listed Jabez Lord, owner of the *Etna* and supercargo, and the captain among the discharged seamen. Dearborn concluded that such action "has on the face of it conspicuous marks of collusion and intentional misconduct as an agent of the United States." Spencer claimed that the captain told him that the vessel was going to Africa for slaves, "but it was necessary to change the colours and get a Portuguese master to evade the laws of the United States. . . ." Spencer was ordered to alter the ship to carry slaves, which he did. At Goree the supercargo agreed for 280 slaves to be delivered in the river Gambia. Spencer was then discharged but observed another vessel, the *Mary Ann* of Charleston under Spanish colours and a brig commanded by Campbell with a supercargo called Cushing, taking in slaves.[53]

Reacting to Dearborn's report and other official complaints, President Madison informed Congress in his second annual message of December 5, 1810, that "it appears that American citizens are instrumental in carrying on a traffic in enslaved Africans, equally in violation of the laws of humanity and in defiance of those of their own country." He hoped that Congress would devise "further means of suppressing the evil."[54]

Although the Secretary of the Navy reported, "I hear not without great concern that the laws prohibiting the importation of slaves have been violated in frequent instances;" the only ship condemned in 1811 was the *Donna La Costa*, forfeited for fitting out for the slave trade and for importing slaves. The President ordered *nolle prosequis* entered in the case of the schooner *Nancy* in North Carolina and the ship *Pennyslvania* in South Carolina.[55]

Only a handful of seizures and condemnations occurred during the War of 1812. The President's inconsistent policy toward the slave trade is revealed in two cases which arose in 1812. In the first instance the Spanish cruiser *General Morla* had been seized at Baltimore with a number of Africans on board. Because the ship had been unavoidably forced into United States waters, the President ordered James H. McCulloch, Collector of the Customs in Baltimore, to release the vessel "provided such a disposition is made of the Africans in question as may be conformable with the laws of the State of Maryland." In no case, however, should they "be exported in the same vessel." In the second case, customs officials seized the schooner *Robert Rich* in the district of North Carolina for bringing certain slaves from Havana. When the parties concerned indicated a willingness to transport the slaves beyond the jurisdictional limits of the United States "provided the President" would "arrest all further judicial proceedings," the President ordered a *nolle prosequi* entered.[56]

The war also created a problem of slaves captured from the enemy. Several privately armed and public vessels late in 1813 captured slaves from British vessels and brought them into Wilmington, North Carolina. Customs officials seized the *Snap Dragon*, a privately armed vessel, and libeled her for an alleged breach of the 1807 act. The collector seized the slaves captured by the public vessel *Saratoga*. The legal question was how far the provisions of the law for capturing the enemy's property may or may not supercede those of the slave act. The President ordered the libel against the *Snap Dragon* for a violation of the Slave Trade Act of 1807 dismissed by having the district attorney enter a *nolle prosequi*. The court dismissed a libel for disposition of the slaves brought in by the *Snap Dragon* upon the grounds that the slave act retained its full force and operation. In still another case, the *United States* v. *Six Negroes, two Boats, Muskets*, etc., April 1814, the court ruled that "enemies" property captured by a land force accrues to the United States and not to the actual captors, and that the Negroes mentioned in the libel were confiscable to the use of the United States."[57]

Toward the close of the session the district attorney, in light of the seemingly conflicting opinions from the courts, requested clarification, indicating to the judge that there were confined in the jail of the city some forty or fifty blacks who had been captured by the public vessels *Rattlesnake* and *Enterprise*. Although no record has been found of the court's answer, no further cases arose in the district at that time.[58]

From passage of the act ending the slave trade until the close of the War of 1812, the courts indicted only one person, John S. Hutton, for participating in the slave trade. Hutton pleaded not guilty in the Pennsylvania circuit court in October 1808. The district attorney apparently dropped the case before sending it to the petit jury.[59]

After the War of 1812, Collector William Ellery of Newport, Rhode Island, continued his running battle with the slave traders, in particular the DeWolf family and the Collector at Bristol, Charles Collins. In December 1816 Ellery identified a number of vessels believed engaged in the slave trade, including the *MacDonough*, the *Brutus*, the *Yankee*, the *Clara*, and the *Cleopatra*. Ellery had little success in getting Collins to take any action. Collins replied to Ellery that the ships had been sold to Spanish owners and that while he regretted

that this State is resorted to for the purpose of carrying on any part of any illicit traffic in slaves . . . I fear that (as long as the public agents abroad, such as consuls at Tenneriffe, Havannah [*sic*] & continue to wink at it, when they have it fully in their power to bring offenders to Justice) all exertions here will be unavailing.

In addition to the problem of Collins in Bristol, Ellery found the district attorney, Asher Robbins, unwilling to prosecute without a witness who could give bond with sufficient security to pay costs in case of acquittal.[60]

An anonymous respondent detailed the precise method of transferring ownerships in a letter to Obadiah Brown in August 1816.

Cargoes suited to the African market are procured here and taken on board vessels suited to the business and cleared for Havanna [*sic*]. The master there effects a nominal sale of vessel and cargo to a Spaniard, takes on board a Spanish nominal Master and proceeds to Africa. A power of attorney to effect the sale is always prepared here before sailing. When the vessel has made one voyage she can proceed on another without returning to the United States. A cargo is usually sent out to her to Havanna [*sic*].[61]

President Madison in his eighth annual message indicated that the interposition of Congress

appears to be required by the violations and evasions which it is suggested are chargeable on unworthy citizens who engage in the slave trade under foreign flags and with foreign ports, and by collusive importations of slaves into the United States through adjoining ports and territories. I present the subject to Congress with a full assurance of their disposition to apply all the remedy which can be afforded by an amendment of the law.[62]

Although both Houses of Congress established committees on the portion of the President's message pertaining to the slave trade, no new legislation emerged.[63]

Shortly after assuming the Presidency, James Monroe commenced receiving a variety of reports from the Secretaries of State, Treasury, and Navy on the problems associated with "piractical" establishments on Galveston and Amelia Islands. The topic of piracy and its treatment before the federal courts has been dealt with in Chapter 7; however, the slave trade involvement will be discussed here. The first concern expressed to the President was a group headquartered on Galveston Island, then claimed by the United States as part of Louisiana and also by Mexico as part of Texas. The leader of the group of Galveston was Commodore Aury, assisted by "refugees from Barrataria and mulattos." Aury claimed authorization from the Mexican government, although various United States officials disputed this claim. Aury established a government including prize courts. Vessels operating from the island commenced seizing vessels in the Gulf of Mexico, principally those with the Spanish flag but "often without much concern as to the national character, particularly when money was in question." Among the cargoes condemned were a number of slaves.[64]

Captain Charles Morris of the U. S. frigate *Congress* reported to the Secretary of the Navy on June 10, 1817,

Most of the goods carried to Galveston, are introduced into the United States, the more bulky and least valuable, regularly through the custom house, the more valuable, and the slaves, are smuggled in through the numerous inlets to the westward, where the people are but too much disposed to render them every possible assistance. Several hundred slaves are now at Galveston, and persons have gone from New Orleans to purchase them.[65]

Beverly Chew, collector at New Orleans, began supplying information to the Secretary of the Treasury in August, listing additional slave cargoes captured and sent to Galveston. He believed that the slaves were sold

to the Lafittes, Sauvinet, and other speculators in this place, who have or will resell to the planters; and the facility offered to smugglers by the innumerable inlets are too obvious, on a view of the map, to doubt; but there either are or will be all introduced into this State, without the possibility of the officers of the revenue being able to prevent or punish them, more especially as a great portion of the population are disposed to countenance them in violating our laws.[66]

Late in August Chew reported some success. The *Boxer*, which commenced cruising off the Sabine river in late June, had captured two small schooners with thirty slaves on board, and the deputy collector of the district of the Teche had seized fifteen slaves.[67]

Aury partially obviated the problem of Galveston when early in the fall he abandoned the island for Amelia Island, but not before disposing of 300 "Africans to agents of some planters on the river." Chew reported that the deputy collector of the district of Teche received information on the passage of a "large gang of Africans . . . near the church of Attacapas on the night of the 14th ultimo, bound for the Mississippi" but heard of it too late to seize them. Chew believed that Lafitte and Lafon were establishing a new base at Galveston and would soon appoint a new "judge and other authorities."[68]

Monroe finally acted in October, posing a series of questions to his Cabinet, among which was the query, "Is it expedient to break up the establishments at Amelia Island, & Galveston, it being evident that they were made for smuggling, if not for piratical purposes, and already preverted to very mischievous purposes to the U. States?"[69] The Cabinet evidently responded favorably since the President in early November ordered a combined navy and army force assembled to seize Amelia Island. [70] In his first annual message to Congress, Monroe explained the problems associated with the two islands, identifying Amelia as a place "being made a channel for the illicit introduction of slaves from Africa into the United States, an asylum for fugitive slaves from the neighboring States, and a port for smuggling of every kind." He stated briefly that with a "just regard for the rights and interests of the United States . . . orders have been accordingly issued" for the suppression of the establishment on Amelia Island. Amelia Island was taken without bloodshed late in December.[71] Monroe still had doubts as to the public's reception of this action, writing to Jefferson that

Amelia Island & Galveston, is also still a cause of concern, thro' the probability is, that the public mind, will discriminate, between a banditti, form'd of adventurers, of all nations, except the Spanish Colonies, plann'd in our own country, & resting for support, on presumed impurity within us, & the cause of the Colonies themselves to which we all wish success.[72]

Although the Galveston-Amelia Island problems presented the immediate difficulties, American involvement in the international trade was still a matter of concern.[73] The House Committee on the African Slave Trade on February 11, 1817, not only recommended that the President enter into a "convention with the Government of Great Britain, for receiving into the colony of Sierra Leone, such of the free people of color of the United States as, with their own consent, shall be carried thither" but also that the President "consult and negotiate with all the governments where Ministers of the United States are, or shall be accredited, or the means of effecting an entire and immediate abolition of the traffic in slavery." The House did not act upon the report or recommendation.[74]

Congress entered into a flurry of activity in the early months of 1818. The Senate initially concerned itself with a petition from the Society of Friends at Baltimore which in part called for the United States to take measures "in concert with other nations for the entire abolition" of the slave trade. The concept of cooperation with other nations, in particular Great Britain, occupied Congress and the President from 1818 to 1825. Lord Castlereagh proposed to Richard Rush in 1818 certain measures, among which was the reciprocal submission to the right of search. In November 1818 Secretary of State John Quincy Adams rejected the proposals on constitutional, practical, and historical grounds. First, Adams pointed out that the conventions reached with Spain, Portugal, and the Netherlands provided "for the establishment of two Mixed Courts, each composed of judges of the two signatory powers." Adams doubted that the United States could constitutionally institute a court for "carrying into execution their penal statutes beyond the territories of the United States—a court consisting partly of foreign judges not amenable to impeachment for corruption, and deciding upon the statutes of the United States without appeal." Secondly, Adams indicated that there were practical difficulties "with regard to the cargoes of negroes who might be brought to the United States on board captured slave traders; the peculiar status of negroes within the different

States of the Union made it impossible that the Federal government should assume any responsibility for their disposal." Finally, Adams replied "that the admission of a right in the officers of foreign ships-of-war to enter and search the vessels of the United States in time of peace, under any circumstances whatever, would meet with universal repugnance in the public opinion of this country. . . ."

Congress attempted to instruct the President beginning in 1820 when the House passed a resolution urging cooperation, but the Senate defeated it by the casting vote of the President of the Senate. In 1821 a House committee responded to Adams's concerns, indicating that a qualified right of search would not be detrimental to the United States and that the problem of disposal of vessels and slaves delivered into the jurisdiction of the United States had been resolved in the Act of 1819. The House did not act upon the committee's report during the session. Another House committee in 1822 concluded that the total suppression could "never be effected by the separate and disunited efforts of one or more states. . . ." Again the House did not act upon the report. Finally in 1823 the House approved a resolution requesting the President

to enter upon and to prosecute, from time to time, such negotiations with the several maritime powers of Europe and America, as he may deem expedient for the effectual abolition of the African slave trade, and its ultimate denunciation, as piracy, under the law of nations, by the consent of the civilized world.

With such encouragement, Richard Rush signed a convention in London in March 1824. The British parliament immediately ratified the convention which declared the slave trade piracy. The United States Senate was less cooperative. Supporters of the Presidental candidacy of William H. Crawford, led by Senator Henry Johnson of Louisiana, so amended the convention as to make it unacceptable to Great Britian. Thus attempts at cooperation were shelved for the remainder of the period.[75]

While the Senate debated the concept of an international concert, the House in 1818 received the report of the Committee on Foreign Relations relative to Amelia Island and the illegal introduction of slaves. The Committee approved of the President's course of action opining

that it is but too notorious that numerous infractions of the law prohibiting the importation of slaves into the United States have been perpetrated with impunity upon our Southern frontier; and they are further of opinion that similar infractions would have been repeated, with increasing activity, without the timely interposition of the naval force, under the direction of the Executive of our Government.

The report concluded,

The experience of ten years has, however, evinced the necessity of some new regulations being adopted, in order effectually to put a stop to the further introduction of slaves into the United States. In the act of Congress prohibiting their importation, the policy of giving the whole forfeiture of vessel and goods to the United States, and no part thereof to the informer, may justly be doubted. This is an oversight which should be remedied.

Also the committee pointed out that "the omission of the States to pass acts to meet the act of Congress, and to establish regulations in aid of the same, can only be remedied by Congress legislating directly upon the subject themselves, as it is clearly within the scope of their constitutional power to do so."[76]

Although the House proposed a bill, the act which emerged from Congress originated in the Senate. Introduced on April 1 and approved on the 10th, the bill evoked little reported debate in the Senate. In the House, however, Eldred Simkins of South Carolina proposed an amendment which provided for "disposing of slaves seized for being illegally imported, by sale, one-half of the proceeds to the benefit of the United States, and the other to the benefit of the officers making the seizure, &c." Simkins and Weldon W. Edwards of North Carolina, who supported the motion, felt that sale of the slaves by the federal government was the only means of executing the laws against the trade.[77] Collector William I. McIntosh of the District of Brunswick, Georgia, pointed out bluntly the failure to provide for the disposition of the slaves.

It is a painful duty, sir, to express to you, that I am in possession of undoubted information, that African and West India negroes are almost daily illicitly introduced into Georgia, for sale or settlement, or passing through it to the territories of the United States for similar purposes; these facts are notorious and it is not unusual to see such Negroes in the streets of St. Mary's, and such too, recently captured by our vessels of war, and ordered to Savannah, were illegally bartered by hundreds in that city, *for* this bartering or bonding (as *it is called,* but in reality *selling,*) actually took place before any decision had [been] passed by the court respecting them. I cannot but again express to you, sir, that these irregularities and mocking of the laws, by men who understand them, and who, it was presumed, would have respected them, are such, that it required the immediate interposition of Congress to effect a suppression of this traffic; for, as things are, should a faithful officer of the government apprehend such negroes, to avoid the penalties imposed by the laws, the proprietors disclaim them, and some agent of the executive demands a delivery of the same to him, who may employ them as he pleases, or effect a sale by way of a bond, for the restoration of the negroes when legally called on to do so; which bond, it is *understood*, is to be *forfeited*, as the amount of the bond is so much less than the value of the property. . . . There are many negroes . . . recently introduced into this state and the Alabama territory, and which can be apprehended. The undertaking would be great; but to be sensible that we shall possess your approbation, and that we are carrying the views and wishes of the government into execution, is all we wish, and it shall be done, independent of every personal consideration.[78]

The amendment failed by a large margin. The bill left the disposition of the slaves illegally imported to the states. The House approved it with minor alterations on the 16th, the Senate accepted the bill on the following day, and the President signed the bill on the 20th.

Under the act informers would get one-half of all forfeitures and fines. The new penalties for violations were as follows:

	Fine	Imprisonment	Forfeiture
Equipping a slave trade vessel	$1,000-5,000	3-7 years	None
Transporting a black from a foreign place	$1,000-5,000	3-7 years	Vessel, tackle, and apparel
Importing a black from a foreign place	$1,000-10,000	3-7 years	None
Buying illegally or selling an imported black	None	None	$1,000 per person bought or sold

To encourage officials to enforce the law, the act placed the burden of proof on the defendant "to the extent that he must prove that the slave in question had been imported at least five years before the prosecution."[79]

Even without new legislation, the government tried to stop the trade through Georgia. Secretary of the Navy Benjamin Crowninshield issued orders to Captain John H. Elton on July 16, 1817, indicating that with the seizure of Amelia Island by MacGregor the possibility that slaves would be illegally introduced into Georgia had increased and directed Elton to "detain and search every vessel under whatever flag which may enter the River St. Mary's or be found hovering upon the coast under suspicious circumstances, and seize every vessel freighted with slaves." The district attorney for Georgia, William Davies, questioned the legality of the orders. Crowninshield in April 1818 appealed to Attorney General William Wirt for an opinion. Wirt pointed out that a seizure could not be made purely because a vessel was found "sailing on the high seas," within the jurisdictional limits of the United States with blacks "on board." The Act of 1807 required that in order to justify a seizure "the purpose to sell them as slaves or to land them within the United States shall also exist." Wirt, however, believed that the orders were in conformity to the law if they placed emphasis upon the "suspicious circumstances" and not merely on the cargo of the vessel.[80]

The number of condemnations and prosecutions in 1818 was small. The district attorney filed an information against Stephen Brown in Louisiana for purchasing an imported slave. The trial resulted in a verdict for the defendant. The Georgia grand jury indicted one person for smuggling blacks into the United States, but the trial jury acquitted him.[81] Although collectors seized twelve vessels—seven in Louisiana,[82] three in Alabama, and two in South Carolina—the various courts forfeited only five. The United States government was encountering many of the same difficulties that the British faced in trying to enforce the navigation acts in the 1700s.[83]

The Alabama cases, involving three vessels—the *Merino*, the *Constitution*, and the *Louisa*—would occupy Congress and the courts for a number of years. The three vessels all owned by citizens of the United States sailed from the United States to Havana where they took on board certain goods and a number of slaves. The *Merino* cleared Havana on June 2 for Mobile; the *Constitution* and the *Louisa* cleared Havana on the 10th for New Orleans. The owners of the vessels, however, engaged to land the slaves at Pensacola, which was Spanish territory, on their respective voyages. The United States ketch *Surprise*, commanded by Lieutenant Isaac M'Keever, seized the *Merino* within a mile and a half of Fort Barancas, inside the bar, and within the harbor of Pensacola. Colonel George M. Brooke of the United States Army took possession of the *Constitution* under the guns at Fort Barancas then in possession of the United States' forces. Lt. M'Keever also captured the *Louisa* outside the bar at Pensacola. The district court of Alabama condemned the vessels as forfeited, but the judge reserved the distribution for the future order of the court. The claimant entered appeals to the Supreme Court in each of the three cases.[84] The appellants contended:

[1.] That the regular admiralty process was not issued in these cases. [2.] That the informations did not conclude against the form of the statute. [3.] That the District Court of Alabama had not jurisdiction, the seizures having been made, not within the waters of that state, or on the high seas, but within the jurisdiction of a foreign nation. [4.] That the acts of Congress, on which these informations are founded, were intended to apply exclusively to the suppression of the slave trade, from the coast of Africa, or elsewhere, for the purpose of holding or disposing of the subjects of the trade, as slaves, and not to the carrying of them, when in a state of slavery, from one foreign country to another.

The Court, in an opinion written by Justice Washington, admitted that the proceedings in these cases "were not conducted with the regularity usually observed in admiralty cases"; however, the parties waived these objections by appearing before the court and filing their claims to the property seized. The second objection the Court found to be without foundation. Washington pointed out that in the case of *The Hoppit* the Court had observed that "technical niceties of the common law, as to informations . . . are not regarded in admiralty informations . . ." The Court rejected the third objection, pertaining to the jurisdiction of the district court in the case. Finally the Court held that carrying slaves from a foreign country to a possession of that country falls within the language of the acts of 1800 and 1818. In the case of the *Constitution* the Court ruled that evidence contained in the information justified the condemnation of the vessel; however, in the case of the *Merino* and the *Louisa* the Court found that the evidence did not justify the condemnation and thus reversed the decision of the district court and remitted the cases to the court "with directions to permit the libellants to amend, it being obvious to the court, from the evidence, that the negroes taken on board of those vessels were transported for the purpose of their being held to service." The Alabama district court reaffirmed its condemnation of the *Merino* and the *Louisa*.[85]

The following year the House requested the record of the district courts' disposition of the Africans. Jeremiah Austell supplied district attorney Henry Hitchcock with the disposition records, indicating that Daniel Walden, who received fifty-four blacks after the apportionment, sold them at auction to the highest bidder, bought twenty-three himself and carried them to New Orleans, and sold the balance to citizens of the United States. The court ordered the slaves in the schooners *Louisa* and *Merino* sold, and local citizens purchased them except for four who were purchased by Allen Glover of Demopolis and James Wade of Claiborne.[86]

Not satisfied with the information supplied, the House Committee on the Suppression of the Slave Trade on March 2 requested permission from the House to be authorized "if necessary to the discharge of their duty, to send for persons and papers." In explaining the resolution, Charles F. Mercer of Virginia said it "would probably . . . be the means of detecting one of the most stupendous frauds which had ever received the inadvertant [*sic*] sanction of a Court of Justice, anywhere, at any time." The House approved the motion. Almost three months later on May 22 Mercer recommended to the House that the committee be discharged from the further consideration of the several documents and that the documents be referred to the President. After a brief objection to sending the documents to the executive, the House concurred in the resolution.[87]

During the committee's process of acquiring and studying the documents, Lieutenant M'Keever petitioned Congress for additional compensation of $3,000 for expenses he incurred in appearing before the various courts trying the cases of the *Merino* and *Louisa*. M'Keever stated that the proceeds from the slaves of the two vessels were $8,830.50, of which one half, or $4,415.25, was distributed among the captors, his share coming to $419.95. The Act of 1819 permitted the proceeds to be distributed among the crew as if the vessel were a prize taken from an enemy. The specific distribution was spelled out in an act of 1800 which granted to sea lieutenants two-twentieths of the proceeds. The Committee on Naval Affairs approved the petition and reported a bill which Congress approved in February 1827. Final congressional action on the Alabama cases occurred in 1828, when as part of a bill appropriating $30,000 for the suppression of the slave trade pursuant to the Act of 1819, Congress permitted the Secretary of the Navy to use part of the money to pay the claim of the administrator of the estate of Taliaferro Livingston, late marshal for the District of Alabama, for the maintenance of the Africans captured in 1818 with the proviso that sums received by Livingston for the hire of the Africans and for the labor performed for him by the Africans should be deducted.[88]

Hardly had the Act of 1818 gone into effect when the House on November 26 and the Senate on December 15, 1818, referred resolutions to appropriate committees to determine if the act needed further amendments or if additional legislation were needed.[89] While the committees were investigating the topic, a series of memorials flowed into Congress requesting revision of the 1818 act. Between December 21 and February 12, Congress received and read twelve memorials from New York, Pennsylvania, Rhode Island, Connecticut, Massachusetts, and New Jersey. Although the content of the Senate memorials is unknown, the one received by the House specifically objected to Section 5 of the 1818 act under which the memorial claimed "persons of color have been illegally introduced into the United States, and have been seized and sold as slaves."[90]

On January 12 Representative Mercer, in the course of introducing a resolution, reported that in a publication which he had seen

the names were given of at least twenty vessels fitted out in the ports of the United States for the obvious purpose of carrying on the slave trade. Appeals had been taken from the decisions which had been made by the inferior tribunals in some of these cases, and the names of American houses and American citizens engaged in this detestable traffic, were to be found on the records of the British court.

Mercer's resolution, which the House approved, requested information from the Secretary of the Navy. The House passed a second resolution which requested similar information from the Secretary of the Treasury. The Secretary of the Navy reported on the 12th; the Treasurer on the 21st. Before the House received the report of the Secretary of the Treasury on January 13, the committee reported a bill. The Senate committee reported one on February 8.[91] The House debated its version on March 1. The *Annals* indicated that much debate arose on the different features of the bill but reported very little of the actual debate. Two changes were made: one a potentially crippling provision that a navy commander should bring a vessel alleged to be in violation of the act to the ports of the state or territory to which the vessel belonged; the second instituted the death penalty for importing an African in violation of the act. With the two amendments the bill passed the House 57 to 45.[92] The Senate received the House version on the 2nd and, after striking the death penalty amendment, approved the bill the same day. The House accepted the change and the bill became law on March 3.[93]

The act provided sufficient authority and incentives to insure that the trade could be dealt with if the appropriate administrative and judicial machinery of government were willing to act. The legislation authorized the President to use naval vessels on any of the coasts of the states or territories, in Africa or elsewhere

where he may judge attempts may be made to carry on the slave trade by citizens or residents of the United States . . . and to instruct and direct the commanders of all armed vessels of the United States to seize, take, and bring into any port of the United States, all ships or vessels of the United States, wheresoever found, which may have taken on board, or which may be intended for the purpose of taking on board, or of transporting, or may have transported, any negro, mulatto, or person of color,

in violation of previous acts.

Numerous incentives were offered:

1. The officers and men would receive half the proceeds from the sale of the vessels, furniture, and apparel to be distributed as in the case of prizes.
2. A bounty of $25 would be paid to the officers and crews of commissioned vessels for each black, mulatto, or person of color who was delivered to the marshal or agent duly appointed to receive them.
3. Any citizen who should lodge an information with the district attorney would receive the normal portion of the penalties and in addition a bounty of $50 for each black, mulatto, or person of color delivered into the custody of the marshal.

To avoid permitting the illegally imported Africans from being sold into slavery, the act contained detailed instructions on the disposition of the blacks. The act instructed commissioned vessel commanders to turn over to the marshal of the district every African found on board a seized vessel if brought into the United States or if elsewhere to such person or persons as the President should appoint and also transmit to the President a descriptive list of such persons. The law permitted the President to

make such regulations and arrangements, as he may deem expedient for the safekeeping, support, and removal beyond the limits of the United States, of all such negroes, mulattoes, or persons of color, as may be so delivered and brought within their jurisdiction: And to appoint a proper person or persons, residing upon the coast of Africa, as agent or agents for receiving the negroes, mulattoes, or persons of color. . . .

Finally, the act appropriated $100,000 to carry the law into effect.[94]

Two cases arose almost immediately, one in Georgia and the second in South Carolina. In Georgia the collector seized a number of Africans and turned them over to the state's agent in accordance with a state act of 1817. The state law provided that the Governor should sell such persons after giving sixty days notice, provided

that if previous to the sale . . . the society for the colonization of free persons of color within the United States, will undertake to transport them to Africa . . . and shall likewise pay to his excellency the Governor all expenses incurred by the state, since they have been captured and condemned, his excellency the Governor, is authorized and requested to aid in promoting the benevolent view of said society, in such manner as he may deem expedient.[95]

Prior to the day of sale, the deputy marshal, acting on orders from the district judge, arrested the Africans from the state's agent. At the same time Reverend William Meade, agent of the Colonization Society, "arrived, clothed with full power to comply with the conditions of the law, and again to transport them to their native country." In light of these events, the Governor determined not to sell the blacks but to hold them until the court's final decree should be made and if they were returned to his jurisdiction to deliver them to the Colonization Society.[96]

Thomas Parker, district attorney of South Carolina, reported to the Secretary of State in July that the marshal was now in possession of four illegally imported blacks. He indicated that the blacks were abandoned "in fright by the Person who had been in possession" and thus no one could be tried or "a verdict arrived at to justify the marshal in taking possession of them." Parker indicated that while the blacks were in confinement, an attorney for one of the seizors persuaded Carnaghan, the seizor for the United States, to apply to a state judge for a sale of the said blacks as slaves. The state judge, unaware of the 1819 act, ordered the blacks to be sold as slaves and the money divided according to certain state acts. Parker convinced the state's attorney that the order could not be carried out, so the attorney put the blacks into custody of the marshal. Parker concluded that if the request for compensation of the marshal were not complied with, the marshal might refuse to act in the future.[97]

Even with the new legislation the illegal activity appeared to reach new heights in 1819. Before Congress acted, the Secretary of State received a report indicating that a company started from Huntsville, Alabama, to Galveston and Trinity Bay to purchase Africans which were imported into that area. William Tate asserted that he had "seen Africans here that I believe have been brought from that unhappy country within twelve months past." James Tallmadge declared in the House in February 1819 that about 14,000 slaves "have been brought into our country this last year." Two other estimates placed the numbers at 13,000 and 15,000 respectively.[98]

In addition, as part of his charge to federal grand juries in Boston and Providence in October and November 1819, Associate Justice Joseph Story devoted considerable attention to the slave trade. After outlining the criminal legislation, Story commented,

It might well be supposed that the slave trade would in practice be extinguished. . . . But unfortunately the case is far otherwise. We have but too many melancholy proofs from unquestionable sources, that it is still carried on with all the implacable ferocity and insatiable rapacity of former times.

He asserted that Americans were involved:

They throng to the coasts of Africa under the stained flags of Spain and Portugal, sometimes selling abroad "their cargoes of despair," and sometimes bringing them into some of our southern ports, and there, under the forms of the law, defeating the purposes of the law itself, and legalizing their inhuman but profitable adventures.[99]

Due in part to the new legislation, but primarily because of the efforts to suppress piracy, government officials brought numerous libels against vessels into the federal courts for condemnation proceedings during 1819. The Georgia district court heard six cases. The three cases decided in 1819 resulted in the restoration of the vessels and slaves.[100] At New Orleans, where three vessels were libeled, the district attorney dropped two of the prosecutions, and the court ordered the vessel condemned and sold in the third. In the two cases that were not prosecuted, the captains of the vessels brought two and five slaves respectively, without knowledge of the owners of the vessel and unaware of the illegality of the slaves. The Secretary of State with the concurrence of the President ordered that the suits not be prosecuted.[101] The Rhode Island district attorney successfully prosecuted the brig *Martha* under the Act of 1818 for transporting slaves from Africa to the West Indies. The attorney dropped a second prosecution against the vessel under the Act of 1819.[102] The President ordered a libel against the schooner *Echo* in the South Carolina district court *nolle prosequied*.[103] In several ways the year 1820 could be considered the capstone for activity in the attempt to suppress the slave trade. The President set about implementing the Act of 1819; numerous seizures occurred; several federal officials were accused of complicity in the illegal trade; and Congress made engaging in the slave trade an act of piracy.

Late in 1819 the President asked both the Attorney General and the Secretary of the Treasury if the Act of 1819 permitted the President to use part of the $100,000 appropriation to purchase land in Africa and carpenters tools for making a settlement or merely paying for transportation to Africa. The Attorney General was of the opinion that the President could not use the money for the above purposes nor pay the salary and expenses of transporting an agent from this country to Africa. He felt that Congress should make the President's powers clearer. William Crawford, Secretary of the Treasury, on the other hand, felt the President could do all the above things without clarification from Congress. The President appointed agents and dispatched them to Africa to receive any persons who might be sent there under the act. On December 17 the President stated his interpretation of the act with the intent that Congress, if it differed, could amend the act. Congress did not act; thus, it tacitly approved of the President's course of action.[104]

The House on December 31 requested the Secretary of the Navy and the Secretary of the Treasury to lay before the House copies of communications since 1816 concerning the illicit introduction of slaves and a statement of the measures each adopted to prevent the same. William Crawford responded on the 11th of January and revealed that "from an examination of the records of this office, that no particular instructions have ever been given, by the Secretary of the Treasury, under the original or supplementary acts prohibiting the introduction of slaves into the United States." He added that the

general practice of the Department has been to confine its attention, and to limit its instructions, to cases arising under the revenue laws, except where, by direction of the President of the United States, the superintendence of other laws has been specially required of it. No such duty has, in relation to the laws prohibiting the introduction of slaves into the United States, been required of the Secretary of the Treasury.[105]

The report should not have evoked surprise. The administrative machinery of the period was small and inefficiently organized. The Secretary of State gave instructions to district attorneys and marshals; the Secretary of the Treasury, to collectors of the revenue. Although the executive encouraged cooperation, it was not guaranteed. The problems Ellery encountered both with the district attorney and other collectors in Rhode Island were more typical than atypical. No Justice Department existed to oversee enforcement of federal criminal statutes. In areas where the people approved of the illicit traffic, a single marshal with a few deputies had the near impossible task of trying to enforce the law.

Congress, in its accustomed deliberative fashion, tried attacking the problem through resolutions and additional legislation. Representative John A. Cuthbert of Georgia introduced on January 19th a resolution "that the Committee on the Slave Trade be instructed to inquire into the expediency of establishing a registry of slaves, more effectually to prevent

the importation of slaves into the United States or the territories thereof.''
Cuthbert indicated that with the extensive coast lines "slave ships might frequently elude the vigilance of the public vessels, and throw their cargoes
amongst our black population, and thus escaping the possibility of being
discovered. . . . '' After a brief objection by John Randolph to granting
additional powers to the national government, the House approved the
resolution. The committee never reported on the resolution.[106]

Later in the session Congress adopted the approach of additional
legislation. On April 6th the Senate commenced considering a bill to
continue in force the act on piracy. On the 16th the Senate approved the bill
and sent it to the House. On May 8th Representative Mercer made a report
from the committee on the subject of the slave trade, recommending the
incorporation of The American Society for Colonizing the Free People of
Color of the United States and an amendment to the piracy bill to define participation in the slave trade as piracy and thus require the death penalty upon
conviction. The House approved the bill with the amendment on May 11;
the Senate concurred on the 13th. Thus the final major piece of criminal
legislation had been passed. Whether the death penalty would deter the
slave trade any more than imprisonment would be revealed later.[107]

While Congress considered the various proposals on suppressing the slave
trade, the President received charges against General D. B. Mitchell, agent
of the United States to the Creek Indians and former Governor of Georgia.
On the 19th and 20th of January, Secretary of State John Quincy Adams
received letters from John Clark, then Governor of Georgia, enclosing
copies of resolutions approved by the Georgia legislature in 1818 and
sundry papers relating to allegations against Mitchell. Adams replied on
March 1 that the papers had been presented to the President and that the
President immediately requested the Secretary of War[108] to investigate the
charges, but the President did not desire to communicate the charges to
Congress at that time. Adams also expressed appreciation from the President for the concern of the state of Georgia about the unlawful entry of
Africans through Savannah. The President, Adams said, was unaware of
the resolutions until receipt of the Governor's letters.[109]

Before Adams responded to Governor Clark he had instructed District
Attorney R. W. Habersham of Georgia, in compliance with the third of the
Georgia resolutions, to

commence the prosecution of every person (against whom testimony adequate to
conviction may be obtainable) or in any way connected with this traffic, or who has
violated the Laws of the United States, by importing, holding, selling, or disposing
of any of the African slaves referred to in the said Resolution.

Adams also told Habersham to communicate with the Governor and use
any evidence he might have and then transmit to the Department of State

the following information: "What is their present condition, in whose possession they are, and what proceedings have been had in the Admiralty Court concerning them." Adams concluded that the President wished "that if they can be recovered, they may be delivered into the custody of the Marshal of the District to be sent to Africa at the expense of the United States and conformably to the provisions of the Laws of the United States."[110]

Habersham responded on March 24 stating that he had contacted the Governor to obtain his support. "The slaves alluded to in the resolutions," he surmised, were "those composing the three Cargoes of the 'Syrena', 'Poltina' and 'Tentative.' " The three vessels were engaged in the slave trade under Spanish authorization and captured by privateers of various South American countries and, while in possession of the captors, were brought by United States' men of war into the district. Claims were filed in admiralty in favor of the original Spanish owners, and the property was finally decreed to them. The blacks were distributed to various people in the vicinity to be be employed on their plantations. In the case of the *Syrena* and the *Tentative*, the court had ordered the slaves turned over to the marshal by April 27. Habersham expected the slaves shortly to be removed from the United States. The district attorney also referred to the Africans introduced into the country by William Bowen and asserted that if sufficient evidence were produced, he would prosecute. The marshal, Habersham reported, had possession of the blacks, one believed to be part of the cargo of the *Tentative* and two whom the marshal had taken from a male resident of the upper part of the state, who now was in the penitentiary.[111]

Although the exchange quieted for a time, on May 10 the grand jury for the federal circuit court issued a general presentment stating their "desire . . . not . . . to cast a shade on the character of any public servant" but feeling that it was their duty

to state that there has been a flagrant violation of the Law of the United States in the introduction of a number of African Negroes into this State; that the perpetrators of this Crime have not been brought to justice and that it now appears from the operation of the Law of the United States limiting the time at which prosecution in such cases should commence, all hope of justice in this case is at an end. Whether the fault in the present instance is in the Law or its execution we do not pretend to determine, but we confess that we feel indignant at the violation of a law whose object is to preserve from shame the character of our country, and we do think the subject worthy of the attention of Congress, as well as the heads of department of the United States government.[112]

Habersham submitted a copy of the grand jury presentment along with correspondence with Governor Clark and evidence assembled against Mitchell and Bowen to the Secretary of State on June 8. The enclosures revealed that Habersham commenced his investigation of Bowen on August 24, 1819, on which date he wrote William McIntosh, Collector of Brunswick, to furnish information and affidavits that would justify instigating a prosecution. Habersham indicated that he had found no papers in his office relative to Bowen except a demand from Bowen to McIntosh to deliver the blacks to McIntosh and a reply from McIntosh. In a letter to Habersham dated December 19, Governor Clark encouraged the district attorney to institute a prosecution against Bowen and Mitchell. The Governor indicated that he possessed key evidence. The Governor also recommended that the prosecution occur in Milledgeville instead of Savannah since witnesses could be procured with less trouble and more certainty at the former location. After assembling the evidence, Habersham wrote the Governor on February 2, enclosing a summary of the evidence and the possibilities of prosecution. Habersham's summary reveals the defects of the law and the difficulty of successfully prosecuting violators.[113]

Captain William Bowen obtained by purchase or otherwise in East Florida a number of Africans and adopted the necessary means to have them forwarded to the Creek nation. While being transported through Georgia, specifically Camden County, a bill of sale for forty-five of the blacks was executed transferring ownership to Gables, an Indian. The sale appeared to have been executed merely to disguise the nature of the transaction. From a permit granted by General Mitchell, it appeared that Bowen intended the blacks merely for settlement in the Alabama territory and not for sale. From the evidence it did not appear how the blacks were brought into the United States, either by boat or other vessel or by land, and there was no evidence of Bowen's intent to sell them. The blacks reached the agency, some in November 1817 and some in January 1818. Habersham then compared the available evidence with the Act of 1807. Based on the facts, he dismissed Sections 2, 3, 7, 8, 9, and 10, leaving 1, 4, 5, and 6. Since Section 1 carried no criminal penalties, it was useless to prosecute for its violation. Section 6 punished purchasers or sellers of blacks which had been brought into the United States. Because of the transfer of ownership there was no actual sale or purchase of the blacks after they had been brought within the jurisdiction of the United States, thus the section did not apply. Section 5 required that the person must not only bring in slaves with the intent to sell but also must have sold them. It did not appear that Bowen had made such a sale. Thus only Section 4 offered possibilities of prosecution. The section required that if any citizen of the United States should, from and after the first day of January 1801, "take on board, receive or transport, from any of the coasts or kingdoms of Africa, or from any other foreign kingdom, place, or country," any black for the "purpose of selling them in any port or place within the jurisdiction of the United States as slaves, or to be held to service or labor, or shall be in any way aiding or abetting therein," such citizen "shall severally forfeit and pay five thousand dollars." Habersham indicated that all the requisite evidence required by this section except two could be met. The two exceptions were the taking on board or transporting in a ship or vessel, from Florida into the United States or the aiding or abetting therein, and the purpose to sell. It might be proved that a vessel was employed to cross the St. Mary's River within the meaning of the act. It would be most difficult to prove the intention of selling blacks within the jurisdiction of the United States. Habersham concluded the analysis of the 1807 act with a comment that the "act certainly appears insufficient for the purpose of correcting the evil."[114]

He pointed out that a subsequent Congress had sought to remedy the defects and thus passed an act on April 20, 1818. The 1818 act repealed the first six sections of the Act of 1807. Section 6 of the 1818 act provided requirements identical to Section 4 of the Act of 1807 except that the punishment had been altered to a fine

not exceeding ten thousand dollars nor less than one thousand dollars, one moiety to the use of the United States, and the other to the use of the person or persons who shall sue for such forfeiture, and prosecute the same to effect; and, moreover, shall suffer imprisonment for a term not exceeding seven years nor less than three years.

Habersham felt Bowen's case would fit the section. He pointed out, however, that the importation had occurred before the act was passed, and thus a prosecution would be *ex post facto*. He also commented that the 1818 act permitted prosecutions to be completed under the 1807 act although it had repealed the first six sections.[115]

During the next several months Habersham and Clark corresponded concerning the evidence the Governor had secured and the desire by Habersham to have the originals of the affidavits rather than copies. On May 8 the Governor turned the originals over to Habersham. Two days later Habersham laid the evidence before the circuit court judges. The judges felt that the testimony submitted would not permit prosecution under the Act of 1807. Even if the case could be brought within the provisions of the Act of 1807, offences committed against the act had to be prosecuted within two years. Thus the statute of limitations contained in the act prevented prosecution at this late date.[116]

While the Secretary of State and the district attorney were concerned with Georgia's Governor, Monroe asked Attorney General William Wirt for an opinion on the manner of disposing of blacks unlawfully brought into the United States prior to the act of March 3, 1819. Responding on February 2, 1820, Wirt believed that proceedings could be instituted against the blacks under the act through a prosecution by information instituted by the district attorney. If it should be ascertained by the verdict of a jury that such negro &c have been brought in contrary to the true intent and meaning of the acts &c then the court shall direct the Marshal of the said district to take the said negroes &c into his custody for safe keeping subject to the order of the President &c.

Wirt also contended that a prosecution should be instituted against General Mitchell. "Such a prosecution," Wirt felt, "will give him an opportunity of acquitting himself, if innocent, and will inflict a just punishment on him, if guilty." Finally Wirt advised the President to submit the Governor's communication to Congress.[117]

On March 8, 1820, the vessel *Isabella* [*Isabelita*] was libeled for a violation of the slave trade in the admiralty court of the district of South Carolina. The source of Bowen's slaves was now revealed. The *Isabelita* was a Spanish vessel owned by Juan Madrazo of Havana. The vessel was dispatched on a slave trading voyage to Africa in 1817. On her return voyage she was captured by the *Successor* under the piratical flag of Commodore Aury, commanded by one Moore, an American citizen. The vessel and slaves were carried to Amelia Island, and there condemned by the pretended Court of Admiralty and sold, under its authority, by the prize-agent Louis Segallis to William Bowen. The South Carolina court ordered the vessel restored to Madrazo. In Georgia, Madrazo entered a libel for the slaves. The Governor of the state entered an information for the slaves. Bowen entered in a claim in both cases. The Georgia district court dismissed the claims of Bowen and the libel of Madrazo, decreeing that the slaves should be delivered to the Governor. Appeals were immediately entered.[118]

Later in the year Wirt, after reviewing the evidence assembled by the district attorney, reported to the President that he perused the documents. Finally on January 21, 1821, Wirt submitted a comprehensive opinion both on the law and the facts of the case. Wirt concluded that Mitchell was "guilty of having prostituted his powers, as agent for Indian affairs at the Creek agency, to the purpose of aiding and assisting in a conscious breach of the act of Congress of 1807, in prohibition of the slave trade—and this from mercenary motives." At the request of the Senate, Wirt's report along with the opinion of February 2 were turned over to Congress on May 6, 1822.[119]

In 1823 the circuit court of Georgia dismissed the libel and claim of the Governor and directed restitution to the libelant. From the circuit court the case went to the Supreme Court. Counsel for Georgia, John M. Berrien, contended that the circuit court did not have jurisdiction since the case involved jurisdiction over the state of Georgia and would thus violate the Eleventh Amendment. Chief Justice Marshall, in an 1828 opinion of the court, agreed with the state, reversed so much of the decision of the circuit court as restored the slaves to Madrazo, but affirmed that portion of the decision dismissing the claim of Bowen.[120]

In conformity to the Act of 1819, during 1820 and 1821 the navy dis-

patched several vessels to the coasts of Africa. In addition the Secretary of
the Navy ordered naval vessels to closely watch the St. Mary's area to prevent illegal smuggling. The *Cyane*, under command of Captain Edward
Trenchard, sailed from the United States in January 1820; the corvette
Horney, under Captain George C. Reed, in June 1820; the corvette *John
Adams*, under Captain H. S. Wadsworth, July 18, 1820; the *Alligator*,
under Captain R. F. Stockton, April 1821; and the schooner *Shark*, under
Captain M. C. Perry, August 1821. Reports from the *Cyane* began
appearing in the newspapers of the United States in May. The *Cyane*
reported capturing four vessels—the schooners *Plattsburg*, *Science*
(formerly a pilot boat), *Endymion*, and *Esperanza*—which it sent to New
York where they arrived in May. The *Cyane* also reported that "the number
of vessels engaged in this inhuman traffic is incredible; not less than 200 at
present on the coast, all of them fast sailers, well manned and armed, and, I
am sorry to add, many of them owned by Americans, although under
foreign flags."[121]

The district court in New York condemned the schooners *Plattsburg*,
Science, *Endymion*, and *Esperanza* in 1821. Juan Marino, a Spanish merchant, appealed the case of the *Plattsburg* to the circuit court, which
affirmed the lower court's ruling, and thence to the Surpeme Court. The
issue in the appeal was his claim that he was owner of the vessel and thus
was engaged in a trade that was legal under the laws of Spain. Story,
speaking for the Court, upheld the condemnation, maintaining that it was
not necessary that the equipments for the voyage should be completed. It
was sufficient if any preparations had been made for the unlawful purpose.
Story also stated that under the Slave Trade Act of 1794 the forfeiture
attaches where the original voyage was commenced in the United States;
whether the vessel belonged to citizens or foreigners and whether the act was
done *suo jure* or by an agent for the benefit of another person who was not
a citizen or resident of the United States. The court had on a number of
occasions approached the issue of the timing of forfeitures. In an opinion
written by John Marshall in 1806 in the case of *The United States* vs.
Grundy and Thornburgh, Marshall distinguished between forfeiture at
common law, where nothing rests in the government until some legal step
had been taken for the assertion of its rights, and forfeitures accruing under
the statute, where the thing forfeited may vest immediately or on the
performance of a specific act. The majority of the court eight years later in
the case of *The United States* v. *1960 Bags of Coffee* ruled that the Non-
Intercourse Act of 1809 declared "that the forfeiture shall take place upon
the commission of the offense." Story entered a dissent, concurred in by
two other justices. Story was worried that if

the secret taint of forfeiture be indissolubly attached to the property, so that at any
time and under any circumstance with the limitation of law the United States may

enforce their right against innocent purchasers, it is easy to forsee that great embarrassments will arise to the commercial interests of the country; and no men, whatever may be his caution or diligence, can guard himself from injury and perhaps ruin.

Story's reversal was consistent with his strong antislavery feeling.[122]

The district attorney brought charges against six crewmen. At the time the clerk of the New York circuit court began to administer the oath to the grand jury, one of the six, Eugene Malibran, came into court and challenged the array, claiming that the "venire under and by virtue of which the Grand Inquest was summoned and is returned" was not made according to law. The court immediately, without giving an opinion on the challenge, discharged the grand jury and the petit jury which had been summoned and ordered the marshal to summon a new grand jury for the 11th.[123]

The new grand jury proceeded to indict six persons for violating the slave trade, among which were Eugene Malibran and Alex M'Kim Andrews, commander of the schooner *Endymion*. After the prosecution and the defense presented the evidence in Malibran's case, the judges charged the jury to acquit the defendant, which the jury did without leaving the court room. The jury in the case of Andrews found the defendant guilty, but the defense objected to the verdict on account of "one of the jurors being seized with fits, which prevents his attendance in Court at the giving of the verdict." The court ordered a new trial. Juries did not convict either Andrews or the other four.[124]

The navy sent the captain of the *Science*, Adolph Lacoste, and the captain of the *Plattsburg*, Joseph F. Smith, to Boston where the grand jury indicted them for violating Sections 2 and 3 of the Act of 1818. Juries convicted both, and the court sentenced them to five years in prison and fined each one $3,000. President Monroe pardoned both men in 1822.[125]

As additional vessels began arriving from Africa, other questions arose. The marshal of Massachusetts inquired of the Secretary of State if he should pay bills for pilotage, custody, dockage, and other necessary charges "on their being examined and approved by the Court"; and he wondered if he would have them allowed in his account in case of an acquittal. Adams replied a month later that the President did not "consider the payment by the marshals of the district the expenses attending the sending in and prosecution of vessels suspected of having been engaged in the slave trade, as authorized by the Law, or that they can be allowed in his accounts on the event of the acquittal of the vessel." Although seemingly insignificant, with the low pay of the marshals, the Presidential ruling made the administration of the act precarious.[126]

The Georgia court was active throughout the year with slave trade cases. The court ordered the *Montevediano*, libeled on May 23, 1820, forfeited in

January 1821; and the court ordered the *Anna Maria*, libeled in August, forfeited in December. Finally the revenue cutter *Dallas* brought a brig under the Artigian flag—the *General Ramirez*—into Savannah with 270 Africans on board.[127]

Shortly after the Georgia district court had rendered its decision in the case of the *Ramirez*, the Massachusetts district court became involved with an equally important and more explosive suit. Lt. R. F. Stockton, commander of the schooner *Alligator*, in the course of patrolling the coast of Africa from May to July 1821, captured four French vessels. Stockton placed prize crews aboard the vessels. Three were recaptured from the prize crew, but the fourth, the *Jeune Eugenie*, arrived at Boston and was libeled in the district court. The French consul immediately filed a protest. By fall the President was sufficiently concerned to suggest to Daniel Brent, chief clerk of the State Department, that the United States "should disclaim all rights to seize foreign vessels, of any & every nation, engaged in the slave trade and forbear to seize those sailing under foreign flags, until an arrangement on that point is made with foreign powers." Concerning Stockton's conduct, the President in the same letter felt that since Lt. Stockton "was not ordered to abstain from seizing vessels which he believed to be American, sailing under foreign flags, I do not think, as at present advised, that he ought to be censured or a Court of inquiry ordered on him." Monroe also expressed a willingness to "give the vessel to the Consul of France. . . ."[128]

After a careful reading of the Act of 1819 the President wrote Brent on the 17th of September that the Act authorized the President "to cause to be seized, &c. all ships of the United States, & of the United States only." Later, after receipt of a letter from Attorney General William Wirt, the President told Brent that public vessels should be able to demand a view of a ship's papers to determine that the flag was not fraudulently assumed.

My own view as heretofore given is not at variance with this, tho' in my anxiety to avoid countenancing in any manner, the British doctrine respecting the right of search, & to avoid also giving just cause of offence to any foreign power, this particular measure did not occur to me. A general order, or instruction, to this effect, to the commanders of vessels cruising on the African coast, would I think be proper. . . .[129]

The case of the *Jeune Eugenie* raised three important questions: first, whether she was an American vessel; second, whether she was engaged in the slave trade; and third, whether if she were French and engaged in the slave trade, the court was bound to restore the property to France. The district court ordered the vessel restored, whereupon the United States appealed to the circuit court with Justice Joseph Story presiding. From the evidence it appeared that the ship was built in the United States, was engaged in the slave trade, but was owned by Raibaud and Labatut, residents of the French Island of Guadeloupe. Daniel Webster, who was assisting District Attorney George Blake, made a unique plea, which Story accepted, that the slave trade was contrary to the law of nations and thus that the court might rightfully condemn the vessel for an infraction of that law. The slave trade violated the law of nations because it "was a violation of the law of nature." It was contrary to the law of nature "because it instigated and encouraged the most atrocious crimes and barbarities, and presented an insurmountable barrier to the advancement of civilization and virtue in that country which was its theater."[130] Although Story rejected the French claim because the President wanted the ship returned to the French, Story ordered the vessel turned over to the French consul.[131] Lt. Stockton precipitated another international incident later in the year. In November 1821 the *Alligator*, after being fired upon by a strange vessel, returned the fire and eventually captured her. Lt. Stockton sent the *Marianna Flora* a Portuguese slaver, to Boston for adjudication. The Portuguese *charge d'affaires*[132] immediately filed a protest.

Lt. Stockton proceeded against the *Marianna Flora* before the district court on the charge of piractical aggression. Upon hearing the cause, the district court ordered the vessel restored and subsequently awarded damages amounting to $19,675 for the act of sending in the ship for adjudication and the consequent detention. Stockton appealed to the circuit court on both decrees. Upon request of the government and with the consent of the libelants, the district court restored the ship and cargo. The further proceedings pertained only to the damages, and the circuit court reversed the award of the district court. Thereupon an appeal was taken to the Supreme Court where in 1826 the Court upheld the circuit court ruling.[133]

During 1821 the government libeled three other ships for violations of the slave trade. The South Carolina district court dismissed the libel against the brig *Francis F. Johnson* in April—although the court certified probable cause. The President ordered a *nolle prosequi* entered in two cases—one the schooner *Coza*, seized by the collector of the customs at Hampton and libeled in the district court for the Eastern District of Virginia, and the sloop *Susan*, libeled in the district court of Louisiana for a defect in the ship's papers in relation to certain blacks conveyed on board the sloop from Pensacola to New Orleans. In the latter case the President indicated that there appeared to have been reasonable grounds for the seizure and made it a condition of the discontinuance that the claimants of the *Susan* pay the costs.[134]

John Low and Robert Hoy were arrested in Georgia on a charge of holding, buying, or selling an illegally imported African. After being bailed in August, the court released them in December when no presentment was issued against them. In Pennsylvania the grand jury indicted Henry

Kennedy for serving on board a vessel employed in transporting a slave from St. Thomas to Cuba. Kennedy appeared to be innocent of intentional violation of the law, and the jury acquitted him.[135]

The House in 1822 continued to be concerned with the inefficiency of the United States' attempts to suppress the slave trade. On January 15 the House instructed the Committee on the Suppression of the Slave Trade to inquire "whether the laws of the United States prohibiting the traffic in slaves have been duly executed; also into the general operation thereof, and, if any defects exist in those laws, to suggest adequate remedies therefor. . . ." On April 12 Representative Joel R. Poinsett reported for the committee, indicating that a bare majority had agreed to make the report. He personally opposed the recommendation of the committee which he "deemed to be injurious to the best interest of the country."[136]

After reviewing the measures taken under the Acts of 1819 and 1820, the report revealed that the committee had found it impossible

to measure with precision the effect produced upon the American branch of the slave trade by the laws above mentioned, and the seizures under them. They are unable to state whether those American merchants, the American capital and seamen, which heretofore aided in this traffic have abandoned it altogether, or have sought shelter under the flags of other nations. It is ascertained, however, that the American flag, which heretofore covered so large a portion of the slave trade has wholly disappeared from the coast of Africa. The trade, notwithstanding, increases annually, under the flags of other nations.

The committee concluded that the total suppression could "never be effected by the separate and disunited efforts of one or more States. . . ." Therefore, the committee resolved "that the President of the United States be requested to enter into such arrangements as he may deem suitable and proper, with one or more of the maritime powers of Europe, for the effectual abolition of the slave trade." The House did not act upon the report during the remainder of the session.

The House demonstrated a stiffening attitude toward the slave trade in the case of the petition of William de la Carrera. Carrera petitioned Congress to be permitted to import into Florida a number of slaves which belonged to him and which were at Havana, having been sent from Pensacola to Cuba to work on an estate of the petitioner. The Committee on the Suppression of the Slave Trade which had been referred to the petition made an unfavorable report which the House ordered to lie on the table.[137]

The House also became interested in the case of *La Pensee*, requesting the President on April 18, 1822, to lay before the House a copy of the judicial proceedings in the district court together with whatever part of the correspondence with the government of France that the executive deemed expedient. John Quincy Adams immediately requested a copy of the judicial proceedings from the district attorney, John W. Smith of Louisiana. Beverly Chew, the collector, supplied the necessary information to William H. Crawford. It indicated that the district court restored *La Pensee* to the original captors and that the vessel was assisted outside the jurisdiction of the United States.[138]

As Congressional interest waned, Secretary of State Henry Clay received reports that Americans were still involved in the trade. Thomas B. Robertson reported on April 20, 1825, from Havana that the slave trade was in the "full tide of operation." "Vessels," he said "are sent out from this port, and our own countrymen have a full share of interest in them—indeed I have heard that an agent of the government has been engaged in the business."[139]

In 1826 the last two criminal prosecutions for engaging in the slave trade came before federal courts. The district attorney in Maine committed a person for a slave trade violation, but the court discharged him. The Maryland grand jury indicted John Gooding for a violation of the slave trade. The trial which lasted into 1827 evoked some public attention. Attorney General William Wirt assisted District Attorney Nathanial Williams in the prosecution. When Wirt had to return to Washington, D. C., for the opening session of the United States Supreme Court, he wrote Henry Clay, indicating that Gooding was being defended by five of the "most eminent counsel at the bar" and "requested that other counsel be employed to assist the district attorney against the host opposed to him." The President also received considerable pressure not to prosecute Gooding. Adams recorded in his diary,

Mr. Meredith, a lawyer, of Balitmore, came with Messrs. Barney, Dorsey, Gale, and another gentleman, and renewed an application heretofore made to me, to direct a discontinuance of a prosecution in the circuit court of the United States against a man named John Gooding for a violation of the laws against slave trading. This Gooding, is what they call a respectable man—that is to say, he has been rich, had a character, and was a warm patriot in the late war with Great Britain. He has a large and helpless family, and, when going to wreck and ruin, speculated in the slave-trade to save himself, was detected, and is under prosecution. The sympathies of many worthy persons in Baltimore have thus been enlisted in his favor, and they petitioned me to arrest the prosecution against him.

Adams also mentioned in the diary that he had "received remonstances against any interposition in his behalf. . . ." The President did not intervene, but the jury acquitted Gooding.[140]

The last libel during the period occurred in 1829 when the government libeled the schooner *May Flower* and cargo in the South Carolina district court for a violation of the Act of 1807. The court dismissed the libel and assessed costs to the defendant.[141]

The enforcement pattern for the twenty-year period is bleak. The government instituted approximately six cases per year or 169 for the period 1801-1829. Of these 135 were libels against vessels which resulted in ninety-five forfeitures. Forty cases were either discontinued, dismissed, or no disposition has been found. Forty-two of the forfeitures were either reversed by a higher court or remitted under the Cuban Remission Act or by a special act of Congress. Thus only fifty-three vessels actually were forfeited. Fourteen suits for penalties were instituted which resulted in seven decisions favorable to the United States and seven cases were either dismissed, discontinued, or ended in acquittal. Finally there were twenty criminal charges brought into the courts resulting in nineteen indictments but only three convictions.

Until the Act of 1819, the Africans forfeited to the United States were turned over to state governments. The Act of 1819 corrected the folly of having the government become a slave trader by turning the Africans over to the United States to be resettled in Africa. From 1819 to 1829 Congress appropriated $284,710 for suppression of the African slave trade. An agency was established early in the 1820s in Africa to handle forfeited Africans. During the 1820s, 158 Africans were returned to Africa as a result of the law.[142]

NOTES

1. 1 *U. S. Statutes at Large*, 347-349; 2 *U. S. Statutes at Large*, 70-71; South Carolina district court, Admiralty Journal C, 1799-1800, p. 127; Charleston *City Gazette and Daily Advertiser*, October 11, 1799; Rhode Island district court, Record Book, 1790-1802; Pennsylvania district court, Minute Book, 1798-1801, pp. 355-357, 387.

2. Elizabeth Donnan, "The New England Slave Trade after the Revolution," *New England Quarterly*, 3 (January, 1930), 256.

3. George Howe, *Mount Hope: A New England Chronical* (New York, 1959), 108-109. Collins continued as collector of Bristol for twenty years. In 1802 James DeWolf defeated Federalist Sam Wardell for a seat in the House of Representatives.

4. Howe, *Mount Hope*, 109.

5. Connecticut 1774, Delaware (Constitution) 1776, Virginia 1778, Vermont 1779, Maryland 1783, New Jersey 1786, Rhode Island 1787, New York 1788, Massachusetts 1788, Pennsylvania 1788, South Carolina 1788 (temporary act, extended by additioinal acts to 1803), Georgia 1793, North Carolina 1794. W. E. B. Du Bois, *Suppression of the African Slave Trade* (reprint, New York, 1965), 223-240.

6. *Annals of Congress*, XIII:992.

7. Howe, *Mount Hope*, 122.

8. *Annals of Congress*, XII:385-386. See also Elizabeth Donnan, ed., *Documents Illustrative of the History of the Slave Trade to America* (4 vols., Washington, D. C., 1930-1935), IV:170-171.

9. *Annals of Congress*, XII:424, 467-472, 534. The fifteen negative votes were

distributed as follows: one each from New Hampshire, Vermont, Rhode Island, and Connecticut; two each from Pennyslvania and New York; three from New Jersey; and four from Massachusetts.

10. *Annals of Congress*, XII:207.

11. 2 *U. S. Statutes at Large*, 205-206.

12. *Annals of Congress*, XIII:820, 992-993.

13. Ibid., 996.

14. Ibid., 1000.

15. Ibid., 1012, 1036. The vote was 56 to 50.

16. Ibid., 223, 240-245, 255-256, 1038, 1186, 1229; 2 *U. S. Statutes at Large*, 286.

17. Du Bois, *Suppression of the African Trade*, 89-90; 2 *U. S. Statutes at Large*, 286.

18. *Annals of Congress*, XV:472-473, 522-523, 878. The Supreme Court neatly set aside the various legislative acts in a decision, *The Brigantine Amiable Lucy* v. *The United States*, in 1810. The Louisiana district court condemned the vessel under the Acts of 1803, 1804, and 1805. The government admitted that the territorial legislature never passed any law prohibiting the importation of slaves. The admission was crucial. Edward Livingston for the owners of the vessels averred that without such a law the Act of 1803 did not apply. The Supreme Court agreed and reversed the condemnation. Cranch, *Reports*, VI:330-332.

19. *Annals of Congress*, XV:274, 346, 374-375, 397, 533. See also Message of Governor Charles Pinckney to the [South Carolina] House of Representatives, November 26, 1806, in Donnan, ed., *Documents Illustrative of the Slave Trade*, IV:519-520. A third attempt by South Carolina to repeal the act opening the trade passed the House, but in the Senate the bill failed to reach a second reading by a tie vote.

20. *U. S.* v. *Brig Favorite* (1803), *U. S.* v. *Nancy* (1803), *Isaac Sherman* v. *Brig Stark* (1803), *Hail Gladding* v. *Brig Eliza* (1803), *John Earle* v. *Ship Amested* (1803), *U. S.* v. *Brig Bayard* (1803). When Benjamin Love and others libeled the ship *Amested* for wages, Judge David Barnes of the Rhode Island district court dismissed the libel ruling that the seamen by voluntarily serving aboard a slave trader forfeited all claim to any wages during the said voyage. Rhode Island district court, Record Book II, 1801-1812, August term 1803; *Ray Sand* v. *Brig Ida* (1801), *U. S.* v. *Brig Sady Nelson* (1803), *U. S.* v. *Schooner Amelia* (1803), Georgia district court, Minute Book, 1799-1809, pp. 86, 179, 189, 190; *Isaac Sherman* v. *Charming Sally* (1803), Massachusetts district court, Record Book IA, 1800-1804, pp., 199-201; *U. S.* v. *Schooner Anna* (1803), South Carolina district court, Admiralty Journal, 1798-1806, p. 62; Charleston *Courier*, April 14, 1804; Maryland circuit court, Minute Book, 1790-1811, May 4, and September 29-30, 1803 (Microcopy 931), reel 1.

21. *Elisha Morrell* v. *The Brig Providence* (1805), New York circuit court, Minute Book, 1790-1808, pp. 281-284; *U. S.* v. *Brig Mary* (1804), *U. S.* v. *Ship Rofamond* (1804), Georgia district court, Minute Book, 1799-1809, pp. 202, 232; *U. S.* v. *William B. Spooner* (1804), *U. S.* v. *José Antonia de Mendoce* (1804), South Carolina district court, Minute Book, 1789-1806, p. 345; *U. S.* v. *Thomas Browne* (1805), Pennsylvania circuit court, Criminal Case Files, Box 4, 1800-1805.

22. G. F. Dow, *Slave Ships and Slaving* (Salem, Mass., 1926), 260, 270-271; Donnan, ed., *Documents Illustrative of the Slave Trade*, IV:531-550.

23. *Annals of Congress*, XXXVII:72-77; Donnan, ed., *Documents Illustrative of the Slave Trade*, IV:504-506, 508-510, 513-516, 521-525.

24. Madison to Attorney for the District of Maine, July 17, 1805, Madison to David Howell, July 2, 1806, Madison to George Blake, July 2, 1806, and Madison to Nathan Sanford, July 2, 1806, (Microcopy M 40), reel 13, pp. 16, 130-131; Benjamin Cowell to Madison, September 27, 1806 (Microcopy M 179), reel 21.

25. *Annals of Congress*, XVI:16, 19, 114.

26. Ibid., 69, 87-88, 167, 270-274, 486-487, 626-627.

27. Ibid., 168, 174-175.

28. Ibid., 200-203.

29. Ibid., 225.

30. Ibid., 225-226.

31. Ibid., 228, 266, 477.

32. Ibid., 189-190.

33. Ibid., 233, 235, 239-240.

34. Ibid., 242.

35. Ibid., 200, 243. On December 23, 1806, the House removed the death penalty by a vote of 60 to 41, with no recorded division; and again on December 31, 1806, 63 to 53, the slave state Representatives favoring the deletion 34 to 16, the free state members opposed 37 to 29.

36. Ibid., 483. The third vote on the deletion of the death penalty occurred on February 12 and a majority approved it 67 to 48, the slave state Representatives favoring 35 to 11, the free states opposing 37 to 31, one vote not recorded.

37. Ibid., 626-627. The vote on the conference report was 63 to 49, the slave states opposing the measure 38 to 12, the free states supporting it 52 to 11. Although the lines between free and slave states generally were not drawn in the early 1800s, the four divisions in the debates over the death penalty indicated the formation of two rather strong blocks. Twenty-five House members voted a consistent antislavery position, including twenty-four from the free states and one from a slave state. Twenty-two members voted a consistent proslavery line, including eighteen from slave states and four from free states.

38. 2 *U. S. Statutes at Large*, 426-430.

39. *Annals of Congress*, XVII:1243.

40. Pennsylvania district court, Information Dockets, 1808-1839; Georgia district court, Minute Book, 1799-1809, p. 328; South Carolina district court, Admiralty Journal, 1806-1814, pp. 52, 75, 86. The *Kitty* is also cited in H. T. Catterall, ed., *Judicial Cases Concerning American Slavery* (4 vols., Washington, D.C., 1926-1936), II:291; and in U. S. District Court, South Carolina, *Reports of Cases Adjudged in the District Court of South Carolina [1792-1809]*, by the Hon. Thomas Bee (Philadelphia, 1810), 252-253.

41. Ibid., 253.

42. Hugh Thomas, *Cuba: The Pursuit of Freedom* (New York, 1971), 75-79, 87-89.

43. South Carolina circuit court, Minute Book, 1790-1809, pp. 366-368; Louisiana district court, Case Files, Box 4.

44. *Annals of Congress*, XX:34.

45. Ibid., 230, 322, 462-465.

46. 2 *U. S. Statutes at Large,* 549-550.

47. Robert Smith to A. J. Dallas, District Attorney, Pennsylvania, July 12, 1809; R. Smith to District Atorney, Georgia, July 19, 1809; R. Smith to T. Parker, District Attorney, South Carolina, July 20, 1809; R. Smith to P. Grymes, District Attorney, Louisiana, July 21, and August 16, 1809; John Graham, Department of State to T. Parker, September 26, 1809 (Microcopy M 40), reel 14, pp. 371-375, 382-384, 400.

48. R. Smith to W. C. C. Claiborne, September 12, 1809, ibid., 389.

49. Louisiana district court, Case Files, Box 4.

50. *Annals of Congress*, XX:705, 738, 1208, 1332; *American State Papers, Miscellaneous*, II:13-14.

51. Louisiana district court, Case Files, Box 4; New York district court, Certificates of Discharge.

52. See Appendix V for complete list of vessels.

53. Henry Dearborn to Albert Gallatin, July 31, 1810, with enclosures, (Microcopy M 179), reel 23.

54. Richardson, ed., *Messages and Papers of the Presidents*, I:470-471.

55. W. E. B. Du Bois, "The Enforcement of the Slave-Trade Law," American Historical Association, *Annual Report 1891 (Washington, D. C., 1892), 166; U. S. v. Schooner Donna La Costa*, Georgia circuit court, Minute Book 1806-1816, p. 270; R. Smith to Robert H. Jones, February 6, 1811, R. Smith to Allen McLane, Collector, Wilmington, Delaware, January 30, 1811 (Microcopy M 40) reel 14, pp. 7, 9.

56. Monroe to McCulloch, Collector of Customs, Baltimore, July 17, 1812, Monroe to Robert H. Jones, district attorney, North Carolina, February 29, 1812 (Microcopy M 40), reel 14, pp. 69, 195.

57. Thomas Cochran to James Monroe, December 15, 1813 (Microcopy M 179), reel 28; Monroe to Robert H. Jones, December 14, 1815 (Microcopy M 40), reel 14, p. 225; Charleston *Courier*, May 16, 1814.

58. Charleston *Courier*, May 16, 1814.

59. Pennsylvania circuit court, Criminal Case Files, Box 5, 1800-1814.

60. Ellery to the Secretary of the Treasury, July 24, August 16, and December 19, 22, 23, 1816 (Microcopy M 179), reel 35.

61. "Rhode Island Slave Trade in 1816," *Rhode Island Historical Society Proceedings*, 6 (January, 1899), 226-227.

62. Richardson, ed., *Messages and Papers of the Presidents*, II:562.

63. *Annals of Congress*, XXX:33, 233.

64. Beverly Chew to William H. Crawford, August 1, 1817, contained in *Annals of Congress*, XXXII:1789-1793.

65. U. S. Navy Department, *Letter from the Secretary of the Navy Transmitting Information in Relation to the Introduction of Slaves into the United States* (Washington, D. C., 1820), 5.

66. *Annals of Congress*, XXX:1789-1793.

67. Ibid., 1793-1794.

68. Chew to Crawford, August 30, 1817, cited in *Annals of Congress*, XXXII:1793-1795; Lt. Commandant John Porter to Secretary of Navy, June 28, 1817, U. S. Navy Department, *Letter from the Secretary of the Navy*, 5.

69. Monroe, *Writings*, VI:31.

70. George Graham, Acting Secretary of War, to Major James Bankhead, Charleston, South Carolina, November 12, 1817, and B. W. Crowninshield, Secretary

of the Navy to Commodore, J. D. Henly, November 14, 1817, cited in *Annals of Congress*, XXXII:1807-1811.

71. Message of President to Congress, January 13, 1818, *Annals of Congress*, XXXII:1801-1803.

72. December 23, 1817, Monroe, *Writings*, VI:47.

73. Governor McCarthy of Sierra Leone wrote in 1817: "The slave trade is carried on most vigorously by the Spaniards, Portuguese, Americans and French. I have had it affirmed from several quarters and do believe it to be a fact, that there is a greater number of vessels employed in that traffic than at any former period." Du Bois, *Suppression of the Slave Trade*, 112.

74. *Annals of Congress*, XXX:939-941.

75. *Annals of Congress*, XXXI:71, 74, 76-77, 109; XXXV:697-700; XXXVI:2216, 2236-2237; XXXVII:440-441, 1064-1071; XL:331-333, 928, 1147-1155; XLII:3001-3036; XLIII:625-628, 696-698, 736, appendix 73-75; Hugh Graham Soulsby, *The Right of Search and the Slave Trade in Anglo-American Relations, 1814-1862* (Baltimore, 1929), 16-18, 27-38; Smith–Thompson, Secretary of the Navy to John Quincy Adams, August 16, 1821 (Microcopy M 179), reel 51.

76. *Annals of Congress*, XXXI:74-78, 646-650.

77. Ibid., 307, 351, 358, 379, 1740.

78. Du Bois, *Suppression of the African Slave Trade*, 114-115.

79. 3 *U. S. Statutes at Large*, 450-453.

80. Opinions of the Attorney General, 1817-1832 (3 reels, National Archives, Record Group 60, Microcopy T 412), reel 1, pp. 50-53.

81. *Statement of Convictions, Executions, and Pardons*, U. S. 20th Congress, 2nd session, House Document 146 (1829), 150b; Louisiana district court, Minute Book, 1815-1819, p. 314.

82. *U. S. v. Sloop Hero*, dismissed by the court; *U. S. v. The Ship or Vessel called the Industry*, and *U. S. v. The Schooner Calypso and cargo*, discontinued; *U. S. v. Sloop Gold Huntress*, dismissed; *U. S. v. The Brig La Nouvelle Enterprise*, dismissed; *U. S. v. Sloop Thorn*, and *U. S. v. The Palacre Brig Josepha and cargo*, condemned and forfeited to the United States. Messrs. Carricabura, Arieta and Co., merchants of Havana, appealed the decision to the Supreme Court. In 1820 the Supreme Court affirmed to the district courts' decision. Prior to the appeal the blacks, in accordance with the act of Congress and a state law of 1818, were sold and the proceeds lodged in the Bank of the United States. After the appeal, Roberts, an Inspector of the Revenue; Messrs. Gardner, Meade, and Humphreys, military personnel; Benjamin Chew, collector at New Orleans; and the naval officer and surveyor of the port of New Orleans, all entered claims for the proceeds. The district court dismissed the claim of Roberts, Humphreys, Meade, and Gardner but upheld the others. The Supreme Court heard a second appeal in 1825. Justice Story, speaking for the court, upheld the district courts' dismissal of the claim of Roberts and others but reversed the decision in regards to the claim of Chew and others. The court ruled that under the Act of 1807 "all the beneficial interest vests in the United States." Louisiana district court, Minute Book, 1815-1819, pp. 298-299, 306, 319, 321, 329-331, 392; Docket Book, 1815-1820, pp. 121, 122, 127, 132, 136; Wheaton, *Reports*, V:338-359; Wheaton, *Reports*, X:312-332.

83. *Statement of Conviction, Executions, and Pardons*, U. S. 20th Congress, 2nd Session, House Document 146 (1829), p. 148, 158. See Lawrence A. Harper, *The*

English Navigation Laws: A Seventeenth-Century Experiment in Social Engineering (New York, 1939), 161-238.

84. Wheaton, *Reports*, IX:393-395.

85. Ibid., 391-408.

86. Austell to Henry Hitchcock, January 28, 1826, Hitchcock to Daniel Brent, January 6, 1826 (Microcopy M 179), reel 64.

87. Congressional Debates II:1491-1492, III:2688-2690, appendix 38-39.

88. U. S. Congress, *American State Papers, Naval,* II:704-705; 4 *U. S. Statutes at Large*, 302; 6 *U. S. Statutes at Large*, 357.

89. *Annals of Congress*, XXXIII:69, 320.

90. Ibid., 77, 88, 90, 97, 113, 162, 167, 173, 176, 189, 197, 426.

91. Ibid., 213, 442-443, 515, 540, 662; *Letter from the Secretary of the Navy Transmitting copies of the instructions which have been issued to Naval Commanders, upon the Subject of the Importation of Slaves* . . ., U.S. 15th Congress, 2nd session, House Document 84 (1819); *Letter from the Secretary of the Treasury . . . in relation to ships engaged in the Slave Trade*, U. S. 15th Congress, 2nd session, House Document 107 (1819).

92. *Annals of Congress*, XXXIII:1430-1433.

93. Ibid., 279-280.

94. 3 *U. S. Statutes at Large*, 532-534.

95. Charleston *Courier*, May 19, 1819.

96. Ibid.

97. Thomas Parker to John Quincy Adams, July 8, 1819 (Microcopy M 179), reel 45.

98. William N. Tate to Burwell Bapett, February 4, 1819 (Microcopy M 179), reel 43; Du Bois, *Suppression of the African Slave Trade*, 124.

99. Story, *Life and Letters of Joseph Story*, I:340.

100. *Mathew Larignia agent* v. *The Procas of the Tantaliva and Slaves of same*, April 1819, also *Charles Mulvey* v. *Tantaliva and Slaves*, and *John Elton* v. *Tantaliva and Slaves*; *U.S.* v. *Miguel de Castro & 95 African Slaves*, April 1819; *In re Madison in behalf of crew of the Brig Montserate*, June 1819 (restored); *Mulvey* v. *109 Africans*, June 15, 1819 (restored), Georgia district court, Minute Book, 1819-1833, pp. 1-4, 22, 28, 47.

101. *Statement of Convictions, Executions, and Pardons*, U. S. 20th Congress, 2nd session, House Document 146 (1829), p. 158; Louisiana district court, Docket Book, 1815-1820, p. 169, Minute Book, 1815-1819, p. 374; John Quincy Adams to John Dick, May 20, 1819, John Quincy Adams to C. W. Ripley, June 11, 1819, John Quincy Adams to John Dick, December 24, 1819 (Microcopy M 40) reel 15, pp. 304-329, 411; Isaac Waldrop to John F. Parrott, December 14, 1819 (Microcopy M 179) reel 46. The President also asked the Attorney General for an opinion in the case of Charles King, a noncitizen, who arrived in New Orleans with a body servant which he intended to carry back with him on his return. The Attorney General felt that King's case fell within the letter of the law as an illegal entry but was not within "its spirit or within the mischief which it was intended to prevent." (Microcopy T 412) reel 1, p. 145.

102. Rhode Island district court, Record Book 5, 1817-1820, August term 1819; *Statement of Convictions, Executions, and Pardons*, U. S. 20th Congress, 2nd session, House Document 146 (1829), 55.

103. D. Brent to Thomas Parker, October 1, 1819 (Microcopy M 40), reel 15, p. 364.

104. William Wirt to Benjamin Homans, October 14, 16, 1819 (Microcopy T 411) reel 1, pp. 67-72; *Annals of Congress*, XXXV:30-31.

105. *Annals of Congress*, XXXV:904-905; *Letter from the Secretary of the Treasury transmitting . . . information in relation to the Illicit Introduction of Slaves into the United States*, U. S. 16th Congress, 1st session, House Document 42 (1820); *Letter from the Secretary of the Navy Transmitting information in relation to the introduction of Slaves into the United States*, U. S. 16th Congress, 1st session, House Document 36 (1820).

106. *Annals of Congress*, XXXV:925-926.

107. Ibid., 693-694; XXXVI:2207-2211, 2231, 2236.

108. Secretary of War John C. Calhoun conducted a preliminary investigation of Mitchell in 1818. Edmund P. Gaines to Calhoun, January 12, 1818, David B. Mitchell to Calhoun, February 3, 1818, Gaines to Calhoun, May 1, 1819, Calhoun to Mitchell, February 26, 1820, Gaines to Calhoun March 19, 1820, Calhoun to Mitchell April 15, 1820, Jared E. Grove to Calhoun, May 19, 1820, Mitchell to Calhoun, November 21, 1820, in John C. Calhoun, *Papers*, ed., Robert Meriwether (vol. I-, Columbia, S. C.; 1959-), II:68, 117-118, IV:45, 687-688, 721-722, V:38-39, 128, 446.

109. John Quincy Adams to Governor John Clark, March 1, 1820 (Microcopy M 40), reel 16, pp. 5-6.

110. John Quincy Adams to R. W. Habersham, February 28, 1820, ibid., 3-4.

111. R. W. Habersham to John Quincy Adams, March 24, 1820 (Microcopy M 179) reel 47.

112. Georgia circuit court, Minute Book, 1816-1823, pp. 135-136.

113. R. W. Habersham to John Quincy Adams, June 8, 1820, with enclosures, (Microcopy M 179), reel 48.

114. Habersham to Clark, February 2, 1820 (Microcopy M 179), reel 48.

115. Ibid.

116. Habersham to Clark, March 24, 1820, Clark to Habersham, April 10, 1820, Habersham to Clark, April 17, 1820, Clark to Habersham, April 22, 1820, Clark to Habersham, May 8, 1820, Habersham to Clark, May 8, 1820, Habersham to Clark, May 10, 1820, (Microcopy M 179), reel 48.

117. Wirt to Monroe, February 2, 1820, (Microcopy T 412) reel 1, pp. 158-160; Wirt to John Sargent, April 24, 1822 (Microcopy T 411) reel 1, pp. 138-146.

118. South Carolina district court, Admiralty Journal, 1819-1833, pp. 76-78; Georgia district court, Minute Book, 1819-1833, p. 75.

119. Wirt to the President, October 17, 1820 (Microcopy T 411), reel 1, pp. 103-104; *American State Papers, Miscellaneous*, II:957-975.

120. Georgia circuit court, Minute Book, 1816-1823, pp. 291, 322, 363, 365; Minute Book, 1823-1834, pp. 21, 61, 83; Peters, *Reports*, (1828)I:110-135.

121. John R. Spears, *American Slave Trade: An Account of the Origin, Growth and Suppression* (London, 1901), 148-149; Charleston *Courier*, June 5, 1820; Providence *Gazette*, June 26, 1820.

122. Cranch, *Reports*, III:350-351; Cranch, *Reports*, VIII: 406; Wheaton, *Reports*, X: 133-146; Catterell, ed., *Judicial Cases Concerning Slavery*, IV:380.

123. New York circuit court, Minute Book, 1819-1828, pp. 77-78, 115, 129; Catterall, ed., *Judicial Cases Concerning Slavery*, IV:376-377.

124. New York circuit court, Minute Book, 1819-1828, pp. 99-101, 105, 207; Charleston *Courier*, September 25, 27, 1820.

125. Catterall, ed., *Judicial Cases Concerning Slavery*, IV:497; Providence *Gazette*, July 13, 1820; (Microcopy T 967) reel 1, vol. III, pp. 155-156, vol. IV, pp. 21-22.

126. James Prince to John Quincy Adams, October 6, 1820 (Microcopy M 179), reel 49; John Quincy Adams to James Prince, November 8, 1820 (Microcopy M 40), reel 16, p. 170.

127. Georgia district court, Minute Book, 1819-1837, pp. 75-78, 92, 100. For a comprehensive study of the case, see John T. Noonan, Jr., *The Antelope: Ordeal of the Recaptured Africans in the Administrations of James Monroe and John Quincy Adams* (Berkeley, 1977).

128. Spears, *American Slave Trade*, 149; Peter Duignan and Clarence Clendenen, *The United States and the African Slave Trade 1619-1862 (Stanford, 1963), 28-30;* Monroe to Daniel Brent, September 15, 1821, Monroe, *Writings*, VI:193-194.

129. Monroe to Brent, September 17, 24, 1821, Monroe, *Writings*, VI:195-202.

130. Catterall, ed., *Judicial Cases Concerning Slavery*, IV:497; Webster, *Works*, XV:278-281; Story, *Life and Letters of Joseph Story*, I:348-356.

131. Adams to Blake, November 13, 1821 (Microcopy M 40), reel 17, pp. 196-197. Adams wrote, "The President desires therefore that at the time assigned for the further argument or sooner if a suitable opportunity should present itself, you would make this suggestion," that the vessel should be delivered to the French Consul, by the court.

132. Story, *Life and Letters of Joseph Story*, I:500, 502.

133. Massachusetts district court, Docket Book, 1820-1826, p. 113, Record Book, 1821-1823, pp. 111-217; Massachusetts circuit court, Record Book 15, part I, 1822, pp. 1-113; Adams to Blake, January 4, 1822 (Microcopy M 40), reel 17, p. 231; Wheaton, *Reports*, XI:1-58.

134. South Carolina district court, Admiralty Records, 1812-1826, p. 143; John Quincy Adams to John W. Smith, October 26, 1821 (Microcopy M 40), reel 16, pp. 171, 173; Catterall, ed., *Judicial Cases Concerning Slavery*, IV:317.

135. Georgia circuit court, Minute Book, 1816-1823, pp. 216-238; Pennsylvania circuit court, Minute Book, 1820-1828, p. 9; Catterall, ed., *Judicial Cases Concerning Slavery*, IV:278.

136. *Annals of Congress*, XXXVIII:1535-1538.

137. Ibid., 1454.

138. Ibid., 1612, 1617, 1743-1744; Wirt to the President, January 22, 1822, Beverly Chew to William H. Crawford, April 24, 1822 (Microcopy M 179), reel 53; John Quincy Adams to John W. Smith, April 27, 1822 (Microcopy M 40), reel 17, p. 311; Louisiana district court, Minute Book, 1819-1825, pp. 204-205, 207-209, 219-220, 232, 234, 238, 240, 247.

139. Thomas N. Robertson to Henry Clay, April 20, 1825, Henry Clay, *Papers*, ed. James F. Hopkins (vol. 1-, Lexington, 1959-), IV:273-274.

140. Wirt to Henry Clay, January 1, 1827 (Microcopy M 179), reel 65; Wirt to Nathaniel Williams, March 19, 1827 (Microcopy T 411), reel 1, pp. 216-217; Adams, *Memoirs*, VII:305, 372; Maryland circuit court, Minute Book, 1823-1828 (Microcopy M 931), reel 1, December 19, 21, 26, 1826, January 4, 1827, May 17, 1827, May 17, 1828; Wheaton, *Reports*, (1827), XII:460-480; Catterall, ed., *Judicial Cases Concerning Slavery*, IV:74.

141. South Carolina district court, Admiralty Journal, 1826-1842, p. 57.
142. Du Bois, *Suppression of the African Slave Trade*, 122n; *American State Papers*, *Naval Affairs*, III:51-52, 77-85, 143-149, 210.

9
Conclusion

A number of factors influenced and shaped the development of federal criminal law from 1789 to 1829, among which were the structure and jurisdiction of the inferior federal courts, the definition of crimes and penalties, the court personnel, and the attitude of the general public to specific criminal acts.

The Judiciary Act of 1789 established the first inferior courts and defined their jurisdictions. The act established three types of lower courts: district courts that would be part of a circuit, district courts that were not part of a circuit, and circuit courts. The three types would remain part of the system through 1829, except for the brief interlude between 1801 and 1802 when the Judiciary Act of 1801 was in force. The 1789 act granted criminal jurisdictions to all three types of courts; however, the Crimes Act of 1790 established punishments which prevented the district courts that were part of a circuit from trying criminal cases.

The Act of 1789 prohibited an appeal to the Supreme Court in criminal cases. Initially each circuit court had three judges, two assigned from the Supreme Court and the district judge where the circuit was being held; and all but two districts were included in a circuit. Congress reduced the number of Supreme Court justices assigned to the circuits to one in 1793. The Act of 1793 stipulated that if the two circuit judges disagreed on a point of law or a punishment, the case would be carried over until the next term when a different member of the Supreme Court would be present. The short-lived Judiciary Act of 1801 increased the number of circuit judges to three and included Kentucky and Tennessee in a circuit. The second Judiciary Act of

1802 returned the system to the 1793 status with several modifications. First, the act assigned members of the Supreme Court to a specific circuit. Second, if the two circuit judges disagreed, upon the request of either part of their counsel, the point of disagreement would be certified to the Supreme Court to be finally decided. Third, Kentucky and Tennessee were excluded from the new circuit arrangement.

The second point was extremely important. From 1802 to 1829 circuit courts referred twenty-one cases to the Supreme Court for an opinion, and those opinions began to form a body of interpretation for the operation of the criminal justice system. In addition, on two of those occasions the Supreme Court, when issuing an opinion, ruled on the constitutionality of a criminal act. In the case of *The United States* v. *Zebulon Cantril* (1807), the Court, speaking through Chief Justice John Marshall, upheld a defense contention that the Act of Congress of 1798, designed to protect the Bank of the United States, was "inconsistent, repugnant, and therefore void." Thirteen years later the Court issued an opinion in the case of *The United States* v. *Smith* (1820) in which it ruled that the Piracy Act of 1819 was a constitutional exercise of the power of Congress to define and punish the crime of piracy.

There was no provision, however, for any type of referral or appeal from the district courts that were not included in a circuit. From 1802 to 1829 Congress added eighteen district courts but only one new circuit, the Seventh Circuit consisting of Kentucky, Tennessee, and Ohio. Political considerations defeated attempt after attempt to expand the number of circuits. Not until 1837 was a partial solution attempted.

The certification system remained intact until 1889 when Congress, by an act of February 6, authorized the Supreme Court to review the final judgment against any person accused of a capital crime. In 1891 Congress permitted the Supreme Court to review cases involving "infamous crimes." When the court adopted a very broad construction of "infamous," Congress deleted the right in 1897. Unfortunately the 1891 act had eliminated the certification process. After 1897 the Supreme Court was divorced from all but capital cases. The Criminal Appeals Act of 1907 finally restored that right.

Because the Supreme Court had no general appellate jurisdiction over criminal cases, the interpretation of procedural safeguards contained in the Constitution, the Bill of Rights, and in the Judiciary Act of 1789 were not consistently applied from court to court across the federal system. A number of these rights came before the courts—the right against self-incrimination, the right to a speedy trial, the use of confessions, the right to be tried by one's peers. The interpretation of what these meant was left to the circuit and district judges. It seems incredible that Congress permitted such a system to exist throughout the nineteenth century. The people had placed tremendous responsibility and trust in the federal judges.

The Judiciary Act of 1789 did not define what would constitute the criminal law of the United States. Almost immediately a controversy broke out over whether or not the common law of England, which most states had adopted, applied to federal crimes. The Supreme Court resolved the issue in 1812, with a repeated certification in 1816, when it declared that the common law had not been adopted, thus all criminal prosecutions in federal courts had to be based upon statutes. Long before the common law was excluded, Congress had adopted a number of statutes defining criminal acts and providing appropriate punishments. The crimes acts of Congress may be divided into three categories: Common crimes, defined with their punishments in 1790 and modified and expanded throughout the period; acts designed to protect federal agencies and institutions, specifically the post office and the two Banks of the United States; and laws enacted to cope with unique problems such as neutrality, Indians, and slave trade. Congress also approved from time to time temporary acts to deal with emergency or allegedly emergency situations, such as a Sedition Act of 1798, the Enforcement Act of 1809, and the various acts prohibiting trade with the enemy and the use of licenses during the War of 1812.

The machinery Congress provided for enforcing criminal laws was detailed in the Judiciary Act of 1789—judges, a district attorney for each district, and a marshal. The quality of personnel appointed to these positions was high. The deficiencies occurred in areas such as salary, compensation, and assistance. The enforcement arm of the court was the marshal, who served both the district and circuit courts in states where the two existed. Marshals not only arrested and detained violators (using state and local jails) for trial but also carried out a number of other judicial and non-judicial functions, among which were impanelling jurors, delivering processes, and taking the dicennial census. Marshals could and did employ deputies. On rare occasions the President would authorize a district attorney to employ an assistant, or an assistant would be sent from the capital. Congress realized from the start that the system was inadequate. Two solutions were apparent: one, the legislature could establish a large number of courts with their attendant officers; or two, the legislature could authorize the state courts and state officials to enforce federal laws.

Throughout the period Congress chose the second alternative. A study needs to be conducted of state court records to determine the effectiveness of this approach. The system prevailed even though a number of states refused to accept the authorization until 1842 when the Supreme Court in the case of *Prigg* v. *Pennsylvania* refused to mandate that the states had to enforce federal laws.

If Congress had adopted the first approach and established a large number of courts, it is doubtful if enforcement would have been altered significantly. The general crimes acts presented few difficulties. The public could identify with murder, perjury, counterfeiting, or forgery. The people could also support acts designed to protect the postal system and the banks of the United States. More difficult for the citizenry to accept were acts that involved ideological, political, or moral issues—neutrality, the embargo, trading with the enemy, and slave trade. Each of these acts encountered opposition, both in their adoption and implementation, usually from a specific location or section of the country. The inability of the federal government to enforce these laws led to numerous frustrations for the Presidents who were in office when the laws were enacted. Jefferson and Madison, in particular, discovered the difficulty of trying to enforce an unpopular law on an unwilling public.

One further complication for effective enforcement was the nature of the punishments established for criminal violations. The only punishment for a person convicted of treason was death. Even when a judge might instruct a jury that treason had been committed, jurors were reluctant to convict when death was the only penalty. The same attitude prevailed toward piracy and slave trade, after they were included in the capital crimes category. The Act of 1825 softened a number of penalties and provided greater variance in the penalties assigned upon conviction. Because of the rigidity of the penalties, the Presidents, with the exception of John Quincy Adams, frequently pardoned persons convicted of capital offences because they did not have the right to commute the sentence to a prison term.

The final problem with enforcement was the lack of coordination between enforcement officials. The district attorneys and marshals reported to the Secretary of State. Customs officials, who were crucial parts of the enforcement system, particularly for neutrality and slave trade, reported to the Secretary of the Treasury. The lack of rapid communications added to the problem.

The system that evolved during the period was not perfect. The system was politicized early and remained that way. Presidents Adams, Jefferson, and Madison attempted to use the criminal law to quash opposition to their measures. The structure was inadequate to permit the development of a true national system. The most unfortunate aspect was that the precedents established in this period would be repeated by future generations. The federal justice system is still politicized. There have been other sedition acts and the incarceration of alien enemies, and other Presidents have used the criminal law to try to limit the opposition. The great balance to the system has been the petit or trial jury representing the people. When a particular law, rather it was the Sedition Act of 1798 in the South or the Embargo Act in New England, was not supported by the people, those acts were violated with as much impunity as prohibition in the 1920s and the marijuana laws in the 1970s.

DISPOSITION OF INDICTMENTS BY CIRCUIT COURTS

	Guilty	Not Guilty	Nolle Prosequis	No Disposition	Quashed	Continued	Dismissed	Defaulted	Settled	No Appearance	Discharged	Escaped	Abated	Discontinued	Forfeited Recognizance	Jurisdiction	TOTALS
Connecticut	6	3	11	2	1	1	0	0	0	0	0	0	0	0	0	0	24
Delaware	1	0	0	0	0	0	0	0	0	0	0	0	0	0	0	0	1
Georgia	36	66	15	71	1	0	0	0	0	0	6	1	0	0	0	0	196
Illinois	3	0	3	0	0	0	0	0	0	0	0	0	0	0	0	0	6
Indiana	2	6	3	1	0	0	0	0	0	0	0	0	0	0	0	0	12
Kentucky	3	2	1	0	0	0	0	0	0	0	0	0	0	0	0	0	6
Louisiana	161	52	74	50	4	0	0	0	0	0	0	0	0	0	0	0	341
Maine	22	12	10	24	0	1	0	0	0	0	1	0	0	0	0	0	70
Maryland	17	16	37	1	0	0	0	0	0	0	0	0	0	0	0	0	71
Massachusetts	73	51	56	30	5	0	1	0	0	0	1	0	0	2	0	0	219
New Hampshire	7	5	0	1	0	0	0	0	0	0	0	0	0	0	0	0	13
New Jersey	4	1	0	0	0	0	0	0	0	0	0	0	0	0	0	0	5
New York	32	37	6	42	1	0	0	0	0	0	2	1	0	0	0	0	121
New York (N.D.)	2	0	0	0	0	0	0	0	0	0	0	0	0	0	0	0	2
North Carolina	19	14	1	2	0	1	0	0	0	0	0	1	1	0	0	0	39
Ohio	6	0	3	0	0	1	0	0	0	0	0	1	0	0	0	0	11
Pennsylvania	82	100	547	389	1	0	0	0	0	0	0	0	0	0	0	0	1,119
Rhode Island	10	8	2	0	0	3	1	0	0	0	0	0	0	0	0	0	24
South Carolina	19	24	28	23	0	1	1	0	0	0	0	0	0	0	2	0	98
Tennessee	8	9	12	0	0	0	0	0	0	0	0	0	0	0	0	0	29
Tennessee (W.D.)	13	3	0	4	0	0	0	0	0	0	0	0	0	0	0	1	21
Vermont	40	50	70	4	2	3	1	10	2	1	1	0	0	0	0	0	184
Virginia	28	19	22	17	10	1	0	0	0	0	1	2	1	1	0	0	102
Virginia (W.D.)	2	1	1	0	0	0	0	0	0	0	0	0	0	0	0	0	4
TOTALS	596	479	902	661	25	12	4	10	2	1	12	6	2	3	2	1	2,718

NUMBER OF CRIMINAL INDICTMENTS BY CIRCUIT COURT AND YEAR

Year	Connecticut	Delaware	Georgia	Illinois	Indiana	Kentucky	Louisiana	Maine	Maryland	Massachusetts	New Hampshire	New Jersey	New York (N.D.)	New York (S.D.)	North Carolina	Ohio	Pennsylvania	Rhode Island	South Carolina	Tennessee	Tennessee (W.D.)	Vermont	Virginia	Virginia (W.D.)	TOTALS
1801	0	0	7	-	-	0	-	0	0	2	0	0	0	-	5	-	7	0	0	0	-	0	1	-	25
1802	0	0	3	-	-	0	-	0	0	2	0	0	0	-	0	-	3	0	0	1	-	1	0	-	10
1803	0	0	2	-	-	0	-	0	3	1	0	0	2	-	1	-	4	0	1	0	-	0	0	-	14
1804	0	0	1	-	-	2	-	-	3	13	0	0	0	-	1	0	11	0	3	5	-	0	8	-	44
1805	0	0	2	-	-	0	0	0	0	10	3	0	7	-	5	0	4	1	7	0	-	0	0	-	39
1806	0	0	2	-	-	0	2	0	0	1	0	1	4	1	2	0	12	0	0	0	-	0	4	-	28
1807	2	0	0	-	-	0	7	2	0	17	1	0	1	-	1	0	10	0	8	0	-	0	14	-	82
1808	7	0	0	-	-	2	0	2	0	7	0	0	0	-	1	2	8	0	0	2	0	5	12	-	48
1809	2	0	0	-	-	0	12	2	1	2	0	0	0	-	0	0	29	0	2	3	0	0	2	-	57
1810	0	0	12	-	-	0	3	3	0	6	0	0	0	-	1	0	6	1	0	3	0	2	1	-	38
1811	0	0	0	-	-	0	11	0	4	12	0	0	2	-	0	0	15	0	1	0	4	4	1	-	54
1812	1	0	1	-	-	0	3	2	2	11	1	0	12	-	0	0	6	0	0	1	7	8	1	-	56
1813	0	0	1	-	-	0	7	0	1	6	1	0	3	-	1	0	8	5	3	1	4	21	1	-	63
1814	1	0	0	-	-	0	0	0	2	6	0	0	1	0	0	0	3	0	1	2	1	27	1	-	45
1815	1	0	3	-	-	1	32	2	0	10	0	1	3	0	0	0	9	1	0	0	1	32	3	-	99
1816	0	0	6	-	-	0	34	2	4	18	3	0	0	0	2	5	11	0	29	3	0	52	8	-	177
1817	0	0	2	-	0	0	1	3	2	8	0	0	2	0	0	1	17	1	2	0	0	18	1	-	58
1818	0	0	8	0	0	0	8	9	31	14	0	0	1	0	5	0	11	0	0	3	0	1	0	-	91
1819	0	0	29	0	0	0	31	6	0	6	0	3	12	0	6	0	17	0	0	0	1	3	0	-	114
1820	5	0	79	0	9	0	36	1	0	11	0	0	13	0	0	0	22	5	15	1	1	4	6	0	208
1821	0	0	24	2	0	0	9	12	0	12	0	0	1	0	3	1	10	2	1	0	1	2	5	0	86
1822	1	0	4	0	0	0	29	3	8	1	0	0	0	1	0	0	7	0	12	0	0	1	6	0	73
1823	0	0	0	0	0	1	0	1	0	1	0	0	2	1	0	1	14	1	2	0	0	0	4	11	30
1824	2	0	8	0	0	0	0	0	5	6	0	0	7	0	0	0	10	0	0	0	0	1	1	22	42
1825	0	0	2	0	1	0	40	1	3	3	0	0	4	0	4	1	713	0	1	2	0	0	19	0	794
1826	2	1	0	0	2	0	7	0	2	17	0	0	24	0	1	0	116	1	3	0	0	0	1	1	177
1827	0	0	0	0	0	0	69	0	0	7	0	0	7	0	0	0	24	5	0	0	1	0	1	0	114
1828	1	0	0	3	0	0	0	0	3	8	4	0	10	0	0	0	12	1	7	4	0	0	1	0	52
TOTALS	24	1	196	6	12	6	341	70	71	219	13	5	121	2	39	11	1,119	24	98	29	21	184	102	4	2,718

APPENDIX III

TYPES OF CRIMES, INDICTMENTS, AND PERCENTAGE OF TOTAL

Unknown		314	11.55
Revenue Offenses		162	5.96
Admiralty and Maritime		820	30.17
Piracy	406		
Assault and Battery	57		
Revolt	140		
Murder	98		
Manslaughter	13		
Miscellaneous	106		
Treason		30	1.10
Bank and Monetary Offenses		357	13.13
Bank Offenses	51		
Counterfeiting	77		
Forgery	229		
Indian		31	1.14
Embargo		25	.92
Offenses Against Public Ministers		5	.18
Military		48	1.77
Neutrality		107	3.94
Slave Act		9	.33
Postal Offenses		97	3.57
General Crimes			
Perjury	27		
Misdemeanors	650		
Miscellaneous	36		
Total		2,718	99.99

APPENDIX IV

PENALTIES FOR CONVICTIONS BY CIRCUIT COURTS

	Hanged	Imprisonment	Fine	Fine and Im-prisonment	Fine and Physi-cal Punishment	Fine and Disabled	Fine, Physical Pun., and Impris.	Fine, Physical Punish.	Imprisonment and Physical Punish.	Physical Punishment	Judgment Arrested	Appealed to Supreme Court Quashed	No Sentence	Escaped	Bail Forfeited	TOTALS
Connecticut	0	2	1	0	0	0	0	0	0	0	0	0	3	0	0	6
Delaware	0	1	0	0	0	0	0	0	0	0	0	0	0	0	0	1
Georgia	15	1	2	4	3	0	1	0	1	4	0	0	5	0	0	36
Illinois	2	0	1	0	0	0	0	0	0	0	0	0	0	0	0	3
Indiana	0	0	0	0	0	0	0	0	0	0	0	0	2	0	0	2
Kentucky	0	2	0	1	0	0	0	0	0	0	0	0	0	0	0	3
Louisiana	19	25	0	102	0	0	0	0	0	3	1	0	11	0	0	161
Maine	0	1	12	5	0	0	1	0	0	3	0	0	0	0	0	22
Maryland	2	1	5	8	0	0	0	0	0	0	0	0	1	0	0	17
Massachusetts	10	14	15	29	3	1	0	0	0	0	0	0	1	0	0	73
New Hampshire	0	0	2	5	0	0	0	0	0	0	0	0	0	0	0	7
New Jersey	0	3	1	0	0	0	0	0	0	0	0	0	0	0	0	4
New York	6	2	0	20	1	0	1	1	0	0	0	0	1	0	0	32
New York (N.D.)	0	0	2	0	0	0	0	0	0	0	0	0	0	0	0	2
North Carolina	0	10	0	8	0	0	0	0	0	0	0	0	1	0	0	19
Ohio	0	5	1	0	0	0	0	0	0	0	0	0	0	0	0	6
Pennsylvania	0	25	5	33	6	7	0	0	2	1	0	1	0	0	2	82
Rhode Island	1	2	6	1	0	0	0	0	0	0	0	0	0	0	0	10
South Carolina	6	4	1	5	0	0	0	0	2	0	0	0	1	0	0	19
Tennessee	0	3	0	3	0	0	0	0	0	1	0	0	0	1	0	8
Tennessee (W.D.)	1	2	3	7	0	0	0	0	0	0	0	0	0	0	0	13
Vermont	0	0	27	5	0	0	0	0	0	4	0	0	4	0	0	40
Virginia	4	14	0	3	0	0	0	2	0	4	0	0	1	0	0	28
Virginia (W.D.)	0	0	2	0	0	0	0	0	0	0	0	0	0	0	0	2
TOTALS	66	117	86	239	13	8	3	3	5	20	1	1	31	1	2	596
% of Total	11.2	19.7	14.4	40.1	2.2	1.3	0.5	0.5	0.8	3.4	0.2	0.2	5.2	0.2	0.3	100.1

APPENDIX V

SHIPS EXEMPTED FROM SLAVE TRADE ACT

STATE	CAPTAIN OR SHIP'S NAME	LOCATION	DATE OF ENTRY	NUMBER OF SLAVES
Georgia	Schooner Nancy White	Cuba	1809	50
Pennsylvania	Brig Speedwell	Cuba	1809	Not Given
New York	Charles D'Espenville	Cuba	1810	Not Given
New York	Francis O'Ries	Cuba	1810	Not Given
South Carolina	Ship Franklin	Cuba	1809	Not Given
South Carolina	Sloop Philadelphia	Cuba	1809	Not Given
South Carolina	Ship Daphne	Cuba	1809	Not Given
Louisiana	Schooner Dispatch	Cuba	1809	50
Louisiana	Schooner L'Esperence	Cuba	1809	40
Louisiana	Schooner Louisa	Cuba	1809	15
Louisiana	Schooner Cerivo	Cuba	1809	60
Louisiana	Schooner Little Mary	Cuba	1809	80
Louisiana	Schooner Clarissa	Cuba	1809	55
Louisiana	Schooner Del Carmin	Cuba	1809	30
Louisiana	Schooner Callinna	Cuba	1809	12
Louisiana	Sloop Polly	Cuba	1809	30
Louisiana	Schooner Thomas	Cuba	1809	50
Louisiana	Brig Francis	Cuba	1809	90
Louisiana	Schooner Swift	Cuba	1809	23
Louisiana	Schooner Triumph	Cuba	1809	20
Louisiana	Schooner Freeman Ellis	Cuba	1809	20
Louisiana	Ship Arctic	Cuba	1809	100
Louisiana	Schooner Milford	Cuba	1809	70

STATE	CAPTAIN OR SHIP'S NAME	LOCATION	DATE OF ENTRY	NUMBER OF SLAVES
Louisiana	The Chebeck or Spanish Vessel Salvador	Cuba	1809	30
Louisiana	Spanish Chebeck or vessel called Venganza	Cuba	1809	50
Louisiana	Schooner Clara	Cuba	1809	30
Louisiana	Spanish Schooner Rosalie	Cuba	1809	10
Louisiana	William Warnow	Cuba	1809	10
Louisiana	Ship Robert	Cuba	1809	Not Given
Louisiana	Sloop St. Francisco	Cuba	1809	13
Louisiana	Schooner Gov. Brisbane	Cuba	1809	Not Given
Louisiana	Schooner Fanny	Cuba	1809	5
Louisiana	Brig Fair American	Cuba	1809	75
Louisiana	Spanish Schooner Carridad	Cuba	1809	180
Louisiana	Ship Beaver	Cuba	1809	130
Louisiana	Ship General Green	Cuba	1809	170
Louisiana	Schooner Santa Rita	Cuba	1809	20
Louisiana	Schooner Nuestra Sendra del Carmen	Cuba	1809	15
Louisiana	Schooner Freeman Ellis	Cuba	1809	Not Given
Louisiana	Schooner Clarissa	Cuba	1809	Not Given
Louisiana	Sloop San Francisco	Cuba	1809	Not Given
Louisiana	Schooner Felucca St. Rita	Cuba	1809	Not Given
Louisiana	Ship Carridad	Cuba	1809	Not Given
Louisiana	Schooner Triumph	Cuba	1809	Not Given
Louisiana	Schooner Clara	Cuba	1809	Not Given

STATE	CAPTAIN OR SHIP'S NAME	LOCATION	DATE OF ENTRY	NUMBER OF SLAVES
Louisiana	Schooner Swift	Cuba	1809	Not Given
Louisiana	Schooner Collina	Cuba	1809	Not Given
Louisiana	Schooner Polly	Cuba	1809	Not Given
Louisiana	Schooner Del Carmen	Cuba	1809	Not Given
Louisiana	Ship Arctic	Cuba	1809	Not Given
Louisiana	Schooner Reporter	Cuba	1809	Not Given
Louisiana	Cargo of Brig Francis	Cuba	1809	Not Given
Louisiana	Cargo of Ship Beaver	Cuba	1809	Not Given
Louisiana	Cargo of Schooner Milford	Cuba	1809	Not Given
Louisiana	Cargo of Little Mary	Cuba	1809	Not Given
Louisiana	Cargo of Brig Fair American	Cuba	1809	Not Given
Louisiana	Cargo of Brig Mary Ann	Cuba	1809	Not Given
Louisiana	Schooner Virginia	Cuba	1809	Not Given
Louisiana	Ship Madison	Cuba	1809	70
Louisiana	Sloop Catalino	Cuba	1809	Not Given
Louisiana	Schooner Lucky	Cuba	1809	Not Given
Louisiana	Brig Joseph Ricketson	Jamaica	1809	5
Louisiana	Spanish Schooner Virginia	Cuba	1809	3
Louisiana	Schooner Victory	Curacoa	1809	6
Louisiana	Schooner Aurora	Jamaica	1809	1
Louisiana	Sloop Hiram	Santo	1809	25
Louisiana	James Medcalf	Jamaica	1810	120
Louisiana	Brig Alexandrine	Cuba	1810	3
Louisiana	Schooner Marie Louise	Jamaica	1810	Not Given

Bibliography

MANUSCRIPTS

Circular Letters of the Secretary of the Treasury ("T" series) 1789-1878. 5 reels. National Archives Microfilm Publication, Microcopy M 735.

Copies of Presidential Pardons and Remissions, 1794-1893. 7 reels. National Archives Microfilm Publication, Microcopy T 967.

Domestic Letters of the Department of State, 1784-1906. 171 reels. National Archives Microfilm Publication, Microcopy M 40.

Letters of Application and Recommendation during the Administration of James Madison, 1809-1817. 8 reels. National Archives Microfilm Publication, Microcopy M 438.

Letters of Application and Recommendation during the Administration of James Monroe, 1817-1825. 19 reels. National Archives Microfilm Publication, Microcopy M 439.

Letters of Application and Recommendation during the Administration of John Adams, 1797-1801. 3 reels. National Archives Microfilm Publication, Microcopy M 406.

Letters of Application and Recommendation during the Administration of John Quincy Adams, 1825-1829. 8 reels. National Archives Microfilm Publication, Microcopy M 531.

Letters of Application and Recommendation during the Administration of Thomas Jefferson, 1801-1809. 12 reels. National Archives Microfilm Publication, Microcopy M 418.

Letters From and Opinions of the Attorney General. 1 roll. National Archives Microfilm Publication, Microcopy T 326.

Letters Sent by the Attorney General's Office. 2 reels. National Archives Microfilm Publication, Microcopy T 411.

Letters Sent by the Department of Justice: General and Miscellaneous, 1818-1904. 81 reels. National Archives Microfilm Publication, Microcopy M 699.

Letters Sent by the Secretary of the Treasury to Collectors of Customs at All Ports (1789-1847) and at Small Ports (1847-1878). 43 reels. National Archives Microfilm Publication, Microcopy M 175.

Microfilm of the Adams Papers, owned by the Manuscripts Trust and deposited in the Massachusetts Historical Society. 608 reels. Boston, Massachusetts Historical Society, 1954-1959.

Miscellaneous Letters of the Department of State, 1789-1906. 1,310 reels. National Archives Microfilm Publication, Microcopy M 179.

Opinions of the Attorney General, 1817-1832. 3 reels. National Archives Microfilm Publication, Microcopy T 412.

United States Circuit Court. District of Connecticut. Docket, 1800-1843, Record Book, 1790-1814. Federal Records Center, Waltham, Massachusetts.

United States Circuit Court. District of Georgia. Minute Books, 1789-1834. Federal Records Center, East Point, Georgia.

United States Circuit Court. District of Maine. Docket Book, 1820-1838. Federal Records Center, Waltham, Massachusetts.

United States Circuit Court. District of Maryland. Minutes 1790-1911. 7 reels. National Archives Microfilm Publication, Microcopy M 931.

United States Circuit Court. District of Massachusetts. Dockets, 1789-1833, and Record Books, 1789-1821. Federal Records Center, Waltham, Massachusetts.

United States Circuit Court. District of New Hampshire. Minute Books, 1790-1830. Federal Records Center, Waltham, Massachusetts.

United States Circuit Court. District of New Jersey. Minute Books, 1790-1950. 186 reels. National Archives Microfilm Publication, Microcopy T 928.

United States Circuit Court. District of New York. Minute Books, 1790-1832, and Criminal Case Files, 1790-1853. Federal Records Center, Suitland, Maryland.

United States Circuit Court. District of North Carolina. Minute Books, 1791-1835. Federal Records Center, East Point, Georgia.

United States Circuit Court. District of Pennsylvania. Minute Books, 1792-1828, and Criminal Cases, 1791-1883. Federal Records Center, Suitland, Maryland.

United States Circuit Court. District of Rhode Island. Minute Books, 1790-1833, and Dockets, 1790-1821. Federal Records Center, Waltham, Massachusetts.

United States Circuit Court. District of South Carolina. Minute Books, 1790-1836. Federal Records Center, East Point, Georgia.

United States Circuit Court. District of Tennessee. Minute Books, 1808-1833. Federal Records Center, East Point, Georgia.

United States Circuit Court. District of Vermont. Dockets, 1792-1833, and Case Files, 1792-1833. Federal Records Center, Waltham, Massachusetts.

United States Circuit Court. District of Virginia. Order Books, 1790-1831, and Record Books, 1790-1832. Microfilm copy, Virginia State Library, Richmond, Virginia.

United States District Court. Albemarle District of North Carolina, Minute Books, 1801-1858. Federal Records Center, East Point, Georgia.

United States District Court. District of Connecticut. Dockets, 1789-1841. Federal Records Center, Waltham, Massachusetts.

United States District Court. District of Georgia. Admiralty Minute Book, 1819-

1833, and Minute Books, 1799-1843. Federal Records Center, East Point, Georgia.

United States District Court. District of Louisiana. Docket Books, 1815-1830, Minute Books, 1819-1829, and Case Files. Federal Records Center, Fort Worth, Texas.

United States District Court. District of Maine. Record Books, 1789-1830, and Minute Books, 1812-1818. Federal Records Center, Waltham, Massachusetts.

United States District Court. District of Massachusetts. Dockets, 1820-1823, Prize Cases, 1812-1816, and Record Books, 1789-1830. Federal Records Center, Waltham, Massachusetts.

United States District Court. District of New Hampshire. Minute Books, 1790-1841. Federal Records Center, Waltham, Massachusetts.

United States District Court. District of New Jersey. Minute Books, 1789-1950. 186 reels. National Archives Microfilm Publication, Microcopy T 928.

United States District Court. District of Rhode Island. Minute Books, 1790-1835. and Dockets, 1800-1835. Federal Records Center, Waltham, Massachusetts.

United States District Court. District of South Carolina. Admiralty Journal, 1789-1826, and Minute Books, 1789-1814. Federal Records Center, East Point, Georgia.

United States District Court. District of Tennessee. Minute Book, 1797-1803. Federal Records Center, East Point, Georgia.

United States District Court. District of Vermont. Dockets, 1801-1830. Federal Records Center, Waltham, Massachusetts.

United States District Court. District of Virginia. Order Books, 1797-1818, and Record Books, 1790-1832. Microfilm copy, Virginia State Library, Richmond, Virginia.

United States District Court. Eastern District of Pennsylvania. Minute Books, 1789-1828, Admiralty Cases, 1789-1911, and Petitions and Discharges from Imprisonment for Debt, 1797-1838. Federal Records Center, Suitland, Maryland.

United States District Court. Southern District of New York. Minute Books, 1789-1826, and Certificates of Discharge. Federal Records Center, Suitland, Maryland.

War of 1812 Papers. 7 reels. National Archives Microfilm Publication, Microcopy M 588.

NEWSPAPERS

Charleston *City Gazette and Daily Advertiser*
Charleston *Courier*
The Commercial Advertiser (New York)
Maryland Gazette (Annapolis)
New York *Evening Post*
New York *Post*
New York *Spectator*
Niles Weekly Register (Philadelphia)
Providence *Gazette*

JUDICIAL REPORTS

The Case of Alien Enemies, Considered and Decided upon a Writ of Habeas Corpus Allowed on the Petition of Charles Lockington, an Alien Enemy by the Hon. William Tilghman, Chief Justice of the Supreme Court of Pennsylvania, the 22nd Day of November, 1813, reported by Richard Bache. Philadelphia, 1813.

Cranch, William. *Reports of Cases Argued in the Supreme Court of the United States, 1801-1815.* 9 volumes, Washington, D.C., 1804-1817.

Dallas, Alexander James. *Reports of Cases in the Courts of the United States, and Pennyslvania, 1790-1800.* 3 volumes, Washington, D. C., 1798-1819.

Federal Cases, 1789-1879. 30 volumes; St. Paul, 1894-1897.

Peters, Richard, Jr. *Reports of Cases Argued and Adjudged in the Supreme Court, 1828-1842.* 17 volumes; Philadelphia, 1828-1843.

Robertson, David. *Reports of the Trials of Aaron Burr in the Circuit Court of the United States.* 2 volumes; Richmond, 1808.

The Trials of William S. Smith and Samuel G. Ogden . . . in July 1806. New York, 1807.

United States circuit court. 4th circuit. *Reports of Cases Decided by the Honourable John Marshall . . . from 1802 to 1833*, edited by J. W. Brockenbrough. 2 volumes; Philadelphia, 1837.

United States district court. South Carolina. *Reports of Cases Adjudged in the District Court of South Carolina [1792-1809] By the Hon. Thomas Bee.* Philadelphia, 1810.

Wheaton, Henry. *Reports of Cases Argued and Adjudged in the Supreme Court, 1816-1827.* 12 volumes, Philadelphia, 1816-1827.

Wilson, Samuel M., ed., "The Court Proceedings in 1806 in Kentucky Against Aaron Burr and John Adair," *Filson Club Historical Quarterly*, 10 (January, 1936):31-40.

PUBLIC DOCUMENTS

Moore, John Bassett. *International Adjudications, Ancient and Modern; History and Documents.* 8 volumes; New York, 1929-1936.

Richardson, James D., comp. *A Compilation of the Messages and Papers of the President.* 10 volumes, Washington, D.C., 1896-1899.

United States. Congress. *American State Papers.* 39 volumes, Washington, D.C., 1832-1861.

United States. Congress. *Debates and Proceedings in the Congress of the United States; 1789-1824. [Annals of Congress]* 42 volumes, Washington, D.C., 1834-1856.

United States. Congress. House. *Letter from the Secretary of the Navy Transmitting copies of the instructions which have been issued to Naval Commanders, upon the Subject of the Importation of Slaves.* U.S. 15th Congress, 2nd session, House Document 84. Washington, D.C., 1819.

United States. Congress. House. *Letter from the Secretary of the Navy Transmitting information in relation to the introduction of Slaves into the United States.*

U.S. 16th Congress, 1st session, House Document 36. Washington, D. C., 1820.

United States. Congress. House. *Letter from the Secretary of the Treasury . . . in relation to ships engaged in the Slave Trade.* U.S. 15th Congress, 2nd session, House Document 107. Washington, D. C., 1819.

United States. Congress. House. *Letter from the Secretary of the Treasury transmitting . . . information in relation to the Illicit Introduction of Slaves into the United States* U.S. 16th Congress, 1st session, House Document 42. Washington, D. C., 1842.

United States. Congress. House. *Process of Execution: United States' Courts.* U.S. 19th Congress, 1st session, House Document 71. Washington, D. C., 1826.

United States. Congress. House. *A Statement of Convictions, Executions, and Pardons.* U.S. 20th Congress, 2nd session, House Document 146. Washington, D. C. 1829.

United States. Congress. *Register of Debates in Congress, 1825-1837.* [*Congressional Debates*] 29 volumes, Washington, D. C. 1825-1837.

United States. Congress. Senate. *Journal.* 5 volumes, Washington, D. C., 1820-1821.

United States. Congress. Senate. *Journal of the Executive Proceedings of the Senate of the United States, 1789-1905.* 90 volumes, Washington, D. C., 1828-1919.

United States. Congress. *Statutes at large of the United States of America, 1789-1873.* 17 volumes, Boston, 1850-1873.

United States. Navy Department. *Letter from the Secretary of the Navy Transmitting Information in Relation to the Introduction of Slaves into the United States.* Washington, D. C., 1820.

STATE LAWS

Connecticut. *Acts and Laws.* Hartford, 1796.

Delaware. *Laws.* 2 volumes. Newcastle, 1797.

Georgia. *Digest of the Laws of the State.* Philadelphia, 1800.

Kentucky. *Statute Law*, edited by William Littell. 5 volumes. Lexington, 1809-1819.

Maryland. *Laws.* Revised and collected by William Kilty. 2 volumes. Annapolis, 1800.

Massachusetts. *The Perpetual Laws.* 2 volumes. Worcester, 1788-1799.

New Hampshire. *Laws of the State.* Portsmouth, 1797.

New Jersey. *Laws of the State*, revised and edited by William Paterson. Newark, 1800.

New York. *Laws of the State.* 3 volumes. New York, 1798.

North Carolina. *Laws of the State*, edited by James Iredell. Edenton, 1791.

Pennsylvania. *Laws of the Commonwealth*, edited by Alexander James Dallas. 4 volumes. Philadelphia, 1797-1801.

Rhode Island. *Public Laws of the State.* Providence, 1798.

South Carolina. *Acts of the General Assembly of the State.* 2 volumes. Columbia, 1808.

Tennessee. *Laws of the State*, edited by Edward Scott. 2 volumes. Knoxville, 1821.

Vermont. *Statutes of the State.* Bennington, 1791.

Virginia. *The Statutes at Large . . . of Virginia*, edited by William Waller Hening. 13 volumes. Richmond, 1823.

OTHER PRINTED SOURCES

Adams, Henry, ed. *Documents Relating to New England Federalism, 1800-1815.* Boston, 1877.

Adams, John. *Works*, edited by Charles Francis Adams, 10 volumes. Boston, 1850-1856.

Adams, John Quincy. *Memoirs*, edited by Charles Francis Adams. 8 volumes. Philadelphia, 1874-1875.

Ames, H. V., comp. *State Documents on federal relations; the states and the United States.* Philadelphia, 1911.

Brackenridge, H. M. *History of the Western Insurrection in Western Pennsylvania, Commonly called the Whiskey Insurrection, 1794.* Pittsburgh, 1859.

Calhoun, John C. *Papers*, edited by Robert Meriwether, et al. In progress, Columbia, 1959-.

Clay, Henry. *Papers*, edited by James F. Hopkins, et al. In progress, Lexington, 1959-.

Donnan, Elizabeth, ed. *Documents Illustrative of the History of the Slave Trade to America.* 4 volumes. Washington, D. C., 1930-1935.

Eliot, Jonathan, ed. *Debates in the Several State Conventions on the Adoption of the Federal Constitution.* 5 volumes. 2d edition. Philadelphia, 1901.

Farrand, Max, ed. *The Records of the Federal Convention of 1787.* 4 volumes. Rev. ed., New Haven, 1937.

The Federalist. Modern Library Edition, New York, 1941.

Findley, William. *History of the Insurrection in the Far Western Country of Pennsylvania, 1794.* Philadelphia, 1796.

Gallatin, Albert. *Writings*, edited by Henry Adams. 3 volumes. Philadelphia, 1879.

Hamilton, Alexander. *Papers*, edited by Harold C. Syrett, et al. 26 volumes. New York, 1961-1979.

Jay, John. *Correspondence and Public Papers*, edited by Henry P. Johnston. 4 volumes. New York, 1890-1893.

"Jefferson Papers." *Massachusetts Historical Society Collection.* 7th series, 10 volumes. Boston, 1900.

Jefferson, Thomas. *Papers*, edited by Julian P. Boyd, et al. In progress, Princeton, 1950-.

_____.*Works*, edited by Paul Leicester Ford. 12 volumes. New York, 1904-1905.

_____.*Writings*, edited by Andrew A. Lipscomb. 20 volumes. Washington, D. C., 1903.

Kent, William, ed. *Memoirs and Letters of James Kent.* Boston, 1898.

Lawson, J. D., ed. *American State Trials.* 17 volumes. St. Louis, 1914-1936.

Livingston, Edward. *A System of Penal Law for the United States of America.* Washington, D. C., 1828.

Maclay, William. *The Journal of William Maclay, United States Senator from Pennsylvania 1789-1791.* 2nd ed., New York, 1927.

Madison, James. *Papers*, edited by William T. Hutchinson, et al. In progress, Chicago, 1963-.
_____. *Writings*, edited by Gaillard Hunt. 9 volumes. New York, 1900-1910.
Marshall, John. *Papers*, edited by Herbert A. Johnson, et al. In progress, Chapel Hill, 1974-.
Monroe, James. *Writings*, edited by S. M. Hamilton. 7 volumes. New York, 1898-1903.
Storing, Herbert J., and Murry Dry, eds. *The Complete Anti-Federalist*. 7 volumes. Chicago and London, 1981.
Webster, Daniel. *Papers*, edited by Charles M. Wiltse, et al. In Progress, Hanover, N. H., 1974-.
_____. *Private Correspondence*, edited by Fletcher Webster. 2 volumes. Boston, 1857.
_____. *Writings and Speeches*, edited by J. W. McIntyre. 18 volumes, Boston, 1903.
Wharton, Francis. *State Trials of the United States during the Administrations of Washington and Adams*. Philadelphia, 1849.
West, Elizabeth H., ed. "Diary of José Bernardo Gutierrez de Lara, 1811-1812," *American Historical Review*, 34 (October, January, 1928-1929): 55-77, 281-291.

SECONDARY WORKS

Abernethy, Thomas P. *The Burr Conspiracy*. Reprint, Gloucester, Mass., 1968.
American Association of Law Schools. *Select Essays in Anglo-American Legal History*. 3 volumes. Boston, 1907.
Anderson, Frank Maloy. "Enforcement of the Alien and Sedition Laws." American Historical Association *Annual Report*, 1912, pp. 115-126. Washington, D.C., 1914.
Aronson, Sidney H. *Status and Kinship in the Higher Civil Service: Standards of Selection in the Administrations of John Adams, Thomas Jefferson and Andrew Jackson*. Cambridge, 1964.
Aumann, Francis R. "The Influence of English and Civil Law Principles Upon the American Legal System during the Critical Post-Revolutionary Period." *University of Cincinnati Law Review*, 12 (June, 1938):289-317.
Baldwin, Leland D. *Whiskey Rebels: The Story of a Frontier Uprising*. Pittsburgh, 1939.
Bassett, John S. *The Life of Andrew Jackson*. 2 volumes in 1. Reprint, Hamden, Conn., 1967.
Beard, Charles A. *Economic Origins of Jeffersonian Democracy*. Reprint, New York, 1965.
Bemis, Samuel F. *John Quincy Adams and the Union*. New York, 1956.
Beveridge, Albert J. *The Life of John Marshall*. 4 volumes. Boston and New York, 1916-1919.
Bishop, James L. "The Jurisdiction of State and Federal Courts Over Federal Officers." *Columbia Law Review*, 9 (May, 1909):397-418.
Bloomfield, Maxwell H. *American Lawyers in a Changing Society, 1776-1876*. Cambridge and London, 1976.

Brant, Irving. *James Madison*. 6 volumes. Indianapolis, 1941-1961.

Bridwell, Randall, and Ralph U. Whitten. *The Constitution and the Common Law: The Decline of the Doctrines of Separation of Powers and Federalism*. Lexington, Mass., 1977.

Brooks, Charles B. *The Siege of New Orleans*. Seattle, 1961.

Chafee, Zechariah, Jr. "Colonial Courts and the Common Law." *Massachusetts Historical Society Proceedings*, 68 (1944):132-159.

Channing, Edward. *A History of the United States*. 6 volumes. New York, 1905-1925.

Chapin, Bradley. *The American Law of Treason, Revolutionary and Early National Origins*. Seattle, 1964.

_____. *Criminal Justice in Colonial America, 1606-1660*. Athens, 1983.

Chitwood, Oliver P. *Justice in Colonial Virginia*. Baltimore, 1905.

Chroust, Anton-Hermann. *The Rise of the Legal Profession in America*. 2 volumes. Norman, 1965.

Conkling, Alfred. *A Treatise of the Organization, Jurisdiction and Practice of the Courts of the United States*. 5th ed., rev. and enl., Albany, 1870.

Cook, Charles M. *The American Codification Movement: A Study of Antebellum Legal Reform*. Westport, 1981.

Cooley, Rita W. "The Office of United States Marshall." *Western Political Science Quarterly*, 12 (March, 1959):123-140.

Cox, Isaac J. "The Burr Conspiracy in Indiana." *Indiana Magazine of History*, 25 (December, 1929):257-280.

_____. "Monroe and Early Mexican Revolutionary Agents." American Historical Association *Annual Report*, 1911, volume I, pp. 199-215. Washington, D.C., 1913.

Crosskey, William W. *Politics and the Constitution in the History of the United States*. 3 volumes. Chicago, 1953-1981.

Cummings, Homer, and Carl McFarland. *Federal Justice: Chapters in the History of Justice and the Federal Executive*. New York, 1937.

Curtis, Benjamin Robbins. *Jurisdiction, Practice and Peculiar Jurisprudence of the Courts of the United States*. 2d ed., rev., Boston, 1896.

Dallas, George Mifflin. *Life and Writings of Alexander James Dallas*. Philadelphia, 1871.

Davis, David Brion. "The Movement to Abolish Capital Punishment in America, 1787-1861." *American Historical Review*, 63 (October, 1957):23-46.

DeConde, Alexander. *The Quasi-War: The Politics and Diplomacy of the Undeclared War with France 1797-1801*. New York, 1966.

Donnan, Elizabeth. "The New England Slave Trade after the Revolution." *New England Quarterly*, 3 (January, 1930):251-278.

Dow, G. F. *Slave Ships and Slaving*. Salem, 1926.

Du Bois, W. E. B. "The Enforcement of the Slave-Trade Law." American Historical Association *Annual Report*, 1891, pp. 161-174. Washington, D.C. 1892.

_____. *The Suppression of the African Slave Trade to the United States of America 1638-1870*. Reprint, Williamstown, Mass., 1970.

Duignan, Peter, and Clarence Clendenen. *The United States and the African Slave Trade, 1619-1862*. Stanford, 1963.

Dumbauld, Edward. *The Bill of Rights and What It Means Today*. Norman, 1957.

Du Ponceau, Peter S. *A Dissertation on the Nature and Extent of the Jurisdiction of the Courts of the United States. . . .* Philadelphia, 1824.

Ehrlich, J. W. *Ehrlich's Blackstone.* 2 volumes. New York, 1959.

Ellis, Richard E. *The Jeffersonian Crisis: Courts and Politics in the Young Republic.* New York, 1971.

Farrand, Max. "The Judiciary Act of 1801." *American Historical Review,* 5 (July, 1900):682-686.

Faulkner, Robert K. "John Marshall and the Burr Trial." *Journal of American History,* 53 (September, 1966):247-258.

Fenwick, Charles G. *The Neutrality Laws of the United States.* Washington, D. C., 1913.

Fish, Carl R. *The Civil Service and the Patronage.* Reprint, New York, 1963.

Foote, Henry S. *Texas and the Texans.* 2 volumes. Reprint, Austin, 1925.

Fortier, Alcée. *A History of Louisiana.* 4 volumes. New York, 1904.

Frankfurter, Felix. "Distribution of Judicial Power Between United States and State Courts." *Cornell Law Quarterly,* 13 (June, 1928):499-530.

Frankfurter, Felix, and Thomas G. Corcoran. "Petty Federal Offenses and the Constitutional Guarantee of Trial by Jury." *Harvard Law Review,* 39 (June, 1926):917-1018.

Frankfurter, Felix, and James M. Landis. "Power of Congress over Procedure in Criminal Contempts in 'Inferior' Federal Courts—A Study in Separation of Powers." *Harvard Law Review,* 37 (May, 1924):1010-1113.

Friedman, Lawrence M. *A History of American Law.* New York, 1973.

Fuess, Claude M. *Daniel Webster.* 2 volumes. Boston, 1930.

Gayarré, Charles. "Historical Sketch of Pierre and Jean Lafitte," *Magazine of American History,* 10 (July, December, 1883): 284-298, 389-396.

Goebel, Julius., Jr. *Felony and Misdemeanor: A Study in the History of English Criminal Procedure.* New York, 1937.

_____. *The Oliver Wendell Holmes Devise History of the Supreme Court of the United States.* Volume I, *Antecedents and Beginnings to 1801.* New York and London, 1971.

Goebel, Julius, Jr., and T. Raymond Naughton. *Law Enforcement in Colonial New York: A Study in Criminal Procedure, 1664-1776.* Reprint, Montclair, N. J., 1970.

Goodenow, John Milton. *Historical Sketches of the Principles and Maxims of American Jurisprudence . . . . Stuebenville, Ohio, 1819.*

Griffin, Charles C. "Privateering from Baltimore during the Spanish American Wars of Independence." *Maryland Historical Magazine,* 35 (March, 1940):1-25.

_____. *The United States and the Disruption of the Spanish Empire, 1810-1822; a study of the relations of the United States with Spain and with the rebel Spanish colonies.* New York and London, 1937.

Haggard, J. Villasana. "The Neutral Ground Between Louisiana and Texas, 1807-1821." *Louisiana Historical Quarterly,* 28 (October, 1945): 1001-1128.

Haines, Charles Grove. *The American Doctrine of Judicial Supremacy.* Reprint, New York, 1959.

Hall, Ford. "The Common Law: An Account of Its Reception in the United States." *Vanderbilt Law Review*, 4 (June, 1951):791-824.

Hall, Jerome. *General Principles of Criminal Law*. 2nd edition, Indianapolis, 1960.

Harper, Lawrence A. *The English Navigation Laws, a Seventeenth-Century Experiment in Social Engineering*. New York, 1939.

Harris, Joseph P. *The Advice and Consent of the Senate; a study of the confirmation of appointments by the United States Senate*. New York, 1968.

Harris, Robert J. *The Judicial Power of the United States*. University, La., 1940.

Haskins, George L. *Law and Authority in Early Massachusetts: A Study in Tradition and Design*. New York, 1960.

_____. *The Oliver Wendell Holmes Devise History of the Supreme Court of the United States*. Volume 2, *Foundations of Power—John Marshall 1801-1815*. New York and London, 1981.

Hatcher, William B. *Edward Livingston; Jeffersonian Republican and Jacksonian Democrat*. University, La., 1940.

Hawes, Joseph M., ed. *Law and Order in American History*. Port Washington and London, 1979.

Heaton, Herbert. "Non-importation, 1806-1812." *Journal of Economic History*, I (November, 1941):178-198.

Henderson, Dwight F. *Courts for a New Nation*. Washington, D. C., 1971.

_____. "Treason, Sedition, and Fries' Rebellion." *American Journal of Legal History*, 14 (October, 1970): 308-318.

Hickey, Donald R. "American Trade Restrictions during the War of 1812." *Journal of American History*, 68 (December, 1981):517-538.

Hindus, Michael Stephen. *Prison and Plantation: Crime, Justice and Authority in Massachusetts and South Carolina, 1767-1878*. Chapel Hill, 1980.

Hitsman, J. Mackay. *The Incredible War of 1812: A Military History*. Toronto, 1965.

Hockett, Homer Carey. *The Constitutional History of the United States*. 2 volumes. New York, 1939.

Hoffman, David. *Course of Legal Study*. Baltimore, 1817.

Horwitz, Morton J. *The Transformation of American Law, 1780-1860*. Cambridge and London, 1977.

Howe, George L. *Mount Hope: A New England Chronicle*. New York, 1959.

Hurst, James Willard. *The Growth of American Law: The Lawmakers*. Boston, 1950.

_____. *The Law of Treason in the United States: Collected Essays*. Westport, 1971.

Ingersoll, Charles Jared. *A Discourse Concerning the Influence of America on the Mind. . . .* Philadelphia, 1823.

Jennings, Walter W. *The American Embargo, 1807-1809, with particular reference to its effect on industry*. Iowa City, 1921.

Kalven, Harry, Jr., and Hans Zeisel. *The American Jury*. Boston and Toronto, 1966.

Kent, James. *Commentaries on American Law*. 4 volumes. Reprint, New York, 1971.

Kettner, James H. *The Development of American Citizenship, 1608-1870*. Chapel Hill, 1978.

King, C. R., ed. *Life and Correspondence of Rufus King. . . .* 6 volumes. New York, 1894-1900.

Knudson, Jerry W. "The Jeffersonian Assault on the Federalist Judiciary 1802-1805; Political Forces and Press Reaction." *American Journal of Legal History*, 14 (January, 1970):55-75.

Lang, Maurice E. *Codification in the British Empire and America.* Amsterdam, 1924.

Lemly, Henry R. "A Forgotten International Episode." *Journal of the Military Service Institute,* 52 (May, 1952):396-408.

Levy, Leonard. *Jefferson & Civil Liberties: The Darker Side.* Cambridge, 1963.

_____. *The Origins of the Fifth Amendment, the Right Against Self-Incrimination.* New York, 1968.

Lewis, Orlando F. *The Development of American Prisons and Prison Customs, 1776-1845; with special reference to early institutions in the state of New York.* Albany, 1922.

Lillich, Richard B. "The Chase Impeachment." *American Journal of Legal History,* 4 (January, 1960):49-72.

Lomask, Milton. *Aaron Burr, The Conspiracy and Years of Exile, 1805-1836.* New York, 1982.

Mackey, Philip English. "Edward Livingston and the Origins of the Movement to Abolish Capital Punishment in America." *Louisiana History,* 16 (Spring, 1975):145-166.

Malone, Dumas. *Jefferson and His Time.* 6 volumes. Boston, 1948-1981.

Martin, François Xavier. *The History of Louisiana, from the earliest period.* New Orleans, 1827-1829.

McCaleb, Walter F. *New Light on Aaron Burr.* Austin, 1963.

McMaster, John B. *A History of the People of the United States, from the Revolution to the Civil War.* 8 volumes. New York, 1893-1913.

_____. *Life and Times of Stephen Girard, Mariner and Merchant.* 2 volumes. Philadelphia, 1918.

McMaster, John B., and Frederick D. Stone, eds. *Pennsylvania and the Federal Constitution, 1787-1788.* Lancaster, 1888.

McRee, Griffith J. *Life and Correspondence of James Iredell. . . .* 2 volumes. New York, 1857-1858.

Miller, John C. *Crisis in Freedom: The Alien and Sedition Acts.* Boston, 1951.

Miller, Perry. *The Life and Mind in America, from the Revolution to the Civil War.* New York, 1965.

Morgan, Donald G. *Justice William Johnson, The First Dissenter; the career and constitutional philosophy of a Jeffersonian judge.* Columbia, 1954.

Mueller, Gerhard O. W. *Crime, Law, and the Scholars; A History of Scholarship in American Criminal Law.* Seattle, 1969.

Nelson, William E. *Americanization of the Common Law: The Impact of Legal Change on Massachusetts Society, 1760-1830.* Cambridge and London, 1975.

Nettels, Curtis. "The Mississippi Valley and the Federal Judiciary, 1807-1838." *Mississippi Valley Historical Review,* 12 (September, 1925): 202-226.

Noonan, John T., Jr. *The Antelope: The Ordeal of the Recaptured Africans in the Administrations of James Monroe and John Quincy Adams.* Berkeley, 1977.

Perkins, Bradford. *Castlereagh and Adams: England and the United States, 1812-1823.* Berkeley and Los Angeles, 1964.

_____. *The First Rapproachment: England and the United States, 1795-1805.* Berkeley and Los Angeles, 1967.

_____. *Prologue to War: England and the United States, 1805-1812.* Berkeley and Los Angeles, 1961.

Pickering, Octavius. *Life of Timothy Pickering.* 4 volumes. Boston, 1867-1873.

Pound, Roscoe. *Criminal Justice in America.* Reprint, New York, 1972.

———. *Organization of Courts.* Boston, 1940.

———. *The Spirit of the Common Law.* Reprint, Boston, 1963.

Prince, Carl E. "The Passing of the Aristocracy: Jefferson's Removal of the Federalists, 1801-1805." *Journal of American History*, 57 (December, 1970): 563-575.

Rackow, Felix. "The Right to Counsel: English and American Precedents." *William and Mary Quarterly*, 3rd series, 11 (January, 1954):3-27.

Remini, Robert J. *Martin Van Buren and the Making of the Democratic Party.* New York, 1959.

"Rhode Island Slave Trade in 1816." *Rhode Island Historical Society*, 6 (January, 1899):226-227.

Robertson, William Spence. "Francisco de Miranda and the Revolutionizing of Spanish America." American Historical Association *Annual Report*, 1907, I: 189-539. 2 volumes. Washington, D. C., 1908.

———. *The Life of Miranda.* 2 volumes. Chapel Hill, 1929.

Rutland, Robert Allen. *The Birth of the Bill of Rights, 1776-1791.* Chapel Hill, 1955.

Sampson, William. *Sampson's Discourse . . .,* edited by Pishey Thompson. Washington, D. C., 1826.

Schachner, Nathan. *Thomas Jefferson, A Biography.* New York and London, 1957.

Scott, Arthur P. *Criminal Law in Colonial Virginia.* Chicago, 1930.

Scott, James Brown, comp. *Prize Cases decided in the United States Supreme Court, 1789-1918.* 3 volumes. Oxford, 1923.

Sears, Louis M. *Jefferson and the Embargo.* Durham, 1927.

Semmes, Raphael. *Crime and Punishment in Early Maryland.* Reprint, Montclair, N. J., 1970.

Smith, James Morton. *Freedom's Fetters: The Alien and Sedition Law and American Civil Liberties.* Ithaca, 1956.

Soulsby, Hugh Graham. *The Right of Search and the Slave Trade in Anglo-American Relations, 1814-1862.* Baltimore, 1933.

Spears, John R. *The American Slave Trade: An Account of the Origin, Growth and Suppression.* London, 1901.

Spivak, Burton. *Jefferson's English Crisis: Commerce, Embargo, and the Republican Revolution.* Charlottesville, 1979.

Stagg, J. C. A. *Mr. Madison's War: Politics, Diplomacy, and Warfare in the Early American Republic, 1783-1830.* Princeton, 1983.

Story, W. W., ed. *Life and Letters of Joseph Story. . . .* 2 volumes. Boston, 1851.

Surrency, Erwin C. "The Judiciary Act of 1801." *American Journal of Legal History*, 2 (January, 1958):53-65.

Tachau, Mary K. Bonsteel. *Federal Courts in the Early Republic: Kentucky, 1789-1816.* Princeton, 1978.

Thomas, Hugh. *Cuba; The Pursuit of Freedom.* New York, 1971.

Thorning, Joseph Francis. *Miranda: World Citizen.* Gainesville, 1952.

Turner, Lynn W. "The Impeachment of John Pickering." *American Historical Review*, 54 (April, 1949):485-507.

Tucker, St. George. *Blackstone's Commentaries: With Notes of Reference, to the Constitution and Laws, of the Federal Government of the United States; and of the Commonwealth of Virginia.* 5 volumes. Philadelphia, 1803.

Turner, Kathryn. "Federalist Policy and the Judiciary Act of 1801." *William and Mary Quarterly*, 3rd series, 22 (January, 1965):3-32.

Walker, Samuel. *Popular Justice: A History of American Criminal Justice.* New York, 1980.

Warren, Charles. "Earliest Cases of Judicial Review of State Legislation by Federal Courts." *Yale Law Review*, 32 (November, 1922):15-28.

_____. "Federal Criminal Law and the State Courts," *Harvard Law Review*, 38 (March, 1925):545-598.

_____. "New Light on the History of the Federal Judiciary Act of 1789." *Harvard Law Review*, 37 (November, 1923):49-132.

_____. *The Supreme Court in United States History.* 2 volumes. Revised edition, Boston, 1926.

Warren, Harris Gaylord. *The Sword Was Their Passport, A History of American Filibustering in the Mexican Revolution.* Baton Rouge, 1943.

Washburne, George A. *Imperial Control of the Administration of Justice in the Thirteen American Colonies, 1684-1776.* New York, 1923.

Wharton, Francis. *A Treatise on the Criminal Law of the United States.* 2 volumes. 5th edition, Philadelphia, 1861.

White, Leonard D. *The Jeffersonians; A Study in Administrative History, 1801-1829.* New York, 1951.

White, Patrick C. T. *A Nation on Trial: America and the War of 1812.* New York and London, 1965.

Wilgus, A. Curtis. "Some Notes on Spanish American Patriot Activity Along the Atlantic Seaboard, 1816-1822." *North Carolina Historical Review*, 4 (April, 1928):172-181.

_____. "Spanish American Patriot Activity Along the Gulf Coast of the United States, 1811-1822." *Louisiana Historical Quarterly*, 8 (April, 1925):193-215.

Williams, Jack K. *Vogues in Villainy; Crime and Retribution in Ante-Bellum South Carolina.* Columbia, 1959.

Younger, Richard D. *The People's Panel; The Grand Jury in the United States, 1634-1941.* Providence, 1963.

Index

About the Author

DWIGHT F. HENDERSON is Professor of History and Dean of the College of Social and Behavioral Sciences at the University of Texas at San Antonio. He is the author of *The Private Journals of Georgiana Gholson Walker* and *Courts for a New Nation*. His articles have appeared in the *Encyclopedia of Southern History*, *Essays on Southern History in Honor of Barnes F. Lathrop*, and *Perspectives on the American Revolution*.